General editor
Peter
Herriot

New
Essential
Psychology

Personality
Theory and
Clinical
Practice

ALREADY PUBLISHED IN THIS SERIES

Applying Psychology in Organizations
Frank Blackler and Sylvia Shimmin

Cognitive Development and Education
Johanna Turner

Individual Differences
Vivian Shackleton and Clive Fletcher

Instinct, Environment and Behaviour
S.E.G. Lea

Learning Theory and Behaviour Modification
Stephen Walker

Selves in Relation
An introduction to psychotherapy and groups
Keith Oatley

Social Interaction and its Management
Judy Gahagan

FORTHCOMING TITLES IN THIS SERIES

Cognitive Psychology
Judith Greene

Cognitive Social Psychology and Social Policy
Kerry Thomas

Experimental Design and Statistics
Second edition
Steve Miller

Information and Human Performance
Paul J. Barber and David Legge

Lifespan Development
Concepts, theories and interventions
Léonie Sugarman

Multivariate Design and Statistics
Steve Miller

Physiological Psychology
Theory and applications
John Blundell

Peter Fonagy Anna Higgitt

Personality Theory and Clinical Practice

Methuen

London and New York

First published in 1984 by
Methuen & Co. Ltd
11 New Fetter Lane, London EC4P 4EE

Published in the USA by
Methuen & Co.
in association with Methuen, Inc.
733 Third Avenue, New York, NY 10017

Typeset by Rowland Phototypesetting Ltd
Printed in Great Britain by
Richard Clay (The Chaucer Press) Ltd
Bungay, Suffolk

British Library
Cataloguing in Publication Data

Fonagy, Peter
Personality theory and clinical practice.
–(New essential psychology)
1. Personality
I. Title   II. Higgitt, Anna
III. Series
155.2   BF698
ISBN 0-416-35630-3

Library of Congress
Cataloging in Publication Data

Fonagy, Peter, 1952–
Personality theory and clinical practice.
(New essential psychology)
Bibliography: p.
Includes indexes.
1. Personality.   2. Psychotherapy.
I. Higgitt, Anna, 1951–
II. Title.   III. Series.
(DNLM: 1. Personality.
2. Personality disorders – Therapy.
3. Psychological theory.
WM 190 F673P)
BF698.F63   1984   155.2'024616
84–18983
ISBN 0-416-35630-3

To our parents

Contents

1   Introduction   1
2   The psychoanalytic approach: classical theory   24
3   Post-Freudian psychoanalysis   40
4   Behavioural approaches   56
5   Humanistic approaches   84
6   Multi-trait and narrow-trait theories of personality   102
7   The controversy over the consistency of personality   120
8   Socio-cognitive models   135
9   The integration of theories and future developments   160
    Suggestions for further reading   168
    References and name index   171
    Subject index   205

1

Introduction

The definition of personality

Why do you want to study psychology?

'I'm interested in what makes people different from each other', 'I want to study the differences between people', 'I want to understand why people react to things differently' – these are typical answers to the above question commonly put to potential undergraduate psychology students at their selection interview. How and why people differ from one another is, of course, the major concern of that part of psychology termed 'personality'.

The word 'personality' has a simple and unambiguous dictionary definition: 'distinctive individual character, especially when of a marked kind' (Fowler and Fowler, *Shorter Oxford English Dictionary*, 1956). In common parlance we use phrases such as 'an aggressive personality', 'an unstable personality', 'a strong personality' or, even more generally, 'a lot of personality'. Within the discipline of psychology, however, personality refers to an area of theorization and research rather than to an aspect of the individual. Wiggins (1979 p. 395) reflects the generally agreed view in stating that personality refers to that branch of psychology 'which is concerned with providing a systematic account of the ways in which individuals differ from one another'.

Beyond agreeing that the study of personality is broadly concerned with establishing reasons for the differences between people, psychologists have not yet produced a universally acceptable definition of the term. Introductory textbooks on personality contain a bewildering array of definitions. Pervin (1980) suggested that personality consisted of those characteristics of the person which account for consistent patterns of response to situations; while Mischel (1981), from a different perspective, would like to widen the definition so as to include all aspects of the person's interaction with his/her environment.

Whilst acknowledging this lack of consensus, we intend to use the term 'personality' in the following way: firstly, to refer to relatively enduring characteristics of behaviour that enable a person to be recognized as an individual distinct from others; secondly, to refer to the overall internal organization of these behavioural characteristics, how they relate to each other and combine to make a complete person; and finally, to cover the nature of the interaction between the internal organization of these characteristics and the external world.

There are enormous disagreements between psychologists as to which behaviour patterns are most important in characterizing people, the organization of these patterns, their origins and ways of altering them. In this book we will consider a selection of the different approaches that psychologists have adopted in their attempts at identifying what is most essential to our understanding of the ways in which people differ from one another.

A theory of personality

A personality theory is an organized set of concepts (like any other scientific theory) designed to help us predict and explain behaviour. According to Smith and Vetter (1982) theories of personality serve two functions. In the first place, they should provide a logical framework for integrating observations which were previously seen as unrelated. Thus, one approach to the problem of agoraphobia links the reluctance to leave the house (a typical feature of an agoraphobic's behaviour) to the comfort obtained from being looked after by members of the family at home. It is suggested that agoraphobics adopt this behaviour because it has desirable consequences for them – because it is rewarded. The theory places the observation of this type of phobic behaviour in the context of a theory of personality based on the principles of learning by reward and punishment. For clinical psychology, this integrative function of personality theory is achieved when it leads to a conceptual framework which helps clinicians integrate and make meaningful the many disparate aspects of their clients' behaviour.

Smith and Vetter's second point is that a theory should generate new hypotheses which lead to the possibility of further research and in turn to extension and development of the theory. The most important index of such scientific productivity for the clinical psychologist is the ability of a theory to generate new ideas for helping individuals with psychological problems. Learning theory explanations, for example, have been particularly productive of new hypotheses in the area of abnormal behaviour and its therapeutic change.

The field of personality has produced many theories, and thus the question inevitably arises as to how we can compare and evaluate them. Broadly speaking, there are two major approaches. First of all, the theory's formal (or structural) properties should be considered. These might include the clarity of its language, the degree to which it leads to clear and testable hypotheses and the number of assumptions it needs to make. Secondly, a theory may also be evaluated in terms of its empirical (scientific/experimental) properties. This refers not only to the degree to which a theory is consistent with existing scientific evidence but also to its ability to stimulate further research. As Hall and Lindzey (1978) point out, a theory is rarely true or false; it is only either useful or not useful. In clinical psychology, the effectiveness of a treatment approach derived from a theory of personality is frequently used as an indicator of usefulness.

The diversity of psychological theories of personality, all of which have substantial professional support, would indicate to historians of science that psychology in general, and the study of personality in particular, is at a very early stage of its development as a science. Thomas Kuhn (1973), in a very influential work on the development of science, pointed out that in the more 'mature' sciences most workers in a field accept 'a point of view' about their subject-matter as they carry out their research. This point of view guides their researches to particular topics and dictates the methods used. Kuhn refers to the point of view shared by a large number of scientists as a *paradigm*. For example, before the First World War most physicists adopted a Newtonian viewpoint in their work, while currently most adhere to an Einsteinian point of view; Kuhn would say that the dominant paradigm in physics has shifted from Newton's to Einstein's theory.

Psychology has never had just one paradigm. As Kuhn points out, in the absence of a paradigm to guide research it is difficult to accumulate data systematically. Research without a paradigm has a haphazard quality: results do not contribute to one single body of knowledge. In clinical psychology, as in other areas of psychology, many theories exist in relative independence of each other and represent quite diverse and frequently contradictory viewpoints despite having a common area of interest, namely human personality.

Varieties of abnormal behaviour

A major task of any psychological approach to personality is to account for behaviour falling outside the range of normality as well as to explain normal variations. Such 'abnormal' behaviours are generally subsumed under the term 'mental disorders'. In evaluating theories of personality the success of any approach in providing useful explanations for a wide range of abnormal behaviours should be an important criterion. Thus in later chapters we will frequently refer to a variety of abnormal behaviour patterns, and a brief introduction to these might therefore be useful.

Any study of mental disorders must start with a careful description of the behaviour patterns considered to be disordered. In the next few pages we will provide brief descriptions of the most common of these patterns and the terms by which they are known. As will become clear, such disorders may be categorized or grouped together in varying ways. For the present we shall follow the system commonly used in the United Kingdom.

The psychoses

The psychoses are the disorders producing most disruption in an individual's life. The term 'psychosis' does not have an adequate definition but can be taken to refer to disorders in which there is such impairment of normal mental functioning that individuals are unaware that anything is amiss and yet are unable to meet many of the demands of everyday life.

One of the most common of the psychoses is known as *schizophrenia*. A schizophrenic may experience a form of thinking that appears disordered: his/her thoughts lack coherence and continuity and his/her speech contains invented words as well as words used in strange contexts. Disorder characterizes the content as well as the form of their thoughts. They may feel that they are being controlled by alien forces or be certain that their most intimate thoughts are known to other people. Delusions (false beliefs held contrary to all the evidence) may also be present. Often such people report hearing voices which may keep up a running commentary on their actions or discuss them in the third person.

The schizophrenias can be subdivided according to the predominant symptoms displayed. A *paranoid schizophrenic* may have a deep conviction of being persecuted by outside forces. A *catatonic schizophrenic* frequently shows movement disturbances and may, for example, remain in what appears to be an uncomfortable position for prolonged periods or occasionally rush about with catatonic excitement. Many other types of schizophrenia have been described, but most schizophrenics have signs and symptoms from more than one category. The lifetime prevalence of schizophrenia is 1 per cent: that is to say we all have a one in a hundred chance of having a schizophrenic episode at some time in our lives.

Affective (or manic-depressive) psychosis is the other common form of psychosis. In this disorder, severe disturbance of mood predominates. The person's mood may swing from severe depression to elation. The *depression* can be so profound that a person believes that he/she is totally evil and responsible for the suffering of all those that come into contact with him/her. He/she may stop eating and drinking (a typical explanation being that the inside of his/her body has turned into stone) and may be at severe risk of making a suicide attempt.

The opposite extreme of mood from depression is *mania*. In this state a person may be excited and elated to a degree not justified by the circumstances. He/she is full of energy, needs very little sleep and may start many new projects which can result in disastrous and costly failures. Frequently the person behaves in socially unacceptable ways. Although, on the whole, a manic person's mood is infectiously happy, he/she may display marked irritability (particularly if someone attempts to interfere with his/her plans).

The community survey conducted by Wing and his colleagues (1981) found that 0.3 per cent of the population in an Inner London borough suffered from what would clearly be considered as psychotic depression; a further 1.5 per cent had severe depression of which perhaps half would be felt to be psychotic, as described above. It must be remembered that these surveys cover only people in the community; a fair proportion of severely affected people with these disorders would be under hospital care and so would be missed by the surveyors.

Both schizophrenia and manic-depressive psychosis are referred to as 'functional' psychoses, the word 'functional' meaning in this case that they are of unknown causation. Considerable evidence has accumulated that such disorders tend to run in families. There is some controversy as to whether it is living with an ill parent (environment) that causes children to be affected in this way or whether it is an inherited liability (heredity). Studies where children of schizophrenics brought up by their ill parent(s) are compared with similar children who were adopted soon after birth have indicated that both heredity and environment are important, but the former more so (Kety *et al.*, 1978). This also applies to affective psychosis. In addition, there is evidence of biochemical abnormalities in each of these disorders, in that there are imbalances in the relative quantities of particular neurotransmitters (the chemicals which pass from one nerve cell to the next and ensure the passage of electrical impulses in the brain). When the imbalances of neurotransmitters are corrected using the appropriate drugs, symptoms of the disorders tend to diminish (MacKay, 1983). In certain individuals with functional psychosis post-mortem examination of their brain has revealed substantial damage to their brain tissue. Those who in life had had symptoms of withdrawal and apathy rather than hallucinations and delusions were the most likely to have such brain changes (Crow, 1983).

Although the psychoses just described are of uncertain origin, very similar symptoms can be seen in patients with clearly recognizable brain disease. These are described as the *organic psychoses*. The similarity of the organic psychoses to the functional psychoses adds weight to the view that the latter may best be understood in terms of abnormal neurophysiological functioning. Even if these disorders do have biological origins, this does not mean that psychological interventions will not be of benefit in their management. In later chapters there will be many examples of ways in which psychologists of different orientations have usefully contributed to the care given to such individuals.

Neurotic disorders

The next group of mental disorders to be discussed are generally considered to be less severe than the psychoses. No underlying organic cause is known for the neurotic disorders. Affected individuals may display markedly abnormal behaviour and report morbid subjective experiences, but they retain sufficient insight to realize that their thoughts, behaviours and feelings are not appropriate to the circumstances.

Some individuals have anxiety as their major problem. When the anxiety is linked to particular objects or situations, the disorder is termed a *phobia. Agoraphobia* is the most common (forming 60 per cent of hospital phobic referrals). It is a seriously handicapping phobia more commonly found in women than in men. The individual concerned is afraid of going out of the house and of being in crowded places (e.g. shops, busy streets and bus queues). These fears can be quite debilitating, sometimes preventing the sufferer from leaving home for many years.

Most of us have some specific mild fear, whether of heights, aeroplanes, pigeons or spiders. This only becomes a serious problem when it interferes with a person's normal functioning, in which case it is referred to as phobic behaviour. A spider phobic, for example, has a substantial problem when he/she needs to check every nook and cranny of a room before being able to settle down. Phobic responses may develop to social situations such as public speaking, parties or meeting members of the opposite sex. Using a systematic and standardized interview Costello (1982) found mild fears in 67 per cent and phobias in 19 per cent of a group of 449 women.

Some people have anxiety which appears not to be related to any specific situation. This is referred to as an *anxiety state*. The anxiety on occasion may fluctuate and become suddenly of such intensity that the person fears he/she might die. This is described

7

as a *panic attack* and may also occur in phobic disorders. In the Wing *et al.* (1981) study, anxiety states were found in 1 per cent of men and 4.5 per cent of women in the general population.

Obsessive-compulsive neurosis is another disorder in the neurotic category. An individual may dwell on an idea or experience or unwanted thoughts which force themselves into consciousness. Individuals may experience almost irresistible urges to do something unacceptable or aggressive (e.g. shout rude words at the top of their voices, or push someone under a lorry), although they seldom succumb. On occasion they are driven to perform certain ritualistic actions as part of an inner struggle to ward off disaster in some 'magical' way. Typical compulsions often observed in such individuals include washing the hands many dozens of times each day in order to avoid infection or checking twenty or more times that the front door is locked before leaving the house.

This disorder is rare, forming about 1 per cent of all mental disorders referred for treatment (Woodruff and Pitts, 1964). Nevertheless, a survey of the general population has shown that obsessional thoughts can be found in many people in a less frequent and more easily dismissible form (Rachman and De Silva, 1978), and children almost invariably manifest obsessive-like behaviours (such as avoiding the cracks between paving stones) as part of normal development (Rutter and Garmezy, 1983). Obsessions frequently appear together with phobias, depression and quite a diverse range of other emotional problems, and in view of this overlap many doubt if obsessions can justifiably be considered as a subcategory separate from the other neurotic disorders (Rachman and Hodgson, 1980).

The other major disturbance of affect (mood), apart from anxiety, is depression. A person with a *neurotic depression* generally has a melancholy mood-state (sometimes attributable to an external event but disproportionate to it). Affected individuals, unlike those psychotically depressed, can generally, with an effort, cheer themselves up for a short while. In addition to their melancholic mood they also, in many cases, have disturbances of sleep and appetite as well as loss of energy.

Episodes of neurotic depression are very common. Bebbington *et al.* (1981) found 10.5 per cent of Camberwell (London) residents had been depressed in the previous year; this figure rose to 15 per cent if women alone were considered. Brown and Prudo (1981) found that women with three or more children under fourteen at home and who lacked a close, confiding relationship were especially likely to be affected.

More dramatic but far less common are disorders involving a disturbance of consciousness. These *dissociative hysterical neuroses* include the *fugue states*, in which an individual wanders away from home and 'comes to' in a different part of the country, not recalling how he/she got there but having apparently behaved quite normally in between. The term 'hysteria' is also used to describe disorders in which the central symptom is a disturbance of function of some part of the body: individuals may become paralysed, develop tremors, seizures, pain, blindness or deafness without an underlying physical basis being found. This diagnosis (*conversion hysteria*) is rarely used nowadays, largely because in a number of instances this turns out to have been a misdiagnosis, with an underlying physical complaint, such as a brain tumour, having been overlooked (Slater, 1965).

Other non-psychotic disorders

Actual physical malfunctions can also have a primarily psychological origin. Such disorders are described as *psychosomatic* and include skin lesions (e.g. eczema) and even high blood pressure and heart disease. In fact, recent studies have demonstrated that psychological factors such as psychosocial stress play a role in modulating human immune responses and are thus likely to be able to influence our susceptibility to infectious diseases (Jemmott and Locke, 1984).

Personality disorder seems always to pose the greatest problems in attempts at classifying mental disorders. Personality-disordered individuals are said to show exaggerations of normal behaviour patterns. The disorder is long-standing, maladaptive and inflexible, and causes impaired functioning and distress. The main feature is one of recurrent disturbance in relationships with other people.

Several different types of personality disorder have been described. A *hysterical* personality, for example, shows excessive displays of emotion, a craving for attention and a lack of sincerity, and has a theatrical air. The speech of such an individual is often full of hyperbole and is quite superficial. Such people are felt by those around them to be manipulative and self-centred. The *antisocial* personality is perhaps the easiest to recognize. People

9

described in this way frequently come into conflict with society because of unsocialized (e.g. aggressive) behaviour. They seem incapable of feeling significant loyalty to groups or individuals, feel little guilt, and may also be untruthful, manipulative and callous.

From these two examples it should be apparent that personality disorders differ only quantitatively (in degree) from normal personality and so it is harder to categorize someone as definitely personality-disordered than to judge them as paranoid or manic. Thus it is not surprising that estimates of the frequency of such disorders vary widely (Widiger and Kelso, 1983).

Mental impairment

Mental impairment includes significant impairment of intelligence and social functioning, and is associated with abnormally aggressive or seriously irresponsible conduct. The distinction between mental impairment and severe mental impairment is one of degree, being 'significant' in the former and 'severe' in the latter. Thus the distinction is one of clinical judgement according to the latest Mental Health Act (Department of Health and Social Security, 1983). The handicap may have various possible causes, such as infection (e.g. German measles), an accident leading to brain damage, or a tumour. Most frequently, however, there is no known cause. There are in addition various inherited disorders such as Down's syndrome (mongolism). Although the causes of these conditions are not relevant to this book, clinical psychologists from certain theoretical traditions have had a profound influence on the care and training offered to individuals with mental impairment.

Categorization of mental disorders

The previous section on the description of mental disorders was based on the classification system currently in use in the United Kingdom (the Mental Disorders Section of the Ninth Revision of the International Classification of Diseases, otherwise known as ICD-9). This document was published by the World Health Organization in an attempt to produce some uniformity in the way diseases are identified in different countries. It is important that there should be an agreed 'common language' to enable the professionals caring for people with psychological problems, whether in the same or in different countries, to be able to communicate with each other. Such a classification system categorizes the problems experienced rather than the people who have them.

In the 1950s and 1960s there was a great deal of criticism of classification systems such as ICD-9. Zubin (1967) reviewed this literature and concluded that the degree of agreement between professionals of similar training and experience was too low to justify the continued use of these systems; in fact, he found that two different professionals could only agree on a client's most important problem in half the cases (and this was without making any allowance for agreements arrived at by chance alone). The category of depression seemed particularly vague and difficult to recognize unequivocally (Klerman *et al.*, 1979).

Classification systems have, however, developed substantially over the past few years. The changes were initiated by psychologists and psychiatrists wishing to do research with individuals with specific diagnoses and resulted in the development of research diagnostic criteria for most psychological disorders. Feighner, for example, described his aim as being one of making psychiatric diagnosis a science rather than a highly idiosyncratic judgemental activity (see Feighner *et al.*, 1978). By specifying very explicit, practical and exact criteria for identifying disorders (so-called operational criteria), the systems of classification used in both the United States (DSM-III) and the United Kingdom (ICD-9) have been made more precise and easier to operate, little room being left for subjective judgement. In defining depressive disorder, for example, the criteria used specify the length of time depression must have been present, indicate the amount of weight loss or gain necessary for the diagnosis and require that the client complains of a number of problems, such as loss of interest and energy, diminished ability to concentrate and excessive guilt (Spitzer *et al.*, 1978).

The use of such specific criteria has resulted in at least 80 per cent agreement among professionals as to the definition of a person's principal problem (Robins *et al.*, 1981), even allowing for chance agreements. The precision of the process of classification has been further improved by the development of structured interviews. Wing *et al.* first published their structured interview, the Present State Examination (PSE), in 1967. This has been revised several times, and clinicians properly trained in its use are able to produce psychiatric diagnoses that are far more precise and definite than formerly. In the United States, Endicott and Spitzer (1978) developed a similar schedule called SADS (the Schedule for Affective Disorders and Schizophrenia). In the past, up to ten times as many people were classified as schizophrenic by American-trained professionals as by their British counterparts (Cooper *et al.*, 1972). The use of improved techniques for diagnosis has resulted in much closer agreement.

Psychologists have been critical of the classification systems for mental disorders. One of the main criticisms has been that the systems implicitly identify psychological problems with medical ones (Eysenck *et al.*, 1983). This issue will be pursued in the next section. Other psychologists objected to what they called the false precision of these categories. Cantor and her colleagues (1980), for example, claimed that we base our classification of most things on prototypes; any conceptual categories used have imprecise boundaries. For example, in the case of psychiatric disorders the experienced clinician's concept of schizophrenia would be based on two or three of the most typical cases he/she had seen. Thus we define the category on the basis of its most typical members. Any other potential members are judged according to how similar they are to this typical example (or prototype); the more similar they are, the more likely we are to place them in the same category. Natural categories are based on broad similarities, not on exact criteria as the psychiatric classification systems claim. (This approach, as we shall see, has also been applied to the categorization of personality types.) In a slightly different vein, Eysenck and his colleagues (1983) object that since the distinction between normality and abnormality is not clear-cut, classification should be not on the basis of separate categories but in terms of continuous dimensions.

Despite such criticisms, there can be no doubt that there have been great improvements in the system of classification and definitions of mental disorder. These will aid the scientific study of psychological abnormality and the theoretical approaches applied to it.

Models of psychological abnormality

Our attitude towards mental disorder, its causation and any possible treatment depends upon the 'model' of abnormality we adopt. The word 'model' is used to describe a system of beliefs about the nature of reality. In the area of abnormal behaviour, the earliest models evolved from the view that these abnormalities could be attributed to evil spirits possessing an individual. The eighteenth and nineteenth centuries were dominated by moral models which saw abnormal behaviour as punishment for deviation from contemporary moral or social standards such as those related to Christianity. Currently the most generally accepted point of view is contained in the *medical model*, which defines certain abnormalities of behaviour and experience as mental illness.

The main features of the medical model are as follows:

1 Psychological problems are regarded as manifestations or symptoms of an underlying illness.
2 Illness is regarded as being totally different from the healthy state.
3 Certain symptoms are found to occur together frequently. These clusters of symptoms form the psychological disease entities described in the previous section. Placing an individual's problems in such a specific category enables us to make predictions about associated features such as the prognosis (or outcome) of the disorder.
4 Illnesses are seen as having a cause. Here, the proponents of the medical model divide. There are those who regard physical (organic) causes as paramount and provide accounts in terms of heredity and biochemical make-up, leaving little room for psychological explanations. The approach known as the psychogenic medical model, however, retains the notion that psychological illnesses can be caused by factors at a psychological level. It remains a *medical* approach because of its assumption of underlying illness (the behavioural abnormalities being regarded as symptoms). Both versions of the medical model suggest that in order to treat an individual we need to attack the underlying cause of the disease rather than the symptoms. Thus the medical model assumes that the problems with which individuals present are not their *real* problems. The real problems of people presenting with hallucinations would be not that they are suffering from hearing voices, but that they have schizophrenia – a disease perhaps caused by an imbalance of neurotransmitters.

The original introduction of the medical model greatly improved the position for those with psychological problems; their previous treatment had tended towards cruelty (in some ways being quite similar to our present handling of criminals). In addition, the inclusion of abnormal behaviours within the framework of medicine opened the way to the scientific study of mental disorders.

The medical model is, however, by no means universally accepted; many have criticized the analogy between mental and physical illness (e.g. Szasz, 1982). It is argued that physical illness is an 'all or nothing' phenomenon which is either present or absent and for which there are usually 'hard' physical signs. Psychological problems, on the other hand, fall on a continuum so that it is difficult to say at what point an individual may be said to be 'suffering from the disease' (e.g. when does unhappiness become a depressive illness?). In other words, it is difficult to define mental illness with any certainty.

Many critics complain therefore that psychiatric diagnosis is frequently superficial and inaccurate because of the subjective nature of the decisions that psychiatrists are asked to make. Rosenhan (1973) reported a spectacular example of this. He and seven colleagues were 'successful' in getting themselves committed to twelve American mental hospitals with a diagnosis of schizophrenia, simply by reporting that they heard voices saying the single words 'empty', 'hollow' and 'thud'. Despite ceasing to simulate any further psychiatric abnormality once admitted to hospital, they remained confined for an average of nineteen days. On being released, they were all given the diagnosis of 'schizophrenia in remission'.

It should also be noted, as Gorenstein (1984) recently pointed out, that the scientific approach to mental disorder which is fallaciously regarded by many as the hallmark of the medical model is in reality a feature not of medicine but rather of the sciences such as physiology, pharmacology and psychology which have played such a key role in advancing our ability to deal with physical disorders over the last hundred and fifty years. A further argument is that physical illness is culture-free, whereas what is defined as psychologically abnormal depends very much upon the culture in question: for example, self-mutilation is regarded as very odd in our present society, although in the Middle Ages flagellation was accepted as evidence of piety and spiritual devotion. Today in the Soviet Union, the holding of certain political and religious views is considered delusional and thus a sign of mental illness requiring treatment. Thus although in practice the boundaries of social acceptability may play a large part in defining mental illness, the acceptance of purely social definitions carries with it implications that are unpalatable and totalitarian.

An additional criticism of the medical model stresses that physical illness is seen as a deviation from a normal, healthy state. In the case of psychological abnormality this is problematic as it is impossible to define objectively a state of psychological health. Even if normality could be established by statistical means, it would be impossible to identify the degree of deviation from the norm required to achieve abnormality. In any case, it is not feasible to specify which dimensions of behaviour would be relevant in assessing normality.

A final point may be that diagnosis of a physical illness carries with it implications as to a specific cause, course, treatment and outcome. In the case of psychological abnormalities, it is difficult to specify any of these aspects without running into major controversies. There is as yet no psychological, physiological or biochemical theory sufficiently comprehensive or widely enough accepted to justify pronouncements concerning the boundaries of normality and abnormality.

The use of the medical model also has certain practical disadvantages. One is that it is felt to encourage a degree of passivity in individuals with problems. This is probably of benefit in the case of individuals with physical problems who need bed-rest; however, just lying around waiting for someone to 'cure' a psychological problem is likely to be counter-productive. A further disadvantage is the implication inherent in the medical model that those with psychological problems are 'patients', best seen in hospital with nurses and doctors caring for them. This state of affairs is really a historical accident: a previously very common form of mental disorder, general paralysis of the insane, turned out to be the result of untreated syphilitic infection which is, beyond all argument, a physical disease. Some would argue that as most psychological problems have little to do with physical illness there is absolutely no reason why specialist teachers in educational establishments should not be in charge of their care. In addition, hospitals are known to have adverse effects in that long-term hospitalization can lead to a passive dependence on the institution and a loss of ability to deal with the outside world (Goffman, 1961).

Finally, it has been pointed out that although the medical model originally aimed to remove the stigma of being labelled as 'immoral' or 'damned' it has instead substituted a stigma of its own. Being labelled as 'mentally ill' elicits prejudice from others. Farina and his colleagues (1965) demonstrated that 'tipping off' subjects that the person they were to work with was 'mentally ill' caused a marked increase in the reports of the workmate being unpredictable, regardless of the actual behaviour.

Recently a British psychiatrist, Anthony Clare (1980) published a defence of the medical model. He argued that the nature of physical illness itself is by no means as clear-cut as critics of the medical model would have us believe; many physical illnesses reflect a continuum from normality to abnormality. (It is a matter of convention alone as to what particular blood pressure reading is regarded as 'high'.) Clare agrees that criticisms of psychiatric diagnosis are justified, but feels that they should be directed at the psychiatrist in question rather than at the process of diagnosis in general. He concludes that the controversy regarding the relevance of a model based on physical illness to psychological phenomena is based on a false dichotomy between body and mind. There are many cases in which the two do, indeed, seem to overlap: psychological factors are very important determinants of the rate of recovery from physical illness, and certain infections can produce abnormal behaviour (delirium).

The critics of the medical model have frequently objected to the long-term hospital-based care of the psychologically disturbed. At least in part under the influence of these critics, a programme of deinstitutionalization of chronic psychiatric patients was commenced in the United States in the early 1970s. A similar programme is currently under way in the United Kingdom. Such undertakings assume that deinstitutionalization of chronic patients is a humanitarian act preventing the onset of chronic dependence and withdrawal from normal social contacts as seen among some mentally disabled people. Evidence is accumulating in the United States that discharge from institutions in most cases results in a deterioration rather than an improvement in the quality of life of those concerned: 50 per cent of the deinstitutionalized live socially isolated lives, are unemployed and receive inadequate health care (Tessler *et al.*, 1982). It is likely that deinstitutionalization has been over-zealous. It is remarkable, as Weinstein (1982) pointed out, that nobody asked the individuals concerned about their attitudes to the institutions; the 'benefits' of community living were thrust upon them (Iscoe and Harris, 1984).

The most likely outcome of the debate concerning the medical model is that although some aspects of psychological disturbance are best considered within a medical context many other, equally important, aspects are not explained by at least those versions of the medical model that attempt to reduce the reality of human experience to a series of neurochemical events. Some would argue that the medical model currently provides the most appropriate framework for the development of social policy concerning the management and planning of services for people with psychological problems. We would argue, however, that this is a separate problem, to be determined by legislators and society and unrelated to scientific questions concerning the nature of mental disorders. The adoption of the medical model to guide social policy does not in itself validate the use of medical concepts as scientific explanations of psychological dysfunction. It is our view that descriptive terms such as anxiety, depression or schizophrenia should be used as theoretical constructs to aid in the making of predictions and the developing of testable hypotheses about psychological disorders rather than to describe diagnostic categories which assume an underlying disease process and other 'medical' concepts.

The assessment of personality and mental disorders

Most of the personality theories to be considered in this volume have developed techniques of assessing or measuring those aspects of behaviour encompassed by them. These include questionnaires, projective tests, interviews, and the systematic observation and recording of behaviour. The generic term used to describe such techniques is 'personality test'. Such tests can be defined as providing a standardized situation in which an individual's behaviour may be sampled, observed and described (Korchin, 1976). Most of them state their findings in numerical terms, giving a single or frequently a whole series of scores.

The most commonly used method is the *questionnaire*. Psychologists have demonstrated that people can be meaningfully differentiated from each other in terms of their agreement or disagreement with certain written statements. Thus an individual who endorses a statement such as 'I sweat easily' or 'I have difficulty sleeping' is more likely to be an individual characterized by anxiety than someone who feels such statements do not have personal relevance. The total number of similar statements endorsed is taken as an indicator of the person's anxiety level or score on a scale of anxiety. This type of questionnaire has been successfully used to identify individuals with substantial psychological problems living in the community who have not previously sought help (Goldberg *et al.*, 1976).

Questionnaires have not only been used to identify people with psychological problems but have also been applied in attempts at quantifying personality differences within the normal range. A person who endorses a question such as 'Do you prefer reading to meeting people?' or 'Do you tend to keep in the background on social occasions?' may be assumed to be less outgoing or extraverted than someone who replies in the negative to such questions. In this way, questionnaires can yield a score relating to the degree to which a person may be well characterized by a term such as 'sociable' or 'outgoing'.

Many workers feel that questionnaire measures where subjects have to reply yes or no to highly intimate and personal questions can hardly be expected to do justice to the complexities of personality. It is neither surprising nor difficult to understand that under some circumstances individuals would tend to endorse items which seem to them to be more acceptable to others and would also tend to deny personal inadequacies. These forms of *response bias* are described as *social desirability effects* (faking good) and *defensiveness* respectively. Another source of response bias in questionnaires is that subjects seem to prefer to reply in the affirmative to questions regardless of content (*acquiescence*). These latter distortions can to some extent be avoided by careful design of questionnaires. More difficult to eliminate are the potentially distorting effects of the individual's motivation (lack of interest producing carelessness in completion of the questionnaire, for example) and the influence of cultural variables which may influence the understanding of items or the person's attitude to such questionnaires (Anastasi, 1982).

Some workers feel that the risk of an individual responding falsely to a questionnaire is too high and that less direct methods are preferable. *Projective tests* try to disguise the nature of a test by making the task as ambiguous as possible. The person may be asked to describe the shapes he or she can discern in an ink-blot (Rorschach test) or to tell any story that comes to his/her mind in relation to a drawing of a family group (thematic apperception test). Someone who sees an ink-blot as two bears fighting or comments on the family group as being just about to have a row might be considered to have problems with aggression. The assumption underlying such procedures is that an individual's perception of these purportedly neutral stimuli will be substantially influenced by his/her internal psychological state. On the whole, evidence supporting this kind of interpretation has not been forthcoming, and there is insufficient support to justify the widespread clinical use of such techniques (Lanyon, 1984). Although on the whole the responses to projective tests are interpreted impressionistically by the clinician, psychologists have recently attempted to quantify subjects' responses (e.g. Exner and Weiner, 1982). The usefulness of such scores remains to be demonstrated. Currently, psychologists tend to use projective test responses as a source of ideas about their clients rather than as a means of formal assessment.

Interviews provide a more generally accepted method of obtaining information about important and intimate aspects of a person's life. The interview is a major vehicle for exploring the concerns, feelings and problems of the client as they are experienced. Although much of the information produced by a client could have been obtained in other ways, the additional information provided by observation of non-verbal behaviours (e.g. the manner of answering) and the feelings aroused in the interviewer are regarded by many as essential to a full assessment. Empirical support for this view is, however, meagre. Early studies demonstrated spectacularly that the desire for social approval could lead to inaccurate reporting in 50 per cent of average subjects on certain questions (Cannell and Kahn, 1969). Psychiatric interviews tend to yield reliable information concerning global functioning (i.e. presence or absence of impairment) but not regarding specific symptoms (Achenbach and Edelbrock, 1984).

It is, therefore, not surprising that judgements concerning an individual's clinical state made on the basis of interviews have on the whole been found to be no better than a judgement based simply on the person's history (Watts, 1980). More recently, several research centres have attempted to improve the quality of interviewing by designing pre-selected sets of questions which clinicians should ask. Such so-called structured interviews have been shown to be a great deal more accurate and useful than those where questions are not standardized or pre-selected (e.g. Spitzer and Endicott, 1978).

In many ways the most rigorous assessments of an individual may be obtained by *observing* and quantifying (counting) his/her behaviour. For example, we may infer the presence of anxiety in an individual whom we see trembling, sweating and avoiding certain objects or situations. A person may be asked to monitor his/her own behaviour: for example, we may learn a great deal about an individual's sleeping habits by asking him/her to keep a sleep diary. These forms of behavioural assessment have become popular since they undoubtedly provide a potentially highly accurate picture of an individual (Nay, 1979). The innovativeness of such techniques derives not only from the systematic way in which an individual's behaviour is quantified and recorded as it happens but also from the noting of the context in which the behaviours occur (the environmental determinants). Information may be obtained concerning what tends to precede as well as what follows the behaviour being assessed. However, the presence of observers recording an individual's behaviour in his/her natural environment is not always practicable and is invariably expensive. Furthermore, certain psychological problems are not available for direct behavioural observation.

Requirements of good psychological tests

In order to be useful all tests must satisfy a number of requirements. In particular, they must be shown to be both *reliable* and *valid*. To be reliable means that the tests should yield replicable data (similar results on re-administering the test). If a test is ideally reliable, then any change of test score should reflect a change in the attribute being assessed. A test is unreliable if chance factors determine an individual's score. Reliability may be assessed in a number of different ways depending on the nature of the phenomenon under investigation, but is sometimes measured by comparing the scores from two administrations of the test (*test-retest reliability*). The degree of similarity between them is established statistically using the coefficient of *correlation* which ranges between 0 and 1: a strong association would be suggested by a value of .7 or greater, while a value of between .4 and .7 would indicate a moderate association and one lower than .4 would be considered low or negligible. If the 'test' we are using involves the observation and description of a person's behaviour, then we must ensure the reliability of the observations by comparing them with observations of the same behaviour made by an independent observer and calculating correlation coefficients between these. The degree of *interrater reliability* can then be calculated. Reliability may also be assessed in terms of the consistency of a number of measures taken. In the case of a long questionnaire, we might be interested to know whether all the questions measure the same thing (*degree of internal consistency*). This can be roughly measured by estimating the *split-half reliability* (correlating the score from one half of the test with that from the other half). More complex assessments might involve the correlation of two or more equivalent forms of the same test (*equivalent forms reliability*). There are many sources of error in all measurement. The quest for reliability is the quest for reducing the contribution of error relative to the person's true score.

Having satisfied ourselves that our test is reliable we next need to know that it is *valid*, in other words that it actually does measure what it purports to measure. That a test should be valid seems like common sense, but the demonstration of validity is a complex process. There are several types of validity. *Face validity*, as the name implies, refers to the degree to which a test *appears* to measure what it was designed to measure. Appearances, however, even in the area of personality tests, can frequently mislead. It is more important for *concurrent validity* to be demonstrated for a test. This refers to the degree of agreement between a test and other measures of the same thing used at the same time. *Predictive validity* indicates the efficiency with which the test results predict future behaviours (e.g. someone scoring highly on a test of neuroticism should be more likely to receive treatment for neurosis at a later stage).

Construct validity is a notion formulated by Cronbach and Meehl (1955). For many measurements there are no good criteria with which the test score can be correlated, either concurrently or predictively. For these, validity depends on the gradual accumulation of evidence from diverse research studies showing a network of relationships between the measure and other concepts which are theoretically relevant. A test may only be said to possess construct validity if a substantial number of studies has yielded results consistent with its underlying assumptions. Kline (1983) illustrates the notion by describing a hypothetical test of anxiety which, in order to attain construct validity, must be shown to relate to the likelihood of admission to a psychiatric clinic and the prescription of tranquillizing drugs. It should also be shown to: correlate with other tests of anxiety (e.g. self-reported mood changes and observer ratings) and not to correlate with variables *not* related to anxiety (e.g. intelligence); be elevated in people with anxiety as part of their symptomatology, under conditions of experimental stress and when people are in life crises; be lowered following appropriate psychological intervention or after taking tranquillizing drugs. Thus construct validity studies frequently involve numerous assessments of both predictive and concurrent validity.

There is no simple way in which we may deem a test as valid or invalid. It may be useful in some situations or for some purposes but turn out to be lacking in predictive power in other instances.

Relationship of theory and therapy

It will soon become apparent on reading this book that most theoretical approaches to personality suggest methods of psychological treatment as well as explanations for and measurement of mental disorders. It could be argued that a good way of examining the adequacy of a theory would be to assess the effectiveness of the treatment derived from it. In the past, the wish to validate psychological theories was the major motivation behind studies of the effectiveness of different forms of psychological treatment. There are, however, serious weaknesses in this form of validation. Even if a theory contains very clear suggestions as to why a particular disorder arises, it does not follow that a method of treatment based on that theory will be developed. To take an example, the medical profession has clear evidence linking coronary heart disease with particular life-styles, but this has not led to effective cures; in fact, doctors are on the whole unsuccessful at persuading people to alter the way they eat, drink and smoke. Conversely, tranquillizers (drugs which reduce anxiety) are often very effective but tell us nothing about why people become anxious – an example of treatment in the absence of a theory.

Similarly, aspirin provides a good treatment for, but so far no explanation of, headaches.

Even if it casts no light at all on the adequacy of the theories which inspired them, it is essential to know which of a number of rival treatments is most cost-effective. Since the 1950s the outcome of psychotherapeutic interventions has been one of the most controversial questions in clinical psychology. The large number of studies comparing the outcome of different methods of treatment has been exhaustively reviewed in the past few years (see, for example, Smith *et al.*, 1980; Landman and Dawes, 1982; Shapiro and Shapiro, 1982; Steinbrueck *et al.*, 1983). The overall conclusion has been that there are only relatively small differences in effectiveness between therapies. Most of the variability in therapeutic outcome is not explained by theoretical orientation. Individual studies frequently produce results favouring one treatment approach or another for particular problems, but the differences are not marked when all the studies are considered together.

There is, however, no general agreement concerning the scientific status of these results. Many psychologists feel that the practical problems in assessing therapeutic outcome are too great to permit any meaningful conclusions to be drawn. Conclusions from outcome investigations may not be applicable to everyday practice, as such studies tend to involve less severely disturbed clients, substantially briefer treatments and a much higher degree of direct control over what the therapist does than is usual in clinical work.

It has also been suggested by workers of very different orientations that the effectiveness of psychological therapies is not specific to a particular theory but is rather based on more general factors such as how firmly the client expects to get better and how warm and caring the therapist seems to be. If this is so, the outcome literature is clearly not worth pursuing from a theoretical standpoint. Thus, although we shall consider the treatments derived from the personality theories we discuss, we will not consider their effectiveness as evidence for or against the theory itself.

2

The psychoanalytic approach: classical theory

'Freud won't go away', despite the disenchantment of the psychological community with many of his views. Jahoda pointed this out in her provocative address to the British Psychological Society in 1972. Watson, one of the first advocates of behaviourism, predicted in 1930 (p. 27) that 'twenty years from now an analyst using Freudian concepts and Freudian terminology will be placed on the same plane as a phrenologist' (a person practising the nineteenth-century art of telling people's characters by feeling bumps on their head). The inaccuracy of Watson's forecast is attributed by Jahoda to the fundamental psychological questions raised by Freud's ideas.

Following the lead of Sandler, Dare and Holder (1972), we shall divide the development of psychoanalytic thought into four phases, the first three of which correspond to models of the mind developed by Freud. The final phase dealing with developments after his death will be outlined in the next chapter.

First phase: the affect-trauma model

Freud's first major psychoanalytic proposal concerned the nature of hysteria (a condition in which the patient experiences physical symptoms, such as paralysis, in the absence of any organic cause). Together with Breuer, he discovered that the symptoms of the hysteric had psychological meaning and could not be attributed simply to the degeneration of the nervous system as had been previously thought (Breuer and Freud, 1895). Freud's model of neurosis at this time assumed that hysterics had experienced some major emotional trauma which, as it was unacceptable to the conscious mind, had been repressed (forgotten). The emotions (affects) induced by the forgotten trauma continue to press for discharge (expression) into consciousness. Freud held that the patient's symptoms were caused by a breakthrough of this 'strangulated' affect. The exact nature of the symptoms could be seen to link them with the forgotten traumatic event. The following real-life example demonstrates all the crucial components of the affect-trauma model of abnormal personality. A soldier developed a bizarre blindness for objects which were either about fifteen or about thirty-five yards away from him. He recalled under hypnosis that his best friend had been shot when he was standing fifteen yards away from him by a sniper who was some thirty-five yards distant. This memory had been unacceptable to his consciousness and needed to be repressed because he had felt responsible for his friend's death (at the time he found himself unable to return the sniper's fire and so protect his friend).

Although the trauma could, as in this example, be a recent event, Freud believed that most involved childhood or early adolescent experiences that had aroused feelings which could not be fully expressed or resolved at the time: for example, sexual seductions in childhood were frequently recalled by his female hysterical patients during treatment. Freud's therapy involved helping them to release the pent-up emotion (catharsis) by bringing the repressed trauma back into consciousness (abreaction), largely through the use of hypnosis.

Second phase: the topographical model

By the turn of the century Freud had discovered that memories of childhood seduction produced by his patients were not real recollections but probably fantasies relating to unconscious

25

wishes. Such repressed wishes may find expression through dreams, albeit in an indirect form: thus the dream of a small child about losing a favourite pet might be an expression of an unconscious wish to 'lose' or at any rate be rid of a sibling. Freud realized that the fulfilment of many of these wishes would be highly threatening and felt that this was one reason why so many dreams were associated with the experience of anxiety. Unconscious wishes may sometimes inadvertently receive direct expression in so-called slips of the tongue, as when, recently, an American woman senator talked in highly indignant terms about ideological repression in the United States 'for feminists, homosexuals and other perversions – I mean persuasions!'

The three systems of the mind

In constructing his psychological model of dreaming, Freud distinguished three layers of the mind. The deepest layer, the *system unconscious*, was thought to be made up of desires, impulses or wishes of a mostly sexual and sometimes destructive nature. The dominating concern of the system unconscious was the fulfilment of these desires or, as Freud called it, the 'pleasure principle'.

The mode of thinking in the system unconscious was assumed by Freud to be fundamentally different from conscious thinking. Such 'primary process' thinking was assumed to be impulsive, disorganized, incomprehensible to rational thought, dominated by bizarre visual imagery and untroubled by considerations of time, order or logical consistency. Freud felt that dreams were to a large extent the product of these primary thought processes. Although frequently bizarre and usually baffling to conscious thought, dreams could be interpreted if the mechanisms of distortion were successfully unravelled.

Freud reported a dream of seeing his sleeping mother being carried into the room by some bird-headed people. Freud interpreted the dream as a disguised expression of his sexual feelings for his mother; the word for bird (*vogel*) is similar to the German slang word for having sex (*vogeln*). Similar instances of play on words in dreams were reported in an experimental study by Berger (1963). In this study sleeping (and dreaming) subjects had the name of a close friend presented to them auditorily and, when awoken, were asked to recall their dreams. The subjects were not aware of hearing the stimuli, but nevertheless the names were often involved in the dreams indirectly, in puns (e.g. the name 'Gillian' was represented in the dream by a woman from Chile – a Chilean) or by association (e.g. the name 'Richard' giving rise to a dream of shopping in a store of that name).

The *system pre-conscious* forms the middle layer within this topographical model and acts to censor forbidden wishes, only allowing access to consciousness if they are so distorted that their unconscious origins cannot be detected. The psychological phenomenon of perceptual defence can be explained in similar terms.

Work in this field, summarized by Dixon (1981), demonstrated that some subjects have higher perceptual thresholds for emotional stimuli (such as the word 'cancer') than for neutral words. A number of experimental studies used the procedure of presenting neutral and emotional words to subjects, initially for such short durations that they were unaware of seeing the word. The exposure of the word is gradually increased until the subject is able to recognize it. These studies and others using more elaborate methodologies found that for some subjects emotional words needed to be presented for longer periods of time in order to be recognized. It is assumed that subjects perceive and evaluate the word pre-consciously but that because of its conflictual nature its entry into consciousness is hindered. This provides some evidence for Freud's suggestion that the motive for censorship is the avoidance of displeasure associated with conflictual ideas.

The uppermost layer of the mind is the *system conscious*, which is organized in terms of logic and reason, its main function being the handling of external reality, the avoidance of danger and the maintenance of civilized behaviour. The conscious part of the mind is dominated by the 'secondary processes' or what Freud also called the 'reality principle'.

Freud redefined the notion of trauma in this model. Trauma was thought to occur if the conscious part of the mind was overwhelmed by irresistible urges to gratify unconscious wishes, by an intolerable feeling of rejection or by extreme punishment.

Psychosexual development

In addition, Freud constructed a view of human life determined by primitive internal urges which the individual needs to master in the course of his/her development in order to conform to the demands of society. These urges or instincts are said to have their source in the body's metabolism. They are represented mentally in terms of wishes and are directed towards external objects for their satisfaction. He called them sexual instincts, although the word 'sexual' was used in a rather special sense to mean something like 'physically pleasurable'.

Freud (1905) identified three stages in the development of these infantile urges. Each was distinguished on the basis of the zone of the body through which the sexual drive manifested itself at the time. The first phase, the oral, is dominated by instinctual pleasure obtained via oral stimulation. After the age of two years, the focus of pleasure shifts to the anus (anal stage) and the child obtains pleasure from defaecation. Between three and four years of age, the focus shifts yet again to the penis in boys and to the clitoris in girls (phallic stage). This stage is followed by a period of relative calm in psychosexual development (latency stage) which lasts until the onset of puberty. Sexuality returns in adolescence, and in normal development all previous stages of libidinal fixation come to be integrated within genital sexuality.

At each of these stages the child is faced with conflicts between instinctual desires and the conscious activities of the mind. The manner in which the child deals with such conflicts was thought by Freud to have a profound influence on the future development of his/her personality. Stages where instinctual desires are either completely frustrated or too readily gratified may become points of 'fixation' in the development of personality, points to which the adult may well return if confronted by intolerable stresses in later life.

The *oral stage* (Abraham, 1927; Glover, 1924) is commonly divided into two phases: the first, during which the baby sucks, and later an 'oral-sadistic' phase of biting. Two types of oral personality corresponding to these two phases have been described. The first is dominated by passivity, relaxation and dependence, corresponding to a perpetuation of the baby's pleasure at being held by mother at the breast along with a confident belief that the milk will arrive. The second personality type, normally associated with the period of weaning, is characterized by activity and aggression, which can be seen as a perpetuation of the pleasure of biting.

These sources of pleasure can be observed to continue in

individuals who are unable to resist using the oral channel for gratification: for example, individuals who persist in sucking their thumbs, chewing on pencils or Biros, who talk all the time or console themselves by eating when unhappy. On the other hand, a person may try to fend off the desire to give in to these pleasures by manifesting extreme independence, impatience or cynicism. Fisher and Greenberg (1977) summarize the oral character as being preoccupied with issues of giving and taking, concerns about independence and dependence, extremes of optimism and pessimism, unusual ambivalence, impatience and the continued use of the oral channel for gratification.

Several studies have examined whether these 'oral characteristics' do indeed appear together in the same individual. Kline and Storey (1978, 1980) found evidence that the qualities of dependency, fluency, sociability and a liking for novelty and relaxation were associated with one another and corresponded well with psychoanalytic descriptions of the individual whose personality is most strongly affected by the first passive, receptive, sucking phase of the oral stage – oral optimism. They further found that the qualities of independence, verbal aggression, envy, coldness, hostility, malice and impatience were highly correlated, suggesting the oral pessimistic attitude of the infant disappointed and dissatisfied at the breast. Despite these encouraging findings, Howarth (1980, 1982) questioned the existence of these personality types and found that oral optimism was more simply accounted for as an aspect of sociability than as anything to do with psychoanalytic theory. Furthermore, there is almost no evidence to link these personality syndromes with particular patterns of breast-feeding experiences.

The second stage of instinctual development is linked to *anal pleasures* (Freud, 1908; Jones, 1923) and the child's conflicts with the parents over potty-training. Anal fixation occurs if conflicts over anal matters were particularly intense, either because of especially strict toilet-training or because of exceptionally intense pleasure associated with this period. In western society, anal pleasures, unlike oral ones, are socially unacceptable and are therefore rarely perpetuated into adult life. Thus fixation in the anal stage leads to the perpetuation of indirect expressions of anal erotic wishes or to attempts to defend against them. The intense struggle between child and caretaker over toilet-training is thought to be perpetuated in the character traits of obstinacy and

29

stinginess: the child refusing to give up his/her valuable possession (the faeces) at the say-so of his/her parents. The child will frequently feel the need to inhibit the wish to make a terrible mess. The defence against this wish is reflected in the opposite desire to be orderly, tidy and meticulous. The so-called anal (or obsessive-compulsive) character is therefore typified by orderliness, obstinacy, rigidity and a hatred of waste.

There is general agreement amongst reviewers that the major qualities that classical psychoanalysts ascribe to the anally oriented personality do tend to be found together (Fisher and Greenberg, 1977; Pollack, 1979; Kline, 1981). Howarth (1982), despite his criticisms of the oral personality, accepted that there is a personality type epitomized by the neat, pedantic, clear, self-controlled and controlling individual who in a methodical and orderly way runs the bureaucracies of most nations. There is no evidence to suggest that individuals of this type received toilet-training that was in any way different from that of less obsessive-compulsive characters. Yet there is evidence which links measures of anxiety over bowel habits on the one hand to measures of orderliness, obstinacy and parsimony on the other. Rosenwald (1972), for example, demonstrated that the amount of anxiety experienced by persons about anal matters predicted how carefully they arranged magazines when requested to do so by the experimenter.

It is in a sense unfortunate that so much psychological research effort has been devoted to the investigation of the above aspects of psychoanalytic theory because since the 1920s few psychoanalysts (including Freud himself in his later years) have considered seriously this extremely simplistic view of character formation. This, of course, does not mean that analysts have abandoned the concepts of psychosexual development, but the relationship between instinctual wishes and personality development is nowadays considered to be a great deal more complex than in Freud's first formulation.

The phallic stage is the third stage of psychosexual development and is the one during which the so-called *Oedipus complex* arises. In the little boy, the phallic stage is thought to commence when, at the age of three to four years, his sexual interest comes to be focused on his penis and he becomes sexually interested in his mother. His masculinity is awakened, and this prompts him to seek to take over his father's role. He now sees his father as a rival whom he would like to push aside. His aspirations are, of course, unrealistic, and this soon becomes apparent even to him. What is more, he fears that his all-powerful, all-seeing father might discover his line of thinking and seek terrible vengeance by depriving him of that part of his body which is the current focus of his sexual interest. Under the imagined threat of castration and following the time-honoured principle of 'if you can't beat them, join them', the boy decides to give up his interest in his mother and to deal with the threat of castration by identifying with his father.

In girls, the Oedipus complex is complicated by two factors. Firstly, girls are forced to change their object of primary affection from the mother to the father as they move into the phallic stage. (With boys, it is the mother who remains the primary object of affection throughout early childhood.) Secondly, the girl's turning towards father is prompted at least in part by her disappointment with mother for not having equipped her with what she sees as a highly desirable and useful organ, a penis. The girl aims to have a penis at her command by seducing father, and later develops the fantasy of having his baby which at an unconscious level she equates with a penis. In girls, the end of the Oedipus complex is prompted not by fear of physical injury but by fear of the loss of mother's love. The fear of retribution is less intense in girls than in boys, with the result that Oedipal attitudes are less strongly repressed in women, the father frequently remaining a sexually attractive figure.

The fascinating illustrations from mythology quoted by Freud cannot be said to constitute scientific support for his formulations. There is scant evidence for the Oedipus complex in the experimental literature. Studies of children's attitudes to parents at the supposedly Oedipal stage do not bear out the predicted shift in positive feelings from mother to father in boys and from mother to father and back to mother in girls (Kagan and Lemkin, 1960). The finding that boys are more concerned about physical injury than girls is consistent with but cannot be held to prove the existence of castration anxiety (Pitcher and Prelinger, 1963).

Investigations of penis envy have found no evidence that women assess their bodies as in any way inferior to those of men (Fisher, 1973); in fact, different lines of evidence suggest that on the whole women feel more comfortable, secure and confident about their bodies than do men. Referring to Freud's speculation that pregnancy is associated with a fantasy of possessing a penis, Greenberg and Fisher (1983) argued that women should experience preg-nancy as a time of heightened 'phallic feelings'. Their measure-ment of phallic feelings was based on the number of penis-like objects women identified in shapeless ink-blots. They found that women during pregnancy tended to report seeing more elongated objects (e.g. arrows, spears and rockets), more body protrusions (e.g. noses, tongues sticking out and fingers), body attachments (e.g. horns, cigars and snorkels) and the like than they did either before or after pregnancy or than did non-pregnant women. The authors claim that this research supports Freud's suspicion that the penis assumes an important role in the unconscious psychic life of women. This kind of evidence is likely to meet with substantial and probably appropriate scepticism and perhaps even with hostility. Evidence based on projective tests such as the ink-blot tests is frequently unreliable, as a large number of alternative explanations could be put forward to account for the data. Certainly, even within the psychoanalytic camp, Freud's rather Victorian attitudes to women have not been accepted without criticism (Mitchell, 1973).

Theory of neurosis

Freud made an important distinction between neurotic symptoms and character traits. Whilst character (personality) traits owe their existence to the successful defence against instinctual impulses, neurotic symptoms come into being as a result of the failure of repression. In normal development, the child progresses through the psychosexual stages with his/her instinctual strivings getting closer and closer to adult genital sexuality. Certain experiences may result in the fixation of psychosexual energy (libido) at these earlier stages. Fixation is likely to occur at stages associated with particularly intense conflicts. If psychosexual development is seen as the onward marching of troops, then fixation resembles the establishment of garrisons at various points with a consequent weakening of the onward marching force. During times of psychological stress the libido may regress to a point of libidinal fixation so that the person comes to be dominated by the associ-ated infantile wishes. The problem is that whereas in infancy these wishes are normal, an adult or even an older child would be greatly disturbed by and thus would be struggling against intense Oedipal, anal or oral wishes. The obsessional patient, for example, who washed his/her hands for an hour and a half after having gone to the toilet was seen by Freud as struggling with instinctual wishes characteristic of the anal stage. His/her symptom represented at one and the same time the wish to soil and the defence against it.

The idea that neurotics experience more intense pre-genital (oral, anal or phallic) impulses received some support from a study by Kline (1979). He demonstrated that a person's oral optimistic, oral pessimistic (first and second phases of oral stage) and anal fixation scores (on questionnaires designed by this author) taken together correlated with their overall degree of neuroticism.

An important development in this model concerned the role of *aggression*. In his early thinking, Freud was preoccupied with the problems of the psychosexual drives and saw aggression as a response to the frustration of these urges. The horrors of the First World War made a profound impression on him, and he began to be aware of the significance of destructive urges in human behaviour. Gradually Freud (1915, 1923) started to view aggression as an impulse every bit as important as sex and also an inherent quality of human nature. Aggression and destructiveness are elicited when a person is sufficiently thwarted or abused, and the pressure for their satisfaction needs to be defended against and controlled in just the same way as do the sexual urges.

Third phase: structural model

Freud gradually realized that his topographical model was too simplistic and unable to provide answers to a number of elementary questions, such as: where do we find a non-sexual instinct capable of repressing the sexual one, and why are people unable to stop themselves from being their own worst enemies?

Structures of the mind

He rethought his model substantially and conceived of three structures in the mind (enduring organizations which were nevertheless to some extent open to change). The first, entirely unconscious, structure, the *id*, was the reservoir of sexual and aggressive drives, as the system unconscious had been in the previous model.

The second structure, the *superego*, was seen as the organized psychic representation of childhood parental authority figures.

33

The child's picture of the parents is naturally not realistic. The internalized authority figure was therefore held to be stricter and harsher than the parents were in reality. The superego becomes a vehicle for the ideals derived from parents and hence from society. It is the source of guilt, and as such is important in normal and pathological mental funtioning. The superego is partly conscious but largely unconscious.

The third component of this model was the *ego*. It was the ego's supposed function to cope with the demands and restrictions of external reality and to mediate initially between the drives and reality and, later on, as a moral sense develops, between the drives and the superego. To achieve this the ego has a capacity for conscious perception and problem-solving to deal with external reality, and it has the mechanisms of defence available to it to regulate internal forces. Although parts of the ego are conscious, much of its struggling with the internal demands placed upon it by the id and superego occurs unconsciously.

Consciousness in the structural model was conceived of simply as a sense organ of the ego. In Freud's view, most sophisticated psychological processes could function without the benefit of consciousness. This is consistent with a viewpoint, now prevalent in cognitive and experimental psychology, that conscious awareness is limited to the products of mental processes and that the processes themselves are beyond the reach of introspection (see Mandler, 1975).

This model of the mind attributed much more significance to external events and less to the sexual motive than the previous one. Anxiety, guilt and the pain of loss were seen as very much more important in explaining abnormal behaviour than were sexual drives. Defences were no longer viewed as simple barriers against unconscious impulses but as ways of modifying and adapting unconscious impulses and also of protecting the ego from the external world. Anxiety, seen by Freud in the previous model as undischarged sexual energy, was here seen as a signal of danger arising within the ego whenever external demands or internal impulses represented a major threat. This might occur under a threat of loss of love or of enormous guilt as well as a threat of physical injury.

These three structures were conceived by Freud as metaphors, as a way of conceptualizing his clinical observations. He never postulated that anatomical structures corresponding to the id, ego or superego could be located. Some neurophysiologists have tried to do so, although none has succeeded in pairing parts of the brain with Freud's three psychic structures (Hadley, 1983). However, there is some psychometric evidence to indicate that the distinction between the three mental structures drawn intuitively by Freud can be demonstrated empirically. In a large rating scale and questionnaire-based factor-analytic survey of motivational factors, Cattell (1957) and Pawlik and Cattell (1964) identified three dimensions of psychological functioning that arguably fitted in well with the id/ego/superego distinction. As it is unlikely that questionnaires can provide access to an individual's unconscious functioning, and as the identification of dimensions in the statistical procedure of factor analysis is in many ways a fairly arbitrary affair, we cannot regard this study as confirmation of Freud's motivational system; we can only say that it provides an interesting but independent alternative perspective.

Defence mechanisms

The identification of defence mechanisms was one of Freud's early achievements, but it was not until the advent of the structural model that their function and organization could be adequately elaborated (A. Freud, 1937). Defences are unconscious strategies serving to protect the individual from painful affect (anxiety or guilt). Such affect may arise in three ways: through conflict over impulses (ego versus id, e.g. a wish to murder a younger brother), moral conflict (ego versus superego, e.g. a prohibition against cheating in an exam) and external threat (ego versus reality, e.g. a violent disagreement between parents).

The first defence mechanism to be described by Freud was *repression*. This is the process by which an unacceptable impulse or idea is rendered unconscious. It has been suggested that repression is the primary form of defence and that it is in response to its failure that other defences are called into operation. *Projection* is the mechanism whereby unwanted ideas or impulses originating in the self are attributed to others. Thus, what was an inadmissible active wish is permitted to appear in a distorted form as a passively experienced outcome. This is how the object of one's anger frequently comes to be feared. The unacceptable impulse ('I hate him') is externalized onto the object ('He hates me').

Reaction formation is a mechanism that serves to maintain

repression by intensifying its antithesis (opposite). For instance, people disturbed by cruel impulses towards animals might find joining the RSPCA helpful. This would protect them from expressing aggressive impulses by channelling all their energies into preserving rather than destroying life. The nature of their efforts may at times give us a clue to the character of the original impulse: an example of this is the ardent animal-lover who published a pamphlet describing fifteen ways of painlessly killing a rabbit.

Other defence mechanisms include *denial* (perceiving but refusing to acknowledge), *displacement* (the transfer of affect from one stimulus to another), *isolation* (feelings split off from thought), *suppression* (the conscious decision to avoid attending to a stimulus), *sublimation* (the gratifying of an impulse by giving it a socially acceptable aim), *regression* (reversion to a previously gratifying level of functioning), *acting out* (allowing one's actions to directly express an unconscious impulse) and *intellectualization* (the separation of a threatening impulse from its emotional context and placing it in a sometimes inappropriate rational framework).

The defence mechanisms have been the subject of intensive experimental research, although little that is conclusive has emerged. Repression, for example, has been studied in the laboratory, usually by creating anxiety in subjects associated with a particular type of material and seeing if the rate of forgetting is affected. In an extensive review, Holmes (1974) found no evidence of repression in these studies. Wilkinson and Cargill (1955), however, found that Oedipal stories were recalled significantly worse than ones with a neutral theme. In his review, Kline (1981) felt this latter study was persuasive, as was the work of Levinger and Clark (1961), which demonstrated that words to which subjects had strong emotional responses were recalled less well than were neutral words.

The theory of neurosis

In the structural model, Freud conceived of the neurotic symptom as representing a combination of unacceptable impulses which threaten to overwhelm the ego and the defences utilized by the individual against them. Anxiety, the hallmark of most neurotic reaction types, was seen by Freud as the reaction of the ego signalling the imminent danger of being overwhelmed and mobilizing its defensive capabilities, in much the same way that a fire alarm set off at the first sign of smoke might be aimed at summoning the assistance of the fire brigade. The neurotic reaction types are distinguished by the manner in which the ego defends itself against the anxiety and guilt engendered by childhood impulses. Thus, in phobias Freud saw the operation of the mechanisms of projection and displacement. A little boy projects his own envious and jealous anger onto his father because of the love and fear he himself is unable to express directly, and ends up by seeing him as a murderously angry man. Yet this also may become too painful and frightening to bear, and the fear is then displaced onto objects with whom he has less intimate ties: thus he may become terrified of burglars whom he fears might come to kill him during the night.

A paranoid person was thought to use reaction formation as a defence against conflictual homosexual impulses. 'I love him' turns into 'I hate him', which by projection becomes 'He hates me'. Experimental evidence from Zamansky (1958) showing that paranoids fixate longer on homosexual pictures than do controls confirmed numerous clinical observations of intense conflict over homosexual impulses in such individuals.

In obsessive-compulsive neurosis, Freud thought individuals defended against aggressive impulses by reaction formation. Thus they may turn the feared wish to murder brutally into endless concern over the safety of the person concerned. Sometimes the aggression was fended off by isolation, individuals continuing to experience the violent images consciously but feeling that they are bizarre, do not belong and are being thrust upon them from outside. The formulation of obsessional neurosis as due to underlying hostility was supported by a study of Manchanda *et al.* (1979), who found increased hostility in obsessional neurotics on a questionnaire measure.

It was believed that depression involved dealing with ambivalent feelings by turning unconscious aggressive wishes against the self. Silverman (1983) reviewed studies appearing to provide substantial evidence for psychoanalytic formulations of depression. In a number of studies it was demonstrated that the subthreshold presentation of stimuli designed to stir up unconscious aggressive wishes (e.g. a picture of a snarling man holding a dagger) led to a worsening of depression on mood-rating scales.

Evaluation

We shall evaluate developments from Freudian theory in the next chapter, but as all those developments are based on Freud's work it might be useful to mention some of the criticisms that have been directed at his original contributions:

1 Freud *ignored spiritual values* and was strongly anti-religious in his outlook.
2 He *neglected the social nature* of humankind and contributed little to our understanding of the psychology of groups and social systems.
3 He thought of human beings as striving constantly to reduce the internal pressure created by drives and thus neglected drives such as *curiosity*, which are associated with increases rather than the decrease of internal tension and thus were not consistent with his theory of motivation.
4 He told us little about the nature of what is perhaps most uniquely human: *consciousness*.
5 He was *unable to predict* the future path of an individual's development, and he only commented on a person's current life in terms of his/her past.
6 Feminists feel that Freud *misunderstood women* and was too strongly affected by prevailing cultural influences.
7 Most criticisms, however, concern *the data base of psychoanalysis*:
(a) his conclusions were based on a *selected sample* of middle-class Viennese;
(b) his data consisted of his *biased recollections* of what patients said to him during a session which he sometimes did not write down until long after the session had ended;
(c) to the extent that he used patients' responses as confirmatory evidence of his interpretations, he may be accused of *influencing his patients* towards accepting his comments.
8 Equally important are the *inadequacies of formal aspects of his theorization*:
(a) his terms are *ambiguous*, with frequently changing meanings;
(b) he uses many *metaphors*, and his tendency to *reify* these (pretend that the metaphors corresponded to real entities) sometimes led to major logical fallacies, such as appearing to talk about parts of a person's mind as if it had all the properties of an entire individual;

(c) his theory *lacks parsimony* (more assumptions are made than are needed to account for the data).

9 The inadequacies of his theorization make the theory *difficult to test* using simple experimental methodology.

We shall return to the status of the evidence supporting Freud's contentions in the next chapter. There can be no doubt, however, that each of these criticisms has some validity and that the conceptual and scientific foundations of Freud's formulations are profoundly inadequate in a number of areas. It is a puzzle why in spite of its obvious flaws Freud's theory has remained amongst the most influential theories of personality in clinical practice. The key is perhaps to be found in the intuitive appeal of psychoanalytic ideas: they provide many clinicians with a framework within which to view aspects of their clients' behaviour which would otherwise appear incomprehensible. Until another theory emerges which addresses the same range of experiences it is likely that a large number of clinicians will continue to treat Freud's ideas seriously despite their poor scientific status.

3

Post-Freudian psychoanalysis

Psychoanalytic thought following Freud's death developed in two fundamentally different ways. In the United States and, to a lesser extent, Britain, certain psychoanalysts grew dissatisfied with the limitations of Freud's approach. These analysts endeavoured to elaborate further the functioning of the ego, focusing on those parts of it not actively involved in the struggles with the id or the superego. Meanwhile, primarily in Britain, another group of analysts concentrated on studying the effects of early relationships, especially that between the infant and his/her mother. There were many other important developments originating from Freud's work, those of Jung, Horney, Sullivan and Adler being examples. At present, however, the most prolific theorists are in the areas of *ego psychology* and *object-relations theory* which we will now consider in turn.

Ego psychology

Heinz Hartmann (1939) originated a new psychoanalytic approach to personality based on the study of the ego which he felt was a notion neglected by Freud. The central theme of Hartmann's conception was that the ego is not solely involved in conflicts with warring internal structures but is also capable of functioning independently of drives or of involvement in conflicts. The ego was seen as capable, given an adequate environment, of perceiving, learning, remembering, thinking, moving, acting, organizing, synthesizing and achieving a balance. These capabilities were referred to as the *autonomous functions of the ego*.

Using this framework it became possible for psychoanalysts to incorporate the developmental ideas of Piaget (1963/9) into their theoretical framework. Malerstein and Ahern (1982), for example, distinguished three personality types on the basis of the predominance of particular Piagetian developmental stages in the character structure of the individual. Research on neonates (Lichtenberg, 1981) suggests the existence of a very early capacity for differentiating, timing, screening, pattern-matching, sorting and discriminating perceptual materials. These findings back up the emphasis ego psychology places on such functions being an independent, conflict-free part of the ego.

From this background, Erikson (1959) proposed a psychosocial model of ego development. He emphasized the notion of *developmental crises*. These were held to occur at each of eight stages of development (partially corresponding to Freud's psychosexual stages but also considering the problems of transition to early, middle and late adulthood) and are brought about by the individual's need to adapt to changed circumstances and social expectations brought about by the power of maturation.

Each crisis is characterized by its own pair of opposing (desirable and undesirable) personality traits (for example, the stage of basic trustfulness versus mistrustfulness from birth to eighteen months). With the resolution of each crisis, the individual acquires a relatively permanent balance between the desirable and undesirable traits designating that stage. Amongst all of Erikson's stages, the stage of '*adolescent crisis*' (the opposition of identity and role confusion) has made most impact. Longitudinal studies of development (e.g. Block, 1981) have recently provided some support for Erikson's developmental model.

A major innovation introduced by Hartmann concerned the gratification available to the organism from the sheer exercise of its functions (e.g. the pleasure a child gains from learning to walk or draw). Additionally, ego psychologists (notably Rapaport,

41

1967) emphasized that the seeking of stimuli, described as a search for novelty (or curiosity), was necessary for normal development. This enabled some psychoanalysts to move away from Freud's severely criticized (cf. Klein, 1976) motivational system, which had tension reduction as its sole aim. In the current psychoanalytic view, the ego is a balance-inducing system striving to find an optimal level of tension using induction as well as reduction.

Ego psychology has undoubtedly been the most influential psychoanalytic model in the United States. Furthermore, of all the major psychoanalytic approaches it has come the closest to achieving a unification with general psychology; yet it has met with a substantial amount of criticism over the past decade. Ego psychology was developed by Hartmann and his colleagues to meet criticisms of formal aspects of psychoanalytic theory such as its logical inconsistency and lack of a systematic approach. However, many psychoanalysts now feel that the improvements were illusory and that the theory remains as confused and conceptually inadequate as the classical approach (Schafer, 1976). In a critical vein, Holt (1976) called instinct theory, which remained a corner-stone of ego psychology, the 'shame of psychoanalysis'; so riddled was it with philosophical and factual errors and fallacies that nothing short of discarding the concept would do. George Klein (1976) recommended the abandonment of all of psychoanalytic theory not directly concerned with the understanding of clinical problems presented by psychoanalytic clients. This would cover aspects professing to identify general psychological structures and mechanisms such as the ego and instincts. Perhaps in response to these inadequacies of the ego psychological approach, American analysts are increasingly turning to the British tradition of psychoanalytic thought.

The object-relations approach

The paranoid-schizoid and depressive positions (Klein)

Initial interest in psychoanalysis was directed towards understanding the importance of drives upon the development of the psychic apparatus and psychopathology. Subsequently the focus shifted to the mediating and controlling functions of the ego, its mechanisms of defence, the characteristics of its normal functioning and the interactions of these with drives. Developments in Britain and most recent developments in the United States represent a movement away from the formal mechanistic framework of structures, forces and energies which characterized Freud's structural model and Hartmann's ego psychology. The movement is towards a more clinically oriented theory primarily concerned with the development of the infant, its sense of self, its relationships with its care-givers (its objects) and the implications of the internal representations of such relationships on future development. Thus psychoanalytic attention has shifted from the microscopic analysis of thought processes to the examination of self-other relationships using a language much closer to that of day-to-day experience. Melanie Klein's (1932, 1948) approach is chiefly distinguished by being the first to emphasize the importance of infants' earliest relationships. Her developments of Freud's ideas were based on primarily her work with extremely disturbed children, in which she discovered that she could interpret children's play in a way similar to that used to interpret the verbal associations of adults.

Perhaps the most far-reaching of her theoretical contributions has been her insistence that neurosis has its origins in the first year of life. She saw as the main source of difficulty at this stage, infants' innate ambivalence about their most important object relationship: that with the nourishing but sometimes frustrating breast. A basic assumption of her theory was that from their earliest times infants' mental lives were dominated by unbearable conflicts between love (the manifestation of the libido) and hate (the aggressive instinct). She assumed that this conflict was reduced by putting or projecting the aggressive impulses into the breast. Infants, she argued, feel temporarily safer in imagining that the anger comes not from them but from the breast. However, in this way the breast could at times become a frightening and dangerous object for them. At other times, especially during periods of extreme pleasure, the breast is felt as good, is cherished and loved.

Thus in normal development infants during the first year of life have initially to work through their fear and suspicion of the breast: this Klein called the paranoid-schizoid position. During the second half of the first year comes the painful discovery that the loved and the hated breasts are one and the same object. Klein maintained that until the infant could become confident of being loved in spite of his/her rage, every frustration, every occasion when the breast is removed and every time the mother leaves would be interpreted by the infant as a loss due to his/her own destructive fantasies. This would be accompanied by feelings of sadness, guilt and regret. Klein believed that all infants go through this repeated experience of feeling sorrow for the loved object, fear of losing it and then longing to regain it. The infant cannot get beyond this 'depressive position' until he/she becomes assured of having his/her mother's love. He/she needs to accept responsibility for the destructive fantasies and follow this by mental acts of reparation (sorrow and sadness); only then will the major hurdle to development, the depressive position, be overcome. Klein's emphasis in explaining later psychological disturbance was not in terms of the child's actual experiences, such as separations, but rather in terms of his/her internal experience of infancy, in which unconscious fantasies and wishes predominate. Those individuals who as infants were unable to adequately negotiate the depressive position will never succeed in establishing a stable internal image of a good and loving object. Such individuals will always be more likely to feel insufficiently loved and are further presumed by Klein to be predisposed to return to the depressive position with consequent feelings of loss, sorrow, guilt, anxiety and low self-esteem: in other words, they are particularly prone to depression and other psychological problems.

Kleinian theory has been very influential in British psychoanalysis and is receiving increasing attention in the United States. In its exclusive emphasis on instincts it is more uncompromising than Freudian theory. Its main impact on psychoanalysis has been its stress on infants' relationships with their mothers and the central importance of the adequate resolution of this ambivalent relationship for later development. It should be noted, however, that Klein attaches little importance to infants' actual experience of mothering. Thus, as her statements about the inner world of children are not linked to anything that may be happening in the external world her views are more or less impossible to verify empirically. In light of the numerous unwarranted assumptions that she makes concerning infants' fantasy lives we must regard her theory with some scepticism. In evaluating Klein's contributions it is perhaps more important to stress the theoretical developments which her ideas have stimulated rather than the content of her ideas *per se*.

The schizoid personality and the good-enough mother
(Fairbairn and Winnicott)

Fairbairn (1952) and Winnicott (1953) were British analysts who were greatly affected by Melanie Klein's views concerning early development. They both found it hard to accept Klein's exclusive reliance on the classical theory of instincts. Fairbairn was the first to point out that the satisfaction of instinctual drives should not be regarded as the person's aim; the main source of motivation was instead to find a suitable person with whom a human relationship could be established through which needs could be safely gratified. Thus Fairbairn reformulated Freud's theory of the libido. No longer was it seen as a system directing the person towards physical pleasure; by contrast, Fairbairn was impressed by its tendency to send individuals in search of relationships, in search of objects.

As one patient of Fairbairn's put it: 'You're always talking about my wanting this or that desire satisfied, but what I really want is someone to look after me, like a father'. The essence of Fairbairn's approach lies in his emphasis on the strivings and difficulties of the ego in its endeavour to reach an object (a person/relationship) from whom it may find support. For Fairbairn, the ego was not a mechanism of control over other physical systems but was conceptualized as a self. He believed that the self was made up of internalized images of past persons of importance to the individual. These internalized early relationships and the feelings that accompanied them, so he claimed, make up our current experience of ourselves.

One of Fairbairn's greatest contributions was the description of the *schizoid personality*. Such a person is sometimes outwardly quite successful but is in fact a solitary, withdrawn figure who cannot relate to people and, even when in a relationship, gives little or nothing to the other person. Fairbairn (1963) linked this personality type to a weak, underdeveloped self produced by the mother's failure to treat the child as real: her failure to love it for its own sake, to give it spontaneous and genuine expressions of affection which it could internalize and use as the basis of a sound ego structure. This leaves the child unsure of the reality of its own ego (self) and therefore constantly playing a role, indulging in exhibitionism and afraid to give in relationships since that may feel like a permanent loss or self-emptying.

Winnicott (1953) was also concerned with the earliest phase of the mother-child relationship and the importance of what he described as '*good-enough mothering*' for the child's personality development. The child's potential for development from absolute dependence to relative independence was, he believed, strongly influenced by the quality of maternal care. In the earliest stages the infant's experience is one of undifferentiated fusion with and attachment to its primary object, most likely its mother. The 'good-enough' mother reflects this and at the child's birth loves the baby as an extension of herself, which allows her to become empathically tuned to the child's inner needs. As the child develops and becomes aware of its own needs and of the separate existence of the mother, the optimal mother-child relationship changes to allow a careful balance between gratification and frustration. Thus, the 'good-enough' mother initially behaves precisely as the infant wishes, allowing the child the fantasy that the mother is just another part of itself: in other words to feel for a time all-powerful. The child only gradually abandons this fantasy as it experiences tolerable degrees of frustration of its needs and separateness from its object (the mother). This separation, however, permits the infant to express its needs and initiative (the basis of its emerging sense of self). A mother who intrudes too much short-circuits the infant's initiatives and restricts the development of the self. A too distant mother creates for the infant anxiety accompanied by the fading of the infant's internal representation of her. Either of these failures at 'good-enough' mothering may result in the development of a 'false self' based on the necessity for compliance with the demands of the external environment. As adults such individuals will relate to the world through a compliant shell: they will be not quite real to themselves or to others.

The transition from a phase of absolute dependence (undifferentiated fusion with mother) to one of relative dependence (awareness of mother's separateness) is accomplished, according to Winnicott, by the development of 'transitional phenomena' of which the most obvious are *transitional objects*. These are often actual objects, such as a blanket, pillow or favourite teddy bear, to which the child becomes intensely attached and separation from which stirs up extreme anxiety. Attachment to the object is an immediate displacement from attachment to the mother and allows increasing degrees of separation from her. Children know that the blanket or teddy bear is not mother, and yet they react emotionally to these objects as if they were her. Giving such external objects the capacity to soothe, comfort and offer security at times of anxiety and danger permits children to explore the world around them more freely (Eagle, 1983).

Currently, object-relations theory as outlined by Fairbairn, Winnicott and other British psychoanalysts is probably the most popular psychoanalytic approach in the United Kingdom. Its fundamental postulate, that the person cannot be understood without a consideration of the relationship between mother and infant during the first year of life, has become generally accepted in the psychoanalytic world.

In terms of object-relations theory, depression can be traced back to the initially ambivalent relationship between the child and its caretaker. As infants become aware of the mother as a separate being, they also become concerned about the effect of their impulses on her. Ambivalent feelings emerge as a wish to destroy the mother whilst at the same time the child is terrified of losing this relationship of dependence. With 'good-enough' mothering, the ambivalent feelings of hate and love are combined and a good internal object is created. If this is not the case, internalization will be deficient and individuals will never be able to sustain an image of a loving and caring object which admires and cares for them and sustains their self-esteem.

Some empirical evidence supports such a contention. Blatt and Lerner (1983) reviewed studies where students were asked to give brief descriptions of their mothers and fathers. It was found that students with relatively high scores on questionnaire measures of depression also tended to give accounts of their parents which differed substantially from those of non-depressed students. They often saw their parents in terms of what they could do for them rather than as individuals in their own right. Their descriptions lacked subtlety and complexity or any reference to internal attributes such as values, thoughts or feelings. Those who were not depressed were able to consider good and bad attributes of their parents and showed greater willingness to attempt to describe the internal world of their parental figures. These studies give some support to the notion that the internal representation of relationships of those prone to depression is in some respects less complete than that of those without psychological problems.

Whereas ego psychology has attempted to improve

psychoanalysis by refining its conceptual framework, object-relations theory introduced many new concepts which, though not in direct conflict with empirical evidence, are none the less open to criticism. Many assumptions are made concerning the inner world of the infant which are difficult, if not impossible, to substantiate and are justified only if no simpler model can be advanced to account for the same data. Sandler and Sandler (1978) suggested that much of Fairbairn's and Winnicott's clinical material could be explained by a far less complex model. They put forward the idea that the fulfilment of wishes (seen by Freud as the gratification of instincts) could indeed be looked at in simpler terms, namely as the wish to repeat interactions which in the past gave pleasure or comfort. They proposed the theory that each partner in every relationship at any given time has a role for the other and explicitly (in real relationships) or implicitly (in fantasy) negotiates with that person in order to get them to respond in such a way as to restore the wished-for feeling of well-being and safety; for example, a young man may develop a relationship with a shy and diffident girl in order to restore the comfort he experienced at the feeling of being totally in control of his mother. Many psychological problems could be looked at as being attempts to repeat comforting or gratifying early relationships. Thus an agoraphobic woman who uses this manoeuvre to restrict her life by staying in bed most of the day may fulfil a wish to have her husband 'mother' her.

The theory of attachment (Bowlby)

John Bowlby has also been concerned with the mother-infant relationship but has retained a biological component in his psychoanalytic approach. Bowlby (1969) and his student Ainsworth (1973) both suggested that the infant has an inborn biological propensity to behave in ways which promote proximity and contact with a caretaker (usually the mother). Attachment then develops as a consequence of parental responsiveness to these innate behaviours during an especially sensitive period in the first years of life. Proximity and contact with a selected figure thus become goals in their own right, independent of other drives. The general tendency to seek proximity with a familiar figure appears to be a universal phenomenon that is almost impossible to extinguish whatever the conditions of rearing. Bowlby firmly believes that this requirement for an attachment figure persists throughout life; moreover, he has suggested that disturbance of attachment relationships in childhood is the cause of a considerable amount of psychological disorder later on.

Tizard and Hodges (1978) showed that infants brought up in institutions which had fast staff turnovers (some fifty different caretakers and hence no chance for the children to form lasting relationships) continue as children to be more clinging, attention-seeking and disobedient. This pattern persisted even if they had left the institution by the age of four years to live in a family. Rutter *et al*. (1984) followed up institution-reared children in their mid-twenties and found substantially more psychiatric, criminal and relationship problems in this group than in a sample taken from the general population. Moreover, outcome was significantly associated with the quality of caretaking during infancy, early and prolonged experience of multiple caretaking having particularly severe consequences. Thus it seems that the absence of stable early attachments may cause long-term problems. However, it has been suggested that the negative consequences of anxious attachment are due to other factors which are likely to be present, such as hereditary differences or disturbed parental relationships prior to institutionalization, rather than the quality of the attachment *per se*. Nevertheless, a study by Dixon (reported in Rutter and Garmezy, 1983) showed that children who were fostered did not show the social and behavioural abnormalities that institution-reared children did, despite the fact that both the groups studied had similarly severely disturbed parents.

Evidence concerning the lasting effects of the absence of early attachment is as consistent with other object-relations theories as with Bowlby's notions. In fairness to Bowlby, however, it should be noted that much of the work was either inspired by him or stimulated by the researcher's scepticism concerning the importance of early development. Although the data could be adequately treated in numerous other theoretical frameworks, they are most consistent with psychoanalytic ideology in that: first, they underline the vital role of early experience; second, they demonstrate the enduring quality of at least some personality attributes despite substantial situational changes; and third, much of the evidence is inconsistent with the notion of rewards and punishments being the major determinants of psychological development.

The narcissistic personality disorder (Kernberg and Kohut)

Individuals currently seeking psychoanalysis tend to have already attempted alternative, less demanding treatments. Their problems are deeply rooted and very resistant to change. Those with narcissistic personality disorder are described as having a rich fantasy life and yet to be very sensitive to criticism. They tend to exploit others in social relationships and to treat their love objects as nothing more than extensions of themselves (Akhtar *et al.*, 1982). Lasch (1978) suggests that this personality type may be characteristic of contemporary western civilization.

Kernberg (1976) put forward an aetiological model to account for the development of such personalities. He suggests that such children were left emotionally hungry by a chronically cold, unfeeling mother. The children protected themselves against feelings of abandonment by taking refuge in an aspect of themselves that the parents, particularly the mother, admired. This became the core of the functioning self which was split off from the unacceptable self-image of the hungry, rejected infant.

Another American psychoanalyst, Kohut (1972, 1977) sees narcissism as a natural part of development. He suggested that when the child's self-love (narcissism) is undermined by the mother's inevitable occasional failure to provide care, he/she defensively develops an even more megalomanic self-image (which Kohut terms the 'grandiose self'). The grandiose self is expected to become more realistic during maturation and in response to changes in the way the parents respond: for example, a two-year-old who is able to ride a tricycle will receive attention and praise in contrast to an older sibling. It is suggested that narcissistic personality patterns are the result of the arrest of this normal developmental sequence. This childish grandiosity may remain unaltered if, for example, the mother's confirming responses were never forthcoming or were, alternatively, unpredictable or entirely unrealistic.

The above descriptions have enriched the psychoanalytic literature but in the absence of more systematic studies must be regarded more as tentative suggestions than as established facts.

Personality assessment related to psychoanalytic concepts

Concurrent with the development of psychoanalysis was the rising popularity of some extremely complex subjective methods of assessment known collectively as projective tests (see Chapter 1). In these, subjects are presented with an unstructured situation where there are no right or wrong answers. They might be asked to describe ink-blots (Rorschach test) or make up stories around pictures depicting ambiguous social situations (thematic apperception test).

The theory behind these tests is that individuals confronted with such stimuli will indicate things about themselves that they would generally be unwilling or unable to reveal. This occurs by bypassing normal defence mechanisms and gaining direct access to pre-conscious or unconscious material. Psychoanalysts generally feel that such an understanding of a person's unconscious motives could only be available to a trained psychoanalyst who had seen a subject over a number of years. This view seems to be supported by the evidence in that projective tests tend to yield unreliable results (see for example, Atkinson, 1981; Kline, 1983). There have been suggestions that more systematic scoring methods might improve these instruments, but on the whole the information yield fails to justify the extensive training that their adequate administration and scoring requires. The tests are still quite widely used in the United States (Wade and Baker, 1977) but no longer form part of the training of British clinical psychologists, who seem to have responded to critical assessments of the technique (Eysenck, 1959). Moreover, on the basis of psychoanalytic theory there is no reason to suppose that a person looking at an ambiguous picture should reveal any more about themselves than they would in any other situation (Holmes, 1974).

In evaluating projective tests we would draw the following conclusions:

1 the value of such tests in relation to external criteria is as yet insufficient;
2 their use is justified as a source of ideas or hypotheses about a client;
3 the extensive use of these instruments is not compatible with current trends in the professional practice of clinical psychologists.

The practice of psychoanalysis and psychoanalytic therapy

Psychoanalysis

Although, as outlined above, psychoanalytic *theory* has changed substantially since Freud's time, the treatment he pioneered remains relatively unchanged. The client (analysand) lies on a couch with the analyst sitting behind, out of the client's field of vision. The client is asked to talk honestly about whatever comes to mind and to follow the thoughts through however embarrassing or trivial they might seem. In the United Kingdom, full psychoanalysis requires attendance for fifty-minute sessions five days per week over several years, although in some other countries three or four sessions per week are regarded as sufficient.

The aim of psychoanalysis is the undoing of repression and other defences, the recovery of lost memories and the achievement of *insight* or a fresh understanding of previously puzzling behaviour. The analysis may also provide a *corrective emotional experience* in that the relationship with the analyst might help to undo the effects of previous deprivation (Alexander and French, 1946). As the analysis proceeds there is a gradual intensification of the relationship between client and analyst, with the analytic situation encouraging the development of strong feelings for the analyst. The analyst gives away little about him/herself; thus the client's thoughts and fantasies about him/her may be strongly influenced by significant features of their earlier relationships. This process is called *transference*. It involves emotions rightly belonging to childhood relationships being transferred onto the analyst.

The analyst's task is to clarify clients' emotional conflicts. This should start with the interpretation of their defences (e.g. the tendency to deal with anger by turning it on oneself). This can then be linked with past events to provide an account of the clients' forbidden impulses (e.g. anger aimed at an apparently uncaring mother). In doing this, the analyst *works in the transference*, allowing the analysand to feel these conflicts in connection with him/her; thus anger towards the analyst for lateness or insufficient attentiveness may well feel frightening and be fended off initially, just as anger with mother was strongly defended against during childhood. In this way clients can work in the here and now with thoughts and feelings that belong in some way to the past. With successful analysis, the clients gain a better understanding of their behaviour in current relationships, in early relationships and in the relationship with the analyst.

Thus psychoanalysis is aimed not at removing particular problem behaviours or symptoms but at a far-reaching and radical restructuring of the personality. How far it is successful in achieving this goal is a point of considerable contention. In a review of thirty-one studies of the effectiveness of psychoanalysis, Goldberger *et al.* (1976) calculated that the rate of improvement with symptom removal as the criterion was 64.5 per cent, which is roughly comparable to the effectiveness of other therapeutic approaches. There is little evidence concerning claims of more fundamental personality changes following full psychoanalysis. Such changes are in any case very difficult, if not impossible, to assess reliably. A tentative indication that full, five-times-weekly classical psychoanalysis may give the client something that alternative therapies do not comes from studies of the client population of psychoanalysts. From a number of investigations it appears that more than half of the patients of most psychoanalysts, at least in the United States, consist of mental health professionals, themselves involved in the administration of forms of therapy which have been advanced as alternatives to psychoanalysis (Kadushin, 1969).

Psychoanalytic psychotherapy

This form of psychotherapy has evolved from psychoanalysis and is practised much more widely. The analyst and client both sit in armchairs in full view of each other and meet only once or twice a week. The therapy tends to *focus* on specific psychological problems, to emphasize interpersonal events in the client's current life and to consider the possible displacement of emotions from earlier relationships to current ones (generally excluding that with the analyst). Malan (1976) strongly recommends, on the basis of some empirical evidence, the use of interpretations emphasizing the similarity between clients' reponses to the analyst and to their parents. Some therapists go so far as to deliberately induce anxiety in their clients by provocative transference interpretations (e.g. 'You want to murder me just like you wanted to murder your father!' – Sifneos, 1972). Many of these approaches aim at substantially shorter treatments than psychoanalysis and focus on

53

a single conflict (e.g. an inability to be assertive with father and hence with other male authority figures). Therapist and patient often make a 'contract' for a particular number of sessions rather than entering an open-ended arrangement.

Such dynamically oriented psychotherapies rely on a distillation of psychoanalytic fundamentals concerning defences, drives and the transference. In a number of studies (e.g. Sloane *et al.* 1975) where the effectiveness of therapies based on psychoanalytic insights were contrasted clinically with that of other therapeutic approaches for neurotic problems, little difference in effectiveness was found. These are important findings since, whilst classical psychoanalysis compares very unfavourably with more modern therapeutic approaches in terms of time and cost, psychoanalytic psychotherapy is substantially less intensive and in most cases takes no longer than do alternative modes of intervention.

Although in principle the practice of psychoanalysis requires lengthy specialist training, including the psychoanalysis of the trainee analyst, many clinical psychologists, as well as psychiatrists and social workers, practise psychotherapy guided by psychoanalytic principles without receiving a full psychoanalytic training.

Evaluation

Finally, it must be asked: What is the value of the psychoanalytic approach? For psychology, its value is synonymous with its scientific status: although the works of William Shakespeare have profound implications for psychology, they cannot be counted as a part of its body of knowledge. Efforts have been made to demonstrate the scientific validity of psychoanalysis by replicating in the laboratory clinical phenomena such as projection, repression and dream symbolism. These attempts constitute a substantial body of evidence, some consistent with and some failing to support psychoanalytic contentions (see reviews by Fisher and Greenberg, 1977; Kline, 1981; Fonagy, 1981). Although of great interest in their own right, such investigations have no real relevance to psychoanalysis as the processes examined in the laboratory may be analogous to, but *cannot* be the same as, those identified in the clinical setting. Attempting to replicate such a complex process as projection is impossible when so many of the factors normally responsible for its occurrence in real life and in the consulting room are absent in the laboratory.

This does not mean, however, that experimental investigations have no relevance to psychoanalysis. Experimentalists can examine the psychological processes which may underlie phenomena described in the clinical situation without attempting to recreate these phenomena in the laboratory. Fonagy (1982) argues that experimental studies cannot ever hope to validate psychoanalytic ideas in the sense of demonstrating their existence to observers not participating in the psychoanalytic encounter. Nevertheless it is quite possible for laboratory studies to demonstrate the existence of psychological processes that underlie the phenomena described by psychoanalysts.

Taking this approach, we can be a little more optimistic about the potential scientific status of psychoanalysis. The rapid expansion of psychological knowledge has already provided much evidence which is consistent with psychoanalytic assumptions; and if this trend continues, more may follow.

Much information concerning the differences in the characteristics of functioning of the two cerebral hemispheres may be consistent with psychoanalytic suggestions concerning differences between conscious versus pre-conscious thought processes. A review of the literature on laboratory studies of dreaming indicates that there is a case for maintaining that whilst the right hemisphere accounts for the irrational, bizarre (primary process) aspects of dreaming, the left hemisphere contributes more to its logical, narrative aspects (Fonagy and Higgitt, 1984). This dichotomy would not verify Freud's suggestion that we should distinguish between these processes, but it would make it a less preposterous postulate.

No final conclusion can yet be made as to the status of psychoanalysis; both psychoanalysis and psychology will continue to develop and grow for a long while yet. Eventually, adequate common ground may emerge so that psychoanalysis may become acceptable as a branch of psychological science. Until such a time, however, psychologists are correct in treating the unique but clinically based psychological models of psychoanalysts with interested and perhaps sympathetic scepticism.

4

Behavioural approaches

'Thought processes are really motor habits of the larynx.' This rather extreme statement comes from Watson (1913), from whom the behavioural approach to psychology originates. It has been one of the most powerful influences on the development of the subject. This approach maintains that the science of psychology should be concerned with objective methods of investigating the influence of the environment on *observable* behaviour. Some of the major developments in this field will be considered here. They all share certain assumptions. Firstly, action (behaviour) is controlled primarily by the environment, in other words by the situations in which individuals find themselves. Secondly, the patterns of behaviour which go together to make up an individual are acquired largely through the processes of learning. Thirdly, the behavioural approach is an associationist one. Whatever the precise mechanism may be, learning takes place through the strengthening of an association between things close together in time. Fourthly, these processes can be studied adequately in the laboratory. Fifthly, the processes of learning in man are similar to those in animals, and so study of the latter is relevant. Finally, complex behaviours (such as speech) may be considered as made up of several simpler sorts of behaviour.

Learning processes have always been central to the behavioural approach, and our coverage of such approaches to personality will be in terms of the most prominent of these theories. Learning theory has progressed substantially over the past few decades, and many of its current ideas are far less closely linked to a behavioural approach (e.g. Roitblat *et al.*, 1983). In this chapter we shall consider work within the so-called 'traditional' learning theory framework, leaving clinical concepts linked with more recent developments in the learning field until Chapter 8. The theories outlined below are by no means mutually exclusive, although of course it is more economical to assume that only one type of learning accounts for any one form of behaviour.

Classical conditioning

The fundamental principle of classical conditioning (Pavlov, 1927) is that if any stimulus (e.g. a bell) is presented at the same time as another stimulus (such as food) which automatically elicits a response (salivation in this case), then that first stimulus will eventually become capable of eliciting the response on its own (i.e. the bell alone will produce salivation). The food is termed the unconditioned stimulus (UCS) and salivation the unconditioned response (UCR). Salivation which is elicited by the bell (not by the presence of food in the mouth), is the conditioned response (CR) and the bell itself has become a conditioned stimulus (CS). Pavlov noted that the effect of a specific conditioned stimulus could *generalize* to other similar stimuli. Thus a bell with a slightly different tone from the original conditioned stimulus may also produce salivation in the dog. In addition, if certain neutral stimuli only are paired with an unconditioned stimulus whereas others are not, the animal will learn to *discriminate* between them. If the food is presented only in conjunction with a ringing bell and never with a buzzer, the dog learns only to salivate to the bell and not to the buzzer. If the conditioned stimulus ceases to be paired with the unconditioned stimulus, the conditioned response rapidly weakens and stops: the response *extinguishes*. After a few presentations of the bell without food, the dog will salivate little and finally not at all in response to the bell.

Watson extended Pavlov's experiments to explain emotional

reactions. He showed that fears could be conditioned. A little boy of eleven months named Albert played fearlessly with rats. When he was reaching out for a rat being presented to him, a loud noise was made behind his head. After a few such presentations, Albert became scared of the rat; he whimpered and cried even in the absence of any noise at all. Watson and Rayner (1920) concluded from this study of one child that many fears, including anxiety, were conditioned emotional reactions.

Eysenck and Rachman (1965) further extended this learning theory explanation of anxiety to account for all forms of abnormal fears. They suggested that any previously neutral stimulus which happened to make an impact on an individual at about the same time that he/she was made to feel frightened could subsequently acquire the ability to evoke fear itself. They also adopted Pavlov's notion of generalization of this reaction to include stimuli similar to the conditioned stimulus. Anxiety would simply be a naturally occurring response to one situation which has become transferred to another by association. Thus, for example, we may come to fear the sound of the dentist's drill because a particularly painful previous treatment is associated with it, and this reaction may generalize to other high-pitched sounds. Likewise, Albert became frightened of white fur coats because of their resemblance to the white rat.

There is considerable evidence to support Eysenck and Rachman's model. Firstly, it is easy to induce conditioned fear in animals (Broadhurst, 1972) or human subjects. A warning tone which is followed initially by an electric shock will soon elicit mild palmar sweating on its own: a conditioned emotional response, since palmar sweating is a manifestation of fear. Secondly, a fear reaction following traumatic events (e.g. in wartime) may continue long after the danger has passed (Lewis and Engle, 1954). Thirdly, phobics can frequently recall an initial traumatic experience associated with the onset of their fears (e.g. a dog phobic recalling being attacked by a large Alsatian, Rimm *et al.*, 1977). Fourthly, laboratory studies with human subjects show that if the unconditioned stimulus is highly traumatic, a single pairing with a neutral stimulus may induce a long-lasting conditioned emotional response. This was illustrated in numerous studies (see Garcia, 1981). In typical experiments, subjects are made to feel nauseated while tasting a particular food. It was normally found that both animal and human subjects developed long-lasting aversions to that food and continued to avoid it, sometimes indefinitely.

There is, however, a substantial amount of evidence concerning emotional responses that is not consistent with such a simple explanation of fears. Firstly, there is no simple relationship between traumatic events (UCS) and the development of conditioned fears (see Rachman, 1977). People may experience profound traumas without developing substantial irrational fears. Anna Freud and Sophie Dann (1951) described such cases in their report on six German Jewish orphans whose parents had perished in Nazi concentration camps. The children had been separated from their parents when only a few months old and spent their first three to four years together in a concentration camp where they were subjected to traumas many times more grave than loud noises. On coming to England at the end of the war they were studied intensively for over a year. Although they appeared to suffer some anxieties which could be linked to the camp (including, in one child, an acute fear of a van of a similar colour to those seen in the camp), none of them developed phobias, either as children or at any time during their twenty-year follow-up (Goldberger, 1972). A similar problem is raised by Valentine's (1946) attempt to induce an acute fear of opera-glasses (instead of the rat) in a two-year-old child, using Watson and Rayner's design, which failed totally. Several studies have failed, despite close questioning, to elicit any history of traumatic experiences in phobics (e.g. Lazarus, 1971). Thus is seems that neither does conditioned fear inevitably follow traumas, nor can traumas invariably be identified in individuals with irrational fears.

A further major problem for the conditioning theory of phobias lies in the assertion that *any* stimulus, if coupled with an aversive event, may lead to the acquisition of conditioned fear. It has been demonstrated experimentally (although we all intuitively knew anyway) that certain fears such as a fear of spiders, of open spaces, etc. are more likely than others (canaries or parasols, for example). In one such study, Bennett-Levy and Marteau (1984) asked subjects to rate twenty-nine small, harmless animals in terms of how frightening they were. Rats, jellyfish, cockroaches, spiders and slugs were consistently rated as frightening and to be avoided; rabbits, ladybirds, cats and lambs, on the other hand, were rated as non-frightening. The study also revealed that perceptual qualities of these animals, such as ugliness, sliminess and suddenness of movement, accounted for most of the differences between the ratings. Whatever the explanation, classical conditioning theory cannot account for the observed uneven distribution of fears across the range of potential stimuli; nor can it explain why males are less likely than females to acquire fears, or why a fear of strangers is particularly common in the third quarter of the first year of life, whilst fears of animals and the dark are particularly likely in children between three and five years of age (Rutter and Garmezy, 1983).

The most crucial weakness of the conditioning theory lies in the very nature of the conditioning process itself. In the laboratory, as we have seen, it is normally found that if the conditioned stimulus is not reinforced – is repeatedly presented without the unconditioned stimulus – the conditioned response is extinguished: the dog stops salivating to the bell. In the case of phobias, there appears to be no extinction: a dog phobia, for instance, may persist for years in the absence of any subsequent traumatic encounters with dogs. Any theory that claimed to provide an adequate explanation for this would therefore need to account for the extinction of laboratory-conditioned responses on the one hand and the apparent absence of extinction in phobias on the other.

Preparedness

Seligman (1971) offered a possible explanation for both the problem of unequal distribution and that of maintenance. Work with animals had shown that some responses were much easier to condition than others: for instance, it is very much harder to teach a pigeon to peck at a key than to move away in order to avoid an electric shock. It seems as though certain responses might be evolutionarily 'prepared': in other words, the survival of the organism, and hence of the species, is promoted if such prepared responses are learned quickly. In the laboratory, such responses are easily learned and hard to extinguish. Seligman suggested that phobias are such prepared responses: not only are they hard to extinguish, but they frequently appear to be associated with objects of 'biological' significance. It is conceivable that it has been to the advantage of the human species to fear snakes and wild dogs or things that are ugly or move rapidly. The lack of evolutionary advantage produced by a fear of opera-glasses may well explain the difficulty in inducing fear of them! In support of Seligman's suggestions Ohman *et al.* (1979) demonstrated that the extinction of laboratory conditioned emotional responses was slower to pictures of snakes (prepared), than with similar induced responses to pictures of flowers (unprepared stimuli). Thus conditioned responses to 'phobic type' stimuli were maintained better than those to non-phobic stimuli.

Challenges to Seligman's theory must however, be noted. Findings such as those of Ohman and his colleagues may be accounted for in terms of the prior experience of the subjects with those types of stimuli. Emerson and Lucas (1981) failed to reproduce even these findings. De Silva *et al.* (1977) showed that phobias of biological objects (snakes, corpses) were no harder to extinguish through treatment than were unprepared phobias (e.g. chocolate) as Seligman (1971) would have predicted. In a review of the published findings, McNally and Reiss (1982) concluded that there was little evidence to support the preparedness theory. Thus for the moment classical learning theory is unable to account for the non-random distribution of fears.

Incubation

An alternative solution to the problem of maintenance was suggested by Eysenck (1979). His model is based on the phenomenon of incubation in which an enhancement of, rather than a decline in, the strength of the conditioned response is seen under certain circumstances in the absence of reinforcement. Incubation is more likely to occur if the original unconditioned stimulus was highly aversive. The food aversion experiment cited earlier may be an example of this. The aversion to the food (CS) conditioned by a drug (UCS) not only continued but in some cases actually increased in strength as time went on. Eysenck argues that this is because the conditioned response (nausea) itself reinforces the associative link between the conditioned stimulus and the conditioned response (food and nausea). Thus, with each presentation of the CS (the food) the strength of the response is further enhanced.

The incubation theory fits the clinical picture in persistent phobias quite neatly. A person who has become fearful of dentists following a single painful treatment will not lose the fear between appointments, despite perhaps a large number of subsequent painless visits; in fact, his/her fear may well escalate. Thus

61

Eysenck appears to be able to account for the maintenance of phobias.

However, Eysenck's theory has not gone uncriticized. Bersh (1980) points to some major difficulties. His review of the literature indicates that incubation is a markedly unreliable laboratory phenomenon which with four exceptions has only been demonstrated in the Soviet Union. A further important problem is that the theory does not predict with accuracy in which situations incubation might take place. Since clearly not all conditioned responses incubate (Paxton, 1983), it is important to attempt to identify the parameters which are likely to predict incubation. In the case of phobias, we can only assume that incubation has occurred because we observe that there is a failure of extinction. There is no independent evidence. Moreover, the criticisms of the conditioning model considered earlier, especially the problem of age trends, sex differences and the non-random distribution of phobias, have not been tackled.

The molar account of classical conditioning

Probably the major contribution to devising a classical conditioning explanation of neurotic behaviour has come from changes in learning theorists' understanding of the psychological processes underlying classical conditioning itself (e.g. Eelen, 1982). In what is known as the 'molar account' of classical conditioning, it is not the simple pairing of CS and UCS but the learning of the *contingent* nature of the relationship between them that is held to define the learning process (Rescorla and Wagner, 1972). Animals will show conditioned responses to a red light if this is paired with an electric shock. If subsequently both a red and a green light are paired with the shock, we would predict on the basis of conditioning theory that the green light would also elicit the conditioned response. This, in fact, failed to occur (Mackintosh, 1978). Thus, the organism seems to have been able to arrive at the conclusion that the green light was not related to the shock in a contingent way.

The molar view might account for a number of the shortcomings of the earlier classical conditioning explanations considered above. Therefore a person might be exposed to a traumatic event but not develop a phobic reaction unless he/she perceived a contingent relationship between the situation and the traumatic event. Yet even the molar view cannot account for neurotic reactions in individuals who cannot identify traumatic events (Lazarus, 1971) or for the extreme resistance to extinction of neurotic fears. Thus, although classical conditioning may be a factor in the acquisition of some emotional responses it is clearly unable to account for the majority of phobic disorders.

Operant conditioning

The most thorough attempt to provide a general account of all human activity within the behavioural framework was made by B.F. Skinner (1974). He suggested that organisms were best studied in terms of the different behaviours they emit. Emitted behaviours are called *operants*, although it would probably have been simpler for everyone if Skinner had just called them 'acts' (Blackman, 1981). They are not elicited by particular stimuli, as in Pavlovian conditioning; they simply occur (as a dog walks or a human baby babbles). The frequency of production of particular operants is by definition affected by its consequences and is said by Skinner to depend on the animal's reinforcement history. A *reinforcer* is an event that follows an operant and increases its probability of recurrence: for instance, a pigeon receiving food immediately after pecking at a disc is likely to repeat the behaviour. Reinforcers are not restricted to primitive rewards such as food or sexual gratification, but may include a wide variety of events such as the achievement of competence or the satisfaction of curiosity.

Skinnerian (or operant) psychologists have studied in detail the relationship of patterns (or *schedules*) of reinforcement to rates of responding (cf. Walker, 1984). They have, for example, demonstrated that if reinforcements do not invariably follow a particular behaviour, that behaviour becomes more firmly established than if reinforcement follows each emission of the behaviour ('*the partial reinforcement effect*'). It has also been shown that complex operants can be developed through the process of *shaping*. In this procedure, initially, any behaviour vaguely approximating to the desired final operant is reinforced; later, a closer and closer resemblance is needed to achieve reinforcement.

Negative reinforcers are aversive events, the removal of which *increases* the probability of the recurrence of the preceding behaviour: for example, a bar press (or operant) leading to

63

termination of electric shock (negative reinforcer). This is to be differentiated from *punishment*, where the aversive event follows a particular response and *reduces* the probability of its recurrence. Skinnerian psychologists have also investigated the effect that withdrawing reinforcement has upon established behaviour (extinction) as well as the enormous importance of external stimuli in eliciting behaviour when certain responses have been reinforced only in the presence of those stimuli (*discriminative stimuli*). Studies of operant conditioning have traditionally employed non-human subjects. Extrapolation of the findings to humans involves the assumption that the laws governing animal and human behaviour are identical in most important respects. The validity of this assumption is, of course, a point of contention. Notwithstanding such controversy, Skinner (1974), in his book *About Behaviourism*, put forward a philosophical framework within which both human and animal behaviour could be studied scientifically.

Skinner suggests that individual differences in behaviour reflect the obvious fact that each of our reinforcement histories is unique. Skinner was interested in determining the precise conditions controlling behaviour and suggested that this could be achieved using a detailed *functional analysis* of behaviour. The essence of this approach is that behaviour may best be understood by relating it to the environmental context within which it occurs. Radical behaviourists seek to understand human behaviour in terms of the functional relationship that exists between the behaviour and the environment. When consequences can be identified which have selective effects on behaviour they can be defined as reinforcers. In this system, then, reinforcers are defined *functionally*. This approach gives rise to questions such as: 'What environmental changes (e.g. parental behaviour) will lead to a change in the frequency of a child's screaming fits?' Within the philosophical framework of radical behaviourism, unobservable cognitive phenomena, such as thinking or dreaming, are considered as behaviours under environmental control just as observable behaviours are (Davey, 1981).

Models of neurosis

Numerous models of abnormal behaviour have been put forward in Skinnerian terms. A central problem for the learning theory analysis of abnormal behaviour is that learning should, in principle, be adaptive; learned behaviour in consequence should be useful. Abnormal behaviour (such as the compulsive checking behaviour of some neurotic patients) is, at least superficially, unwanted and maladaptive. The self-perpetuating nature of such apparently self-defeating behaviours was, rather dramatically, labelled by the learning theorist Mowrer 'the neurotic paradox'. Working in the tradition of operant psychology, Ullman and Krasner (1975), however, refused to accept neurosis was in any sense 'paradoxical'. They felt that neurotic behaviour, like all forms of behaviour, followed basic learning principles; they did not see a sharp division between 'normal' and abnormal behaviour. Thus phobic behaviour may sometimes be seen to be maintained by its reinforcing consequences. The socially phobic person succeeds in avoiding social situations in which he/she would not be able to perform adequately. This successful avoidance is itself reinforcing. Furthermore, others too may reinforce the neurotic avoidance behaviour. A caring husband taking cups of tea to his agoraphobic wife whenever she is too anxious to get out of bed may only be helping to maintain the behaviour. Freud (1926) also noticed this and labelled it a 'secondary gain' from neurotic symptoms.

Rather than searching for elusive 'intrapsychic' causes of depression, Skinnerians take the actual behaviours associated with depression as the focus of their investigation. In their view it is the socially withdrawn behaviour, the overall lack of activity and the slow rate of performing tasks that need explanation, not some hypothetical underlying disease or malfunction called depression. It is thus the frequency rather than the content of such behaviours that concerns these workers. Lewinsohn (1974), for example, suggested that depressed people lack the social skills to obtain sufficient positive reinforcement from those around them. This would result in a reduction (or extinction) of their social behaviour. Diaries kept by depressed individuals did indeed reveal that the occurrence of pleasant activities (positive reinforcers) and episodes of depression were unlikely to coincide (Lewinsohn and Graf, 1973).

In general, however, behavioural formulations of depression find only limited support in the research literature (Eastman, 1976). One general problem with the behavioural approach, particularly clear in the case of explanations of depression, is that the meaning of the behaviour is not considered: elderly people, for instance, may do relatively little but are not necessarily considered to be depressed. Although current operant approaches accept the importance of such internal events as emotions and thoughts, Skinnerian theory offers no explanation of how reductions in total amounts of behaviour may lead to the cognitive and emotional changes associated with depression.

A further problem of a functional analytic approach to psychological disorder is the identification of those aspects of the environment that have a functional relationship with the problem behaviour. Skinner, on scientific grounds, refused to go beyond his observations to identify specific classes of events as reinforcing. His wish to describe the 'facts' and nothing but the facts leaves his model open to criticism on the grounds of circularity. Positive and negative reinforcements are defined simply by their consequences (whether they increase or decrease the behaviour that preceded them). Nevertheless, it is precisely these consequences which the reinforcers are supposed to be accounting for. For example, how do we know that the parents of a school-phobic child, who are clearly sorry for their offspring, are actively reinforcing the illness behaviour? We assume this to be the case because the illness behaviour persists despite the fact that it was this persistence we wanted to account for in the first place! Eysenck (1976) concluded that Skinner and Freud rivalled each other in their lack of scientific status. These are, perhaps, overharsh words: both these psychologists, in not entirely dissimilar ways, recommended the open-minded, unprejudiced, detailed observation of contingencies governing human behaviour which, as we shall see in subsequent sections, has paid off handsomely in clinical practice (at least in the case of behavioural analysis).

The combination of classical and operant principles

Many influential learning theorists of the 1950s and 1960s suggested that combined knowledge gained from both operant and classical conditioning may provide a more adequate account for neurotic behaviour than either theory alone. To explain neurotic behaviours characterized by anxiety (phobias and obsessional neurosis) these theorists used the laboratory model of shuttle-box conditioning. Miller and Bugelski (1948) found that if rats were given electric shocks in a compartment painted white but were able to escape to the black half of the box, they would persist in running into the black section long after the shocks had been discontinued. They thus appeared to have a 'phobia' of the white compartment. They would also learn new behaviours, such as turning a wheel to open a door, in order to be able to escape from the apparently feared white compartment; again, they would continue to do this long after shocks stopped being administered. Similar work on dogs by Solomon and Wynne (1954) showed that once the animals had learned to avoid a shock, by lifting a paw when a light came on, the behaviour would be performed up to 500 times without a further shock. This behaviour is clearly analogous to certain neurotic behaviour patterns: obsessional rituals, for instance, could be seen as an attempt to avoid some now irrelevant but once powerful aversive event.

The two-stage theory of avoidance

Even now there is no totally satisfactory explanation of the persistence of avoidance behaviour. Many (e.g. Walker, 1984) consider Mowrer's (1969) two-stage (or two-process) model the most likely candidate. Mowrer suggested that initially the animal acquired a conditioned fear response to some aspect of the situation in which it was shocked (e.g. the white colour of the compartment). He saw this conditioned fear as an aversive state, the removal of which would be a positive reinforcer. The second stage of the model then referred to the performance of the avoidance behaviour which led to a reduction in fear and so to the positive reinforcement and strengthening of the avoidance response.

Mowrer's model has been heavily criticized. Rachman (1976) and Eysenck (1981) reviewed these criticisms. Firstly, the theory cannot adequately account for the resistance to extinction of the avoidance behaviour. If jumping from the white side of the box was really maintained by classically conditioned anxiety associated with that environment, then when the shocks were discontinued the avoidance response should extinguish along with the gradual extinction of the classically conditioned emotional response. We might in fact expect the classically conditioned anxiety to extinguish completely within about forty trials, whereas the avoidance response has been observed to occur for as many as 650 unreinforced trials.

Other information also indicates that classically conditioned anxiety plays no part in the avoidance response. It seems that once animals have acquired the avoidance response they are no longer fearful anywhere in the shuttle-box. They eat normally, quite unlike anxious animals, and show no physiological signs of fear (see Mineka, 1979). Seligman and Johnston (1973) suggest that fear is extinguished but that the avoidance behaviour is continued through 'expectancy' on the part of the animal that it will prevent a shock occurring. This may provide a more useful lead, which we will take up again in the context of cognitive theories in Chapter 8.

The above arguments concerning the adequacy of Mowrer's account of shuttle-box avoidance are in any case probably some-what academic since it is clear that it is certainly unable to explain clinical compulsions or phobias. Rachman and Hodgson (1974) argue persuasively that fear and the avoidance response in phobias do not by any means always go together: in the treatment of phobias, for example, patients who have avoided a particular situation for many years may show surprisingly little fear when they actually find themselves confronting it. It seems we avoid many things we are not scared of (such as puddles!), which makes it unlikely that conditioned anxiety should be the motivator of our avoidance. Rachman (1978) therefore suggested that fear should be considered as made up of several loosely linked components (including behavioural avoidance, physiological signs of arousal and the subjective experience of fear) not all of which are necessarily manifested to the same degree on a particular occasion. He stated that we should abandon assumptions of causal links between these components, thereby countering claims that avoidance behaviour can be explained by a reduction of anxiety.

Safety-signal revision of the two-stage theory

A possible explanation for the lack of association between fear and avoidance was put forward by learning theorists who wished to retain the combination of classical and operant approaches as explanations of avoidance behaviour (see Gray, 1971). It was proposed that avoidance was motivated not by the reduction of anxiety but rather by the positive feelings of safety associated with the 'safe' compartment of the shuttle-box. It serves as a con-ditioned stimulus predicting the absence of shock. This experi-ence of safety positively reinforces the avoidance behaviour every time the animal arrives in that compartment.

The safety-signal hypothesis provides a better fit with the clinical picture of many phobias than does the original anxiety-based explanation. Rachman (1984) presented convincing arguments in favour of construing agoraphobia as motivated not by the avoidance of fear but by the seeking of signals of safety. Contrary to popular belief, agoraphobics are not frightened by open spaces; in fact, as Hallam (1978) found, it is not at all easy to identify what stimuli may be associated with their fear. Using the safety-signal account, some previously unexplained facts about agoraphobia became interpretable. Agoraphobics, for example, find it easier to go out with or be driven by someone they trust or to take certain routes, etc. – perhaps trusted individuals or certain situations act as safety signals. This perspective may also explain why the loss of a close relative (perhaps a signal of safety) might so often mark the onset of a phobia.

There can be no doubt of the clinical meaningfulness of Rachman's account. It is unfortunate, however, as he himself admits, that the learning theory bases of safety conditioning are by no means well established. Mineka (1979), in her review of avoidance learning, pointed out that it has never been demonstrated that the safety signal remains a reinforcer when it is no longer in the fear-eliciting situation: in other words, there is no evidence that agoraphobics prefer the company of the same individuals after the problem behaviour has subsided.

Operant explanations of avoidance learning

Reinterpretation of avoidance behaviour in terms of operant theory overcomes many of the objections levelled against two-process theories. Such views assume that avoidance behaviour is maintained because it reduces or eliminates negative consequences. In this framework fear is no longer a necessary part of the explanation of avoidance behaviour, which makes it more consistent with the evidence (Wilson, 1982). The absence of extinction is easy to account for, since this would only take place if the contingency between avoidance behaviour and the outcome (no shock) was broken. For this to happen, the organism needs to be able to discern that the contingency has changed and that avoidance is no longer necessary to eliminate whatever the negative consequences were previously.

This explanation also fits clinical phobias fairly closely. Thorpe and Burns (1983) found that almost 60 per cent of 900 agoraphobic subjects reported a fear of becoming ill. The avoidance behaviour of agoraphobics could therefore be interpreted as a way of avoiding fainting, a heart attack or mental illness.

Although this account of avoidance fits some phobic patterns better than does the two-factor theory, in reality phobic patients are frequently confronted with their feared situations and none the less obstinately retain their avoidance behaviour. In such cases the contingent relationship between their behaviour and its consequences should have been broken as, clearly, no objectively aversive event occurred; yet clinical experience shows that such occasional encounters tend to strengthen rather than weaken avoidance. Having reviewed some of the most prominent learning theory formulations of neurotic disorder, we find that none of them offers a complete explanation for neurotic behaviour as we see it in clients or even for the laboratory-based analogues suggested as models for abnormal behaviour.

Behavioural treatment

The term 'behaviour therapy' covers a wide range of therapeutic techniques which make use of psychological principles (especially principles of learning) derived from laboratory investigations. It has as its aim the constructive changing of human behaviour. Behavioural therapies became a prominent part of the clinician's armamentarium in the 1950s and have since developed rapidly, both in terms of the number and the sophistication of techniques available.

The diversity of approaches under the general heading of 'behaviour therapy' is such that it is difficult to identify a set of principles which underlies all the methods. There are, however, a number of assumptions to which most behaviour therapists would probably subscribe (Davey, 1981; Yates, 1981).

1 Psychological problems need to be '*operationalized*', (i.e. described in terms of observable behaviours) before we embark on efforts to change them.
2 Psychological problems are most usefully conceived of as maladaptive behaviour patterns acquired through traumatic or inappropriate learning.
3 Whatever the history of the problem, they are most usefully conceived of in terms of a functional analysis of current

environment-behaviour relationships rather than by making assumptions about possible past or present internal underlying factors.

4 The most useful guide-lines for intervention are ones derived from experimental psychological principles, especially those relating to operant or classical conditioning.

5 Scientific evaluation of the efficacy of a mode of intervention should be a constant feature of all behavioural treatments.

Behavioural assessment

In line with the general assumptions of the behavioural approach concerning observability and the functional relationship of the environment and behaviour, the clinical assessment of psychological problems has become a procedure of great scientific rigour within behaviour therapy. The aim of behavioural assessment is *the identification and measurement of meaningful response units and their controlling variables for the purpose of understanding and altering human behaviour* (Nelson *et al.*, 1981).

Behavioural measurement

As this definition indicates, the first step of behavioural assessment is the careful description and measurement of the problem behaviour. Contrary to popular conception and despite their insistence on objectivity, behaviour therapists tend to be sophisticated and subtle in their assessment of psychological problems. They are not satisfied by global statements such as 'This person is over-anxious' or 'That person is depressed'; they insist, instead, on examining in detail a number of *response systems* which might be involved in the problem (Lang, 1970; Lazarus, 1976). Anxiety, for example, may be associated with simple *motor behaviours* of avoidance or observable tension of the musculature. A *cognitive/verbal* response system is also involved in that the individual 'feels' anxious and can report this subjective experience. A further important component is naturally a *physiological* one, as the arousal of the autonomic nervous system (e.g. heart racing, experience of nausea) is an integral part of the experience. Behavioural measurement must include at least these three response systems as the correlations between them tend to be modest (Johnson and Melamed, 1979).

As behavioural assessment includes the measurement of these multiple modalities, it follows that no single method of measurement can fulfil the task. Thus, in addition to indirect methods of data-gathering such as interviews and questionnaires which are used in the context of many other forms of assessment, behavioural assessment frequently incorporates: firstly, the *direct observation* of the client by an independent observer in a naturalistic situation; secondly, the client's own long-term monitoring (*self-monitoring*) of his/her problem in the form of diaries kept over a long period; and thirdly, *physiological measures* of the client's emotional state, most frequently measured in terms of heart rate (Cone, 1978).

The collection of such detailed information is a worthy but over ambitious aim. Nelson (1983), one of the originators of the behavioural approach to assessment discusses the disillusionment of many behaviour therapists with the usefulness of the approach. The procedure of the ideal behavioural assessment is time-consuming and often inefficient. It requires extensive co-operation from the client which is frequently not forthcoming (Ford and Kendall, 1979). The techniques used (e.g. direct observation) are frequently unreliable and prone to various forms of bias such as prior expectations on the part of the observer (Harris and Lahey, 1982a,b)

Functional analysis

The aim of behavioural assessment is not simply the accurate multi-modal description of the client's problem but also the identification of internal and external variables which control it. Two sets of variables are normally considered in this context:

1 The conditions associated with increases or decreases in the frequency, intensity or duration of the problem behaviour (in other words, its antecedents or, in learning theory terms, its discriminative stimuli).
2 Internal and external consequences which tend to follow the occurrence of the problem behaviour and which may play a part in its maintenance or exacerbation (Slade, 1982). This way of formulating an individual's difficulties is termed *functional analysis* and consists of three components, the antecedents, the actual behaviour and its consequences.

One example of such an analysis is that of a 65-year-old woman diagnosed as suffering from agoraphobia. Careful monitoring of her behaviour demonstrated that although she insisted on remaining in her house, and in fact on staying in bed almost all the time, her avoidance of going out appeared not to be linked to the subjective experience of anxiety. Examining the antecedents of her behaviour revealed that at certain times of the day her agoraphobic behaviours diminished, with her not only leaving her bed but also going out of the house for short periods. Her puzzling behaviour was explained only after a number of interviews when she finally revealed that she found her husband's sexual advances intensely unpleasant. Her strategy for avoiding such advances seemed to be retiring to her bed and claiming to be ill.

This case illustrates that a formulation of problem behaviours in terms of functional analysis is aimed at explaining the behaviour of that particular individual and is not compatible with traditional systems of diagnosis (see Chapter 1) where individuals are classified according to the category of problems with which they present (Owens and Ashcroft, 1982). Whilst for many individuals the phobia may indeed serve the function of avoiding a feared situation, for others, as in the above case, the function may be subtle and idiosyncratic.

Functional analysis also has the advantage of making suggestions as to possible methods of intervention. Agoraphobia is normally treated by reducing anxiety associated with streets, queues, etc. In the case described above, functional analysis revealed that this would have been inappropriate. Once this client learned the skill of saying no politely but firmly to her husband's sexual advances, her agoraphobic problems disappeared. Assessment, formulation (in terms of functional analysis) and reformulation form an integral part of behavioural treatment.

Treatment methods

It was stressed in the previous section that the various behavioural treatments should not be regarded as specific to particular psychological problems; a treatment programme is individually designed to combat the unique functional relationship existing between an individual's problem behaviour and aspects of the environment. Nevertheless, most behavioural analysts acknowledge the existence of common patterns of responses (which within the medical model would be referred to as syndromes or diagnostic categories). This permits the identification of typical controlling variables and consequently also typical modes of intervention. The following sections are organized on the basis of these categories of problem behaviour.

Behavioural treatment of fear

Perhaps the best known method of behavioural treatment for fear is *systematic desensitization*. This technique has three components. Initially, clients are taught a method of relaxation which permits them to experience feelings of tranquillity. (This is usually achieved through tensing and relaxing the skeletal musculature.) The clients also construct a hierarchy consisting of a number of increasingly threatening situations connected with the source of their fear: for example, in the case of a spider phobic such a hierarchy may range from seeing a picture of a spider through seeing a live spider shut safely in a jar right up to handling a large live spider him/herself. Finally, desensitization proper takes place when clients confront, while relaxed, the items on the hierarchy. This typically occurs over several sessions, in which clients work gradually up the hierarchy until they are facing the most anxiety-provoking item. Clients confront each level of their hierarchy either in their imagination (e.g. imagining that they are sitting in an aeroplane just as the doors are about to shut) or in reality (e.g. climb up to greater and greater heights). It is important that the therapist ensures that clients can cope with one level without anxiety before proceeding to the next.

The method was introduced by Wolpe (1958). He assumed that relaxation, which is a response incompatible with anxiety, comes to be paired with the feared stimulus. In this way the conditioned link between the phobic object and anxiety may be replaced by the association of the previously feared stimulus with a state of relaxation. Any behaviour incompatible with anxiety may serve this purpose. Wolpe, for example, suggested that behaving assertively might also serve to counteract anxiety. Thus helping people to stand up for themselves and speak their minds in interpersonal encounters could remove the anxiety previously associated with such situations (*assertiveness training*).

Of all the behavioural treatments, systematic desensitization has been applied to the widest range of problem behaviours. It has been reported to improve anxiety-related speech difficulties (e.g. Osberg, 1981), hallucinations (Slade, 1973) and insomnia (Steinmark and Borkovec, 1974) amongst other disorders, but its major field of application has been in the treatment of mild phobias. The principle underlying the use of systematic desensitization is that the particular problem behaviours arise out of fear in a specifiable situation to which the individual may be desensitized. Reviewers agree that the technique is beyond doubt of therapeutic value (Rachman and Wilson, 1980; McGlynn *et al.*, 1981). It has also been demonstrated that the procedure is most effective for individuals who have minor phobias (say, animal phobias rather than agoraphobia), who are able to learn relaxation skills and who have sufficiently vivid imaginations to be able to conjure up the sources of their fear (Rimm and Masters, 1979; Emmelkamp, 1982).

So far no general agreement has emerged amongst researchers as to the relative importance of specific features of systematic desensitization. Some studies, for example, have demonstrated that clinical phobias may be as effectively treated by subjects imagining gradually more and more fearful stimuli in the absence of relaxation as by traditional systematic desensitization (e.g. Gillan and Rachman, 1974). This may prove to be of more than passing interest, as recently a number of studies have produced systematic as well as anecdotal evidence that in at least 5 per cent of clients relaxation leads to increased rather than decreased anxiety (Heide and Borkovec, 1984).

Exposure or flooding is another useful treatment for fear. It involves direct exposure of the client to the feared situation without relaxation or assertiveness. Clients face immediately what would be at the top of their hierarchy: for example, a spider-phobic client might be asked to take hold of a spider and allow it to run from one hand to the other until all anxiety subsides. The rationale of this treatment may be loosely based on the two-stage avoidance theory (Mowrer, 1960). In flooding, the client is thought to be presented with the conditioned stimulus without being able to perform the avoidance response. This allows the conditioned response to extinguish.

An alternative rationale in terms of habituation to anxiety-provoking stimuli could also explain the effectiveness of this procedure (e.g. Linden, 1981).

Marks (1981a) reviewed studies of exposure treatment and

found it to be the most universally effective of all the techniques used to treat fear. There is general agreement amongst clinicians that prolonged, uninterrupted exposure (thirty minutes to two hours) is more effective than brief or intermittent forms (Mathews and Shaw, 1973). Exposure in the actual situation is more effective than exposure in imagination (Mathews *et al.*, 1981; Emmelkamp and Wessels, 1975). Finally, just as inducing low levels of anxiety via relaxation does not seem essential to systematic desensitization, neither does the arousal of high levels of fear seem to increase the effectiveness of exposure treatments (Hafner and Marks, 1976).

An excellent example of effective exposure treatment is provided by Mathews *et al.*'s (1981) programmed practice for agoraphobic clients. Each day, *for at least an hour*, clients are asked to practise returning to the situations they were previously avoiding. The therapist only accompanies the client on his/her first journey and subsequently merely acts as an advisor. The programme provides for intense participation by the client's partner. A manual describing the treatment procedure is distributed for the joint use of the client and his/her partner. In a well-controlled study the authors found that clients receiving this form of exposure treatment improved significantly more than a control group not offered exposure; what is more impressive is that the treated clients continued to improve during a six-month follow-up period in which no treatment was given. Other studies have demonstrated that therapeutic gains following exposure treatment are maintained for 2–9 years without the appearance of additional ('substitute') problems (Munby and Johnston, 1980; Cohen *et al.*, 1984). *Modelling* has also been used in the treatment of anxiety (Bandura, 1971a). It consists of the client observing the therapist (the model), who approaches and experiences the phobic situation in a controlled and calm manner. In some modelling treatments (participant modelling) the client approaches the feared stimulus (e.g. coming close to and stroking a large dog) having observed the therapist doing so beforehand. Some workers claim that modelling of responses is an important component in the treatment of phobic disorders. This may be true for the treatment of simple phobias (e.g. fears of animals) and for child clients. However, there is no good evidence to indicate that modelling is any more than a useful tool for persuading children to expose themselves to the situation they fear (Marks, 1978).

Exposure with response prevention is the most widely used treatment for compulsive behaviour problems. It follows a procedure similar to flooding, which should not surprise us since compulsions and obsessions are frequently interpreted as avoidance responses maintained by learning processes similar to those presumed to underlie phobic behaviour. Clients are exposed to the stimuli which usually elicit their rituals but are prevented from performing them: for example, clients may be asked to hold 'contaminated' objects which previously elicited severe compulsive hand-washing.

Marks (1981b) reviewed three studies where treated and untreated groups were compared as well as several uncontrolled investigations involving a total of 200 clients with compulsive problems. The studies showed that exposure and response prevention leads to significant improvements in about two-thirds of quite severely affected cases. This improvement is maintained at two-year follow-up. Treatments using relaxation procedures offer but little help. To be effective the treatment sessions must be accompanied by homework assignments carried out independently by the client. Clients who do not comply with therapists' instructions or who are depressed are somewhat less likely to improve. Compared with other non-behavioural methods, however, exposure with response prevention is markedly successful.

Obsessional thoughts (recurrent, intrusive ideas which distress the client) are much more difficult to treat, even using behavioural methods. The *satiation* technique, which involves encouraging people to think the obsessive thought continuously for periods of up to an hour, has had some success. It is presumed that subjects will become habituated to these internal stimuli, which will then cease to arouse anxiety in them. Stern (1978) reports only two out of seven patients being helped by this technique. *Thought-stopping* is another technique for helping clients with obsessional thoughts. In this procedure, the client is relaxed and then asked to think the obsessive thought. When the client signals that he/she has achieved this, the therapist shouts 'Stop!' and at the same time makes a sudden noise. Gradually the client takes over responsibility for the thought-stopping, at first shouting out 'Stop!' in a similar fashion, then whispering it and eventually employing a silent command. This technique also yields variable results.

Likierman and Rachman (1982) compared the effectiveness of satiation and thought-stopping, finding little therapeutic advance with either method. Thus, there are as yet no reliable behavioural methods available for treating obsessive thoughts.

Why fear-reduction techniques are effective

A large number of theories have been put forward within the framework of classical learning theory to account for the effectiveness of fear-reduction techniques. The evidence is too intricate and complex for us to review, and only some of the less complex ideas will be presented here. The simplest of all learning procedures, habituation, may be one of the processes involved. Exposure and other features of behavioural treatments may promote the habituation of sympathetic responses to clinically pertinent stimuli (Lader and Mathews, 1968; Watts, 1979). Others suggest that fear-reduction techniques facilitate the extinction of a conditioned fear response (Wilson and Davison, 1971; Boyd and Levis, 1983). Yet others believe that the response of anxiety is inhibited by the learning of alternative and incompatible responses (Wolpe, 1981).

As Marks (1982) noted, all these accounts based on learning theory suggest that exposure is the crucial element in fear-reduction techniques. He proposed that any aspects of the treatment which lead to prolonged exposure to the fear-evoking stimulus will result in a decrement of the fear response. This clinical statement, sometimes flatteringly referred to by the term 'exposure theory', of course only explains what technique results in fear reduction but not why it might do so.

Some behaviour therapists (e.g. Bandura, 1977) suggest that in order to understand the mechanism of fear reduction we need to look beyond learning theory. If exposure turned out not to be a *necessary* condition for fear reduction, this would imply that factors other than conditioning may be involved in some or perhaps all such treatments. De Silva and Rachman (1981, 1983) in proposing an argument along such lines summarized seven sources of evidence in support of the contention that fear reduction could take place in the absence of exposure. One line of evidence is the so-called expectancy or placebo effect. Marcia *et al.* (1969) reported a study where snake-fearful subjects were led to believe that very brief 'subconscious' exposure to pictures of snakes was going to reduce their anxiety. During this 'treatment' their anxiety (as indicated to them by audible heartbeats) appeared to decrease. (This was 'rigged' and unrelated to their actual pulse rate.) Although in reality these subjects were exposed to nothing more than a tropical beach scene a significant improvement took place.

In order to understand an effect such as this it may be easier to think of fear reduction in the context of clients' ideas and thoughts rather than in that of traditional conditioning accounts (Critelli and Neuman, 1984). De Silva and Rachman (1984) also carried out a clinical investigation which was inconsistent with the well-accepted learning theory accounts. They demonstrated (in an admittedly small sample) that agoraphobics who were instructed to *leave* the feared situation as soon as their anxiety increased to a criterion point did just as well as those who were told to expose themselves to the fear-evoking stimulus until their anxiety decreased by at least by 50 per cent (the usual treatment consistent with exposure theory).

All in all, it seems that as findings accumulate learning theory may find it increasingly difficult to incorporate results from the fear-reduction literature.

Behavioural procedures with mentally impaired and chronic psychiatric clients

Undoubtedly the most important contribution of behaviour therapy has been in areas where before its introduction no systematic psychological interventions could be offered. One such area is that of mental impairment. In the early sixties there was an atmosphere of great optimism: it was hoped that behavioural treatments would radically change the lives of these individuals. This optimism was perhaps premature, but nevertheless there are striking examples of successful modification programmes. (Burgio *et al.*, 1983).

A large-scale study showed substantial improvement in the eating behaviour of profoundly impaired adults (IQs 20–49). They used peer and therapist modelling of the behaviours, social reinforcements and verbal prompts to shape eating, use of utensils, table manners, etc. (Matson *et al.*, 1980). Reinforcers included being allowed to go to the meals early, having their own mat at table, etc. The rewards were made in front of their peers. There was a significantly greater improvement in the treated group even four months after the end of treatment as compared with a control group.

Another controlled study demonstrated that the social abilities of mentally impaired individuals could be substantially improved using behavioural methods of social skills training (Senatore *et al.*, 1982). In this procedure, the therapist initially modelled appropriate social responses in a number of situations and used social reinforcements to shape these behaviours in mentally impaired adults. In this case the treatment effects were apparent even six months after the treatment.

Operant methods for mentally impaired individuals are beset by problems of generalization as are frequently found in the case of children. The in-patient operant conditioning of autistic children (autism is a form of childhood psychosis often associated with mental impairment in which children tend to have particular difficulties with language) frequently shows highly encouraging results for teaching speech to these children (see Harris and Milch, 1981). These hospital-based improvements often fail to generalize to the child's home setting (Rutter, 1982). However, comparable behavioural methods based in the child's home environment with parents working as behaviour modifiers appear to be of both short- and long-term benefit (Howlin, 1981).

A method of reinforcement frequently used with children, mentally impaired and chronic psychiatric clients involves the issuing of tokens which may be exchanged for desired rewards at specific times. Such *token economy programmes* have been successfully applied in many long stay settings (Ayllon and Azrin, 1968). Amongst the advantages of these programmes is the ease with which they can be adapted to address individual problems, including self-care, participation in group activities and domestic skills, (Kazdin, 1977).

Nevertheless, few studies have been able to demonstrate durable effects for these techniques. Woods *et al.* (1984) provided data the implications of which go beyond this particular procedure. The programme had therapeutic effects (produced behaviour change lasting beyond removal of the tokens) for those patients whose newly acquired behaviours were '*trapped*' by natural social reinforcers. For example, some patients who were incapable of performing in a socially appropriate way were avoided by staff prior to the programme. The programme produced changes in their social behaviour that were so marked that the staff now invited them home for tea. Such reinforcement was sufficient to maintain the newly acquired social interaction behaviour.

A further implication of this study is that an important level of intervention with chronic clients may be at the level of caretaking staff rather than the clients themselves. Using behaviour therapy to change the contingencies of staff behaviour has been demonstrated by controlled studies (e.g. Bernstein, 1982) to be highly effective. A study by Burgio *et al.* (1983) demonstrated that if staff were selectively reinforced for verbal interaction with residents a reliable improvement in client behaviour could be observed. As this example shows, it follows from the functional analysis approach that frequently changing the environment may be the most efficient way of achieving behavioural change. Melin and Gotesman (1981) demonstrated that moving clients' chairs away from the walls to around small tables resulted in a manifold increase in social interaction.

Evaluation

There can be no doubt about the general success of behaviour therapy. As Marks (1981a) concluded, behaviour therapy appears to be the treatment of choice for phobias, obsessive-compulsive disorders, social skills problems, marital and sexual difficulties – in other words, for about 25 per cent of all non-psychotic complaints. Furthermore, it is the only viable mode of psychological intervention in a number of other areas (many of which we have had no opportunity to discuss), such as mental impairment, the rehabilitation of chronic psychiatric patients, the treatment of brain-injured individuals and other medical problems, including psychosomatic disorders, etc.

The usefulness of the procedures is evidenced by the increasing number of new treatment techniques applied to an ever-expanding range of psychological, educational and medical problems. Active clinical behavioural research has resulted in substantial increases in technique, know-how and versatility as well as a greater sophistication in research methodology. It is this richness of technique that represents perhaps the greatest strength of the behavioural approach to treatment: it allows treatment to be flexible. Therapists can modify their approach to replace techniques that seem ineffective with a particular individual with other tools from their therapeutic armamentarium. Moreover, the judicious application of functional analysis gives therapists a sound empirical base from which to judge the success or otherwise of their interventions.

The problem of the behavioural approach is not at all at the level of practice, rather at the level of theory. Numerous reviewers have pointed to the way theoretical developments have lagged behind the proliferation of behavioural techniques. Learning theory, the source of most behavioural procedures, provides an over-used yet probably inadequate framework for such interventions for a number of reasons. Learning theory is derived largely from laboratory animal studies, and extrapolation from these to human problems and their solution involves making assumptions concerning commonalities which are probably unjustified (Marks, 1982; Gelder, 1982). There are a number of ways, for example, in which laboratory experiments differ from human problems:

1 Laboratory experiments last a few days, whereas human phobias or obsessions are established and practised over many years.
2 Animal demonstrations concern 'all or none' phenomena; clinical neuroses have a complex, fluctuating course of waxing and waning.
3 The assignment of labels such as 'conditioned stimuli', 'reinforcement' and 'discriminative stimulus' is unambiguous in the laboratory because these variables are manipulated. Clinically, we assign these labels *post hoc* (after the event), a practice which inevitably has a certain arbitrariness, in our selection and labelling of the crucial variables.
4 There are no explicit rules for extrapolation, so literally any principle of conditioning could be applied to behavioural work.
5 There is no reason to assume that principles discovered in animal learning apply to humans. One spectacular example of this is offered by Bijou and Baer (1966) reporting the case of a young child who responded for a considerable time during extinction. When asked why he continued responding, he replied: 'You didn't tell me to stop!'

Thus, although behavioural interventions are very effective the reason for their effectiveness may be quite unrelated to learning theory principles. Many find these principles inadequate when trying to use them to conceptualize important psychological functions such as self-regulatory behaviour (as the child above) and social or cognitive processes that may be central to behavioural change (e.g. Bandura, 1977; Bower, 1978; Erwin, 1978; and see Chapter 8). Perhaps, then, it is not surprising that there is as yet no adequate learning theory account of psychological abnormality and its treatment. If self-control and social or cognitive processes underlie these, the implication must be that we have to look outside learning theory for a satisfactory account.

5

Humanistic approaches

The common philosophical perspective to the humanistic approaches to personality and psychotherapy is that both consider individuals not as objects of study but as experiencing beings whose awareness of themselves should be the point of departure of any psychological investigation. The humanistic approach aims to consider life as it is experienced by the whole person, not to split people into unrelated parts, nor to reduce them to physiological principles or laws of learning. This emphasis on phenomenological experiences is focused on the *here and now* rather than on distant historical causes in the person's childhood. Furthermore, people are seen as masters of their own lives, capable of making free and responsible choices. Compared with other theories of personality, humanistic approaches see people as unique and noble creatures who need meaningful activity, responsibility and the opportunity to express themselves creatively.

The client-centred approach

Humanistic psychology was undoubtedly a reaction to the reductionism and determinism of the psychoanalytic and behavioural schools. Rogers' approach embodies all the fundamental tenets of humanism. It is based on the assumption that the individual lives within his/her own experiential or phenomenal field. This field, according to Rogers (1959), includes all that is going on within and around the organism at any given moment and which is potentially available to awareness. Thus it includes, in addition to external events, the psychological representations of physiological drives such as hunger and the momentary influence of memory. For good psychological functioning this experiential field should be maximally available to awareness.

Rogers recognizes only a single motive: the actualization tendency (or 'organismic enhancement'). This is an innate desire on the part of all living organisms to extend the range of their phenomenal fields to seek to learn new things and thus enrich their experience. Actualization drives the organism to realize positive capacities that will maintain and enhance the organism itself and contribute to its personal growth. It also pushes the organism towards autonomy (i.e. independence from the environment via the internalization of control). In Rogers' view, the organism evaluates all experiences from the viewpoint of the actualizing tendency.

At the heart of Rogers' theory is the development of the *self*. During the course of development, a portion of the individual's experience becomes separated off and is represented as self-awareness – the actual experiences of being and functioning. Through interaction with important others these initial experiences grow into an organized pattern of perceptions which refer to 'me' or 'I' (Rogers, 1980). Along with this development of the self-concept out of the total experience of the organism, the actualizing tendency also differentiates to produce a *self-actualizing tendency*. The aim of self-actualization is the maintainance and enhancement of the self rather than of the total organism. With increased awareness of the self the need for positive regard from others develops. Such positive regard is essential for maintaining the self-concept. The positive regard of significant others may, at times, be more important even than the individual's own view of him/herself. As development progresses further, individuals learn to experience and to satisfy this need for positive regard on their own, without reference to others. Thus an experience may be evaluated as positive or negative either because it is more or less worthy of self-regard or valued by others:

for example, a child may feel angry with his/her mother but will try to avoid the feeling in order to be regarded as a 'good boy' or 'good girl'.

To summarize, Rogers considers that two dynamic systems make up personality. The organismic system is motivated by the actualizing tendency which aims at realizing the organism's capacities. The second system, the self system, is motivated to maintain a consistent self-image and to enhance the self. Enhancement of the self depends both on the positive regard of others and on positive self-regard (called 'condition of worth').

Psychological disorders

The organism interacts with the environment via both conscious and unconscious processes. An experience at variance with the need for self-regard threatens the consistency of the self-concept and may be either denied to awareness (made unconscious) or distorted so as to suit the self-image. Thus it is assumed that experiences which are distorted or denied to awareness in this way are in fact represented subconsciously in accordance with reality. The tension between the accurate, subconscious representation and the distorted concept of which the self is aware is the *incongruence* which Rogers refers to as the basis of his model of psychopathology. Incongruence is thus the discrepancy which can come to exist between the experience of the organism and the concept of self.

Rogers regards a certain amount of incongruence between self and organismic experience as natural, but, should this incongruence become too great, maladjustment can result. This incongruence between the self and experience will lead to behaviour that is not consistent with the self-concept. To maintain congruence these behaviours will in their turn be either distorted or simply not recognized. People may not even notice that they are behaving in a sexist or prejudiced way because the experiences are not consistent with their self-concept.

Anxiety occurs when underlying incongruence approaches awareness. In the case of more serious maladjustment, the defences will be tightened and distortions of reality will become even more evident. For example, a man who organismically experiences homosexual impulses but whose self-concept cannot admit of such desires may initially experience anxiety, but as the incongruence between self and experience grows he will resort to more complex defences. In a study of 250 people for whom congruence or genuineness (closeness to inner emotional experiences) and neuroticism were independently assessed, it was individuals with high degrees of *incongruence* who were most likely to manifest neurotic symptoms (Tausch, 1978).

Rogers postulates defensive behaviours very similar to those of psychoanalytic theory, including rationalization, projection and fantasy. Nevertheless, Rogers' view differs from Freud's in that for the former the defences *are* the neurotic symptoms: they are the problematic processes separating the self from the experience of the organism. Rogers extends the definition of defences beyond that used by Freud. They are not seen as expressions of unconscious impulses. Rogers, for example, includes extreme withdrawal (as seen in chronic psychosis) amongst the possible defences and thus he extends the concept of defence beyond the neuroses to account for psychotic behaviour as well. In his view, the basis of psychosis is not fundamentally different from the neuroses: it is merely incongruence of a more extreme degree than that found in neurosis.

Application of person-centred psychology

Client-centred therapy

In common with that of many personality theorists since Freud, Rogers' view of the person developed largely during the treatment of neurotic patients. In outlining his treatment model it will become clear how his specific therapeutic techniques have led him to the model outlined above.

The central hypothesis of client-centred therapy is that the person has within him/herself an inherent capacity for and tendency towards self-understanding and for constructive change or actualization (Rogers, 1980). The therapist, therefore, need not control or manipulate the therapeutic process by setting goals or otherwise imposing his/her judgement. Given suitable conditions, clients are able to make their own decisions based on what is intrinsically satisfying and actualizing. Hence the therapy became known as *non-directive therapy*.

The second distinguishing characteristic of this approach concerns the importance of the therapeutic relationship. The therapist's main task is to provide a *therapeutic atmosphere* in which clients can be more open to their own organismic experience, to return once again to their basic nature and judge for themselves which course of life is most intrinsically gratifying. In this climate (Rogers, 1959) the client can learn to reduce the incongruence between self and experience. In contrast to the psychodynamic pursuit of hidden meaning and insight into unconscious processes, Rogers believes that personality is revealed fully in what clients say about themselves.

Thirdly, the principles of the psychotherapy do not differ according to the client's presenting problems, be they labelled psychotic, neurotic or normal: Rogers (1977) firmly rejects all such distinctions.

Finally, Rogerian therapists have recently emphasized the usefulness of actual experience in preference to verbal exploration. The involvement of the therapist in a *real relationship* with his client is increasingly encouraged.

Rogers regards change in psychotherapy as occurring along a number of dimensions. There may be an increased recognition of feelings and of incongruence on the part of clients. Therapy may also enhance clients' ability to communicate self-awareness or their ability to be themselves when relating to others. Clients may also become clearer about who they are and what they want.

Rogers (1980) remarked that in the development of client-centred therapy it has gradually emerged that therapeutic success seems to be more dependent upon the presence of certain 'attitudes' in the therapist than upon technical training. Rogerians hold that the effective communication of these attitudes is both necessary and sufficient for therapeutic change.

According to Rogers (1957), the most important attitude is *genuineness* or congruence. Genuine therapists are themselves without sham or façade. They are congruent in that their organismic experience is present in their awareness and can be directly communicated to the client (when appropriate). Such direct communication could involve therapists in disclosing their reaction to the client, saying, for example: 'I feel quite frustrated by the way you watch so carefully what you say to me, because I feel I will never get to know what you are really thinking.' Genuineness turns psychotherapy into a direct personal encounter with the client.

The second attitude necessary for therapeutic change is that of *warmth* (unconditional acceptance or unconditional positive re-gard). This implies the communication of a deep and genuine caring for the client as a person, much like that of a parent for a child. This is offered unconditionally, not because the therapist necessarily approves of everything a client may do, but because his/her caring is total.

The third attitude is *empathic* understanding. By conveying such acceptance the therapist enables clients to attend gradually to conflicts between their actual self and what they are capable of being. This implies that therapists enter into clients' inner worlds and, having become thoroughly at home there, are able to sense moment-to-moment changes and meanings of which the latter are scarcely aware. Therapists demonstrate their understanding by restating or reflecting the emotional aspect of what clients say rather than the content. It is this need to be sensitive to the emotional tone of clients' verbalizations that makes the work of client-centred psychotherapists such a skilled endeavour (Barker, 1983). If these therapeutic conditions are established, clients will talk in more honest ways about themselves and, according to Rogers, the re-establishment of such congruence is sufficient to lead to changes in behaviour.

Considerable evidence has accumulated concerning the im-portance of these three therapist variables (or facilitators). In studies of therapist facilitativeness, transcripts or tape-recordings of sessions are rated by trained judges who assess the therapist for each of the three interpersonal dimensions: namely empathy, warmth and genuineness. Early studies by Truax and Mitchell (1971) were very encouraging. They indicated that highly facili-tative therapists were much more likely to produce favourable outcomes than those who rated low on these dimensions. Furthermore, therapists rated as low on empathy, warmth and genuineness were actually much more likely to produce negative therapeutic effects, in other words a worsening of the client's condition by the end of therapy.

More recent studies, however, have produced mixed results. A review by Mitchell *et al.* (1977) found that more than half the studies failed to find the expected association between therapist facilitativeness and results of treatment. The authors suggested that this might be accounted for by methodological problems such as unreliable ratings of empathy, warmth and genuineness, markedly low mean levels of facilitativeness in all the therapists participating in some studies, and so on. In addition, many critics question the assessments made by judges from these taped sessions. Therapists are likely to show empathy, warmth and genuineness with great discretion – to choose their moment – and an accurate assessment of their therapeutic importance would need to assess not only how extensively these qualities were used but also how appropriately.

There has been a great deal of controversy concerning the degree to which therapist facilitativeness can be trained. A number of psychologists have tried to break down these skills into component parts and have designed special programmes to teach helping skills (Egan, 1982). Others (e.g. Plum, 1981) have commented that these skills are an integral part of the individual and so any attempt to teach them as an entity will be unsuccessful. In the light of the equivocal status of Rogers' facilitativeness variables, the investment of major effort in teaching them as skills is probably ill-advised. Nevertheless, as Barker (1983) pointed out, despite their questionable empirical basis Rogers' ideas about optimal therapeutic environments have become part of the accepted clinical wisdom of psychologists of all theoretical orientations.

Rogers' psychotherapeutic model was initially used only with neurotic clients. In the 1960s, however, Rogers made a brave attempt to treat schizophrenics using client-centred therapy. In a report of this systematic study (Rogers et al., 1967), it was recognized that treated groups made only marginal gains relative to untreated controls. Furthermore, only the schizophrenic clients' (not the independent assessors') ratings of therapist facilitativeness correlated substantially with outcome – and this type of evidence is weak to say the least.

Encounter groups

During the 1970s Rogers extended many of his concepts to *encounter groups*. These are concentrated therapeutic experiences, often extending over one or more weekends, in which individuals meet to experience impulses, feelings and fantasies. Although many encounter groups rely primarily on verbal procedures, participants are also encouraged to act out emotions in the group rather than just talk about them. Such 'acting-out' is facilitated by body contact (designed to increase awareness of body or organismic feelings) and by games (encouraging the expression of affection and feelings). Exercises, such as a member allowing the rest of the group to carry or catch him/her, are thought to enhance group trust.

There is some evidence to suggest that encounter groups are effective in changing the degree of self-actualization (the degree to which a person makes choices on the basis of current experience and pays attention to inner feelings). The Person Orientation Inventory (Schostrom, 1966) was designed as a questionnaire measure of self-actualization. Smith (1980) reviewed controlled studies of the effect of encounter groups on this measure and found that most of the studies showed increased self-actualization after the group experience. Smith (1981), however, went on to suggest that the 'improvements' might have been due to an alteration in the subjects' vocabulary after participation in the groups rather than to a fundamental change in self-concept. Furthermore, there is much doubt about the degree to which the openness and frankness learned in a group will or can generalize to everyday situations.

Evaluation

Rogers' approach has made a tremendous impact on clinical psychology in the United States and Britain. Clinical psychologists who like neither the dynamic nor the learning theory-based approach have been provided with an alternative. Rogers himself accounts for the widespread influence of his theory thus: 'I had expressed an idea whose time had come' (Rogers, 1974). In the late 1960s and early 1970s, there was a strong movement towards oriental philosophies, and Rogers' ideas had much in common with them. Two examples which illustrate this are the emphasis on experience as the main avenue of learning in Zen teaching, and some of the sayings of Lao-tse, such as 'If I keep from imposing on people they become themselves'. Rogers has also provided a powerful impetus to research into the psychotherapeutic process.

Rogers' influence, however, has not been as marked as might have been expected. In 1980 he himself noted that his ideas and research findings (at least those concerning education) were 'not being taken seriously'. There are a number of probable reasons for this. Firstly, there are major omissions in the theory: for example, although he postulates the existence of unconscious processes, he has never provided a psychology of the unconscious which could clarify what happens to incongruent experiences which are denied to awareness. Paradoxically, the theory also fails to tackle the nature of personality differences in normal people: the question of why, for example, one individual may be more ambitious, quiet and tidy than another. In brief, Rogers' theory is weak in terms of its outline of the psychological mechanisms which play a role in the formation and functioning of personality.

Secondly, in the past few years many clinical psychologists have become disillusioned with the experiential (encounter-group-type) approach to psychotherapy. Despite initial enthusiasm, the thin dividing line between legitimate clinical experimentation and frank exploitation of people's miseries has become obscured. A theory such as Rogers', with its heavy emphasis on experience and putting people in touch with previously unexplored parts of themselves is open to being used to justify questionable events. The potentially harmful consequences are only just beginning to be documented (see, for example, Higgitt and Murray, 1983).

Thirdly, some of Rogers' concepts contain major epistemological problems and are probably impossible to define empirically. The process of actualization has never been adequately measured. The logic of postulating such an innately given drive or motive without the possibility of independent assessment is always in danger of becoming circular. Rogers infers the self-actualization motive from his observation that people seek out situations that will offer fulfilment; he then proceeds to put forward self-actualization as an explanation of the behaviour which led him to formulate the concept in the first place.

Rogers' concept of self faces similar difficulties of operationalization and measurement. The self is a phenomenal construct: in other words, we use it to account for certain experiences. Rogers and his followers, however, consider the self as an entity and a causal agent able to consider and integrate perceptions. These, of course, are unjustifiable assumptions which make the concept of the self as vulnerable as that of the Freudian concept of the ego. A more promising approach to the self was taken by Markus (1977). He regards the self as a frame of reference schema in which cognitions about oneself are stored. Nevertheless, this revised model cannot be treated as equivalent to Rogers' formulation.

In line with these difficulties of measurement, empirical research on Rogerian concepts has been vigorous but has yielded little in the way of substantive findings. In fact, Rogers himself expressed general disappointment about the outcome of empirical investigations: 'I'm not really a scientist. Most of my research has been to confirm what I already felt to be true . . . Generally I never learned anything from research' (Rogers in Bergin and Strupp, 1972, p. 314).

The personal construct theory approach

In 1955, George Kelly advanced his theory of personality. In 1956, Bruner referred to it as the single greatest psychological contribution of the decade. In 1970, Appelbaum assessed Kelly's contribution as containing little that was new and regarded his eminence as a historical accident of his time. Which of these assessments is closer to the truth?

Kelly, like Rogers, aimed to provide an alternative to the behavioural and psychoanalytic schools. He viewed all mankind as scientists. Science, he claimed, is concerned with the prediction and control of phenomena. Scientists propose general theories from which they make predictions about specific events which are subsequently tested empirically. Thus Kelly considered that each person formulates hypotheses about the world, makes predictions from these hypotheses, tests them and, if necessary, revises the hypotheses in the light of his/her 'experimental results'.

Kelly's *fundamental postulate* lay in this concept. He maintained that we interpret or construe events rather than observe them directly. There is not one single correct way of viewing the universe; all interpretations are subject to revision or replacement. He labelled this position *constructive alternativism*. This is a fundamentally cognitive viewpoint. The cognitive position concerns itself with the processes whereby we interpret information from the sense organs, integrating it with our knowledge of the world (Mandler, 1975). Kelly's emphasis on cognitive processes mediating between the environment and the organism's response to it places his theory close to current socio-cognitive approaches (see Chapter 8).

In Kelly's view, construing events involves investing them with meaning, and this helps us to organize our experiences and activities in relation to them. The individual's system of personal constructs determines the way the world is construed. Constructs are bipolar dimensions created by an individual to discriminate between things and so to make sense of the world. As Kelly put it: 'A construct is a way in which some things are construed as being alike and yet different from others' (1955, p. 105). As an example, if one tried to think in what way Hitler and Mussolini were alike, and yet different from Churchill, one might suggest constructs such as: 'fascist–democrat', 'dishonest–honest', 'cruel–humane', 'lost the war–won the war', etc. These could all be constructs used to differentiate historical figures.

Kelly likened constructs to transparent templates through which a person views the world and attempts to distinguish its elements. The most important function of constructs is to provide the basis for predictions about the world and to anticipate and thereby influence events. Actions, in Kelly's view, are ways of testing the predictions (1969). They represent a series of experiments based on a person's expectations. The outcome of the actions may, of course, modify the original theory.

Construct systems are made up of constructs which have interlocking relationships with each other. The construct system is hierarchical, some constructs being subsumed by others: thus, for example, the construct 'attractive–unattractive' may subsume constructs about size of face, size of nose, colour of hair, etc.

Kelly 'reconstrued' several psychological concepts within his theory. He avoided the conception of a self but assumed the formation of *self-constructs* which are used to construe our own identity. As a person construes other people he/she formulates the construction system which governs his/her own behaviour; thus when people talk about others they reveal the construct system within which they also see themselves. An individual who distinguishes between people in terms of 'powerful–not powerful', 'important–not important', 'has to be obeyed–does not have to be obeyed' reveals him/herself as a somewhat authoritarian person whose most important dimension of construing individuals is in terms of the power they have over him. Someone else who differentiates between people in terms of constructs such as 'likes me–does not like me', 'is nice to me–is nasty to me', 'I can rely on–I cannot rely on' is clearly very concerned about the emotional reactions he/she will elicit from other people and the extent to which these may threaten his/her dependence on them.

Interpersonal relationships were seen by Kelly as our attempts to construe the construction processes of others; we hypothesize about what others may be thinking about us and test this out by altering our behaviour as necessary. For example, we stop talking if our audience starts to yawn excessively because we construe from their response that they are beginning to construe us as incredibly boring.

Kelly suggested that constructs develop purely through repeated exposure to and interaction with the environment, which occurs simply by the fact of our being alive. When constructs lead to accurate predictions or anticipation, they may be considered to be validated. This is not the same as reinforcement, since highly aversive events (such as breaking a leg) may validate a construct such as seeing skiing as dangerous. When a construct fails to predict accurately, the person will either turn to another construct upon which to base predictions or undertake a revision of the construct system. Thus in the latter case new constructs are formed out of the failure of old ones to achieve validation (Bannister and Fransella, 1981).

New constructs will only emerge if they do not pose a 'threat' to the individual's construct system: in other words, if they are not incompatible with an essential construct higher up in the construct hierarchy. Thus a man may be 'threatened' by construing women as strong and capable as opposed to weak and incompetent because this would lead him to see his wife as too powerful and he would not then be able to exercise control over her in his usual manner (Fransella, 1981a).

If a person fails to perform according to expectations, he or she invalidates constructs concerning him/herself and thus may become threatening. Individuals with manifest psychotic behaviour are often perceived as a threat to the community, perhaps because they threaten most people's central constructs about human behaviour; those in the helping professions do not perceive this threat because they have developed special constructs. Our construct system concerning people not only determines our reactions to them but also affects the way we conduct our own social behaviour (see Button, 1983). According to Kelly, we tend to play roles that fulfil and thus validate other people's constructs of us.

Kelly maintains that not all constructs can be verbalized. Preverbal construing refers to the use of constructs for which there are no verbal labels, their existence being surmised from the person's behaviour. Behavioural signs of the existence of preverbal constructs include confusion in verbalization, the re-membering of events about whose actual occurrence the person is unsure, dreams the person is unable to recollect clearly, etc. This is the closest that Kelly came to considering unconscious pro-cesses. He totally rejected the dynamic concept of the uncon-scious (the repression of what is intolerable) and saw repression as the cessation of the process of construing.

Kelly explains individual differences solely with reference to the functioning of construct systems: to understand a person we need to know how he/she typically construes life. In line with this, Kelly's understanding of abnormal behaviour is also based on problems in construing.

Psychological disorders

Kelly (1955) offered clinicians a whole range of constructs which they could use in understanding their clients. These constructs were not disease entities, types of people or dimensions of personal characteristics; they were tantamount to a set of co-ordinate axes with respect to which it becomes possible to plot any person's behavioural changes in terms of his/her psychological processes. Kelly called these *diagnostic constructs*. We shall illus-trate these diagnostic constructs by reference to a number of well-known disorders.

Psychological disorders, Kelly felt, resulted from the repeated use of constructs that had already been invalidated. He suggested that all symptoms serve to give structure and meaning to the chaotic experiences which arise out of the use of invalidated constructs (Landfield and Leitner, 1980).

In the case of anxiety, the individual is thought to face events which lie outside the *range of convenience* of his/her construct system. This means that the person's constructs do not apply to (are inadequate for) the events he/she faces. The person may respond to this by a *loosening* of constructs which will help him/her to deal with the ambiguities. As a result of loosening, the con-structs become less specific in their predictions. Of course, the extreme form of loosening (psychotic thought disorder) is also highly maladaptive: 'When anything goes, nothing goes any-where.' Bannister (1963, 1965) suggested that schizophrenic thought disorder reflected the loosening of construct rela-tionships to a point where constructs that are usually reliably and firmly linked come to relate to each other in a more or less random way. He proposed that this degree of construct-loosening occurred as a result of repeated invalidations of predictions. Higgins and Schwarz (1976) and Lawlor and Cochran (1981) showed experimentally that repeated invalidations of the judgements of normal subjects may cause them to loosen their conceptual organization. When subjects were repeatedly told they were incorrect in their judgements, the degree of interrelationship between their constructs decreased. Button (1983), from a Kellian perspective, proposed that all symptomatology, whatever its nature, is the consequence of a person's failure to anticipate people accurately. Problems such as agoraphobia, delusions or alcoholism may all be seen as different strategies for coping with invalidation. Thus a post-pubertal girl faced with social invalidation may turn to the popular hypothesis that for women to be acceptable they must get their weight right. This could set them on the road to pathological dieting and ultimately anorexia nervosa (a disorder in which the dieting turns into a veritable mania to be thin).

When the anxiety engendered by the inadequacy of the construct system is dealt with by *tightening* of constructs obsessive-compulsive symptoms can result. Obsessional rituals represent an extreme attempt at making totally unvarying predictions. These constructs are also completely *impermeable*: in other words, no new elements can be introduced into them. Fransella (1972) used Kellian diagnostic constructs to identify the central problem of stutterers. She felt that stuttering could become a *self-construct*. Stutterers construe themselves as stutterers and would have difficulty in dealing with relationships if they were to abandon this construct without replacing it with an alternative.

The use of the repertory grid in validating Kelly's ideas

The technique involves eliciting a sample of the individual's personal constructs by asking the individual to consider people he/she knows who might fit a number of given roles (including father, brother, employer, most successful person). He/she is then presented with randomly chosen sets of three of these so-called elements and asked to think of a way in which two of these are alike and differ from the third. This produces one pole of a construct (e.g. 'loving'), and the individual is then quizzed as to a possible opposite to this word in order to derive the other pole (e.g. 'rejecting'). Accordingly, a number of bipolar constructs (usually between ten and twenty) can be elicited. The subject is then asked to place all the people he suggested for the roles along all the construct dimensions. In this way a matrix of the rating of all elements on all constructs (the grid) is obtained. Statistical analysis permits reduction of the grid data to a number of dimensions indicative of the construct system of a particular individual.

Winter (1982) makes a case for using the grid in order to assess improvement following psychotherapy. He found that the inter-relations between constructs altered with successful therapy: clients came to view themselves more positively by the end of their treatment. Also, the relationship between symptom constructs (e.g. 'has obsessions–does not have obsessions') and the desirable pole of constructs (e.g. 'attractive' in the construct 'attractive–not attractive') decreases. The importance of this can be seen in the following example: if obsessions are associated with being a 'feeling' person, then it may be difficult for the individual to lose the obsession without running the risk of becoming an 'unfeeling' person.

Personal construct psychotherapy

Personal construct psychotherapy is directed towards a reconstruction of the client's system of personal constructs. Bannister (1983) and Fransella (1981a) summarize the ways in which personal construct therapists help the client to revise their construct system or develop new constructs.

Therapists work with their clients in the way that research supervisors work with their students. The clients are the only experts on their problems; the therapists can contribute their general familiarity with ways of evaluating experience and formulating strategies for exploration. Thus the basic task of the therapist is to *elaborate* the personal construct system in which the client functions and within which his/her difficulties lie. Self-description through *self-characterization* may be used as a way of elaborating the person's life-role structure. Here clients are asked to write a character sketch of themselves in the third person as it might be written by a *very sympathetic* friend who knows him/her *intimately*, perhaps better than anyone ever really could. Elaboration may also be achieved by *prescribed activities* in the occupational or social sphere. A socially inhibited client may well need to elaborate his constructs about people by joining in activities that involve meeting others. The client's constructs may also be elaborated by the therapist *enacting* the client's role, thus allowing him to elaborate on his constructions concerning the way other people construe him. Thus conversation between therapist and client may lead to real-life ventures which test the hypothesis they have been examining. Further discussion may ensure that the implications of the behavioural experiment are reflected upon and made sense of (Epting, 1982). *Fixed-role therapy* (Bonarius, 1970) is a brief form of psychotherapy which involves the client in producing a self-characterization sketch as above. The therapist develops a fixed role sketch which suggests behaviours that are drastically different from those elaborated by the client. The client plays this role for a fixed period of about a fortnight. He/she sees the therapist frequently and is treated as if he/she were the person in the fixed-role sketch, thus validating the new construct.

The mode in which change is achieved via such validational experiences is through a continuous cycle of loose to tight to loose construing. The *loosening of constructs* allows the client to vary the classification of an element from one pole of a construct to the other. An individual determined to construe all people he/she likes, including him/herself, as meek, passive, lacking in aggression and hating violence may need these constructs loosened in order to be able to construe the world usefully. Aspects of the therapeutic situation such as relaxation, free association, reporting of dreams and the uncritical acceptance of the therapist may all contribute to such a loosening process. At other stages of therapy, the need is for the *tightening of constructs* to make predictions from them more stable and thus to facilitate the organization of the construct system. This may be achieved by asking clients to summarize either in words or in writing the things he/she told the therapist. Alternatively, the therapist may challenge the clients' constructs by expressing confusion or asking for evidence or even by labelling the clients' construing as nonsense, thus forcing them to tighten their construing in an argument (Bannister, 1982). Kelly repeatedly stressed the similarity of psychotherapy to scientific research (Bannister, 1982) in that it consists of a series of experiments. These experiments, formulated in the context of personal construct theory, may frequently appear as very similar to behavioural procedures.

In summary, personal construct psychotherapy is directed towards the reconstruction of the client's system of personal constructs. The therapist is active and responds to the client in a wide variety of ways. Enactments, behavioural experiments and role-playing are all important in the procedure, but more traditional psychotherapeutic techniques, such as free association, may also play a part. Naturally, the flexibility and variability of the technique, although in some ways commendable, make a systematic attempt at assessing its effectiveness difficult – in fact, no such attempts have yet been made.

Evaluation

Kelly's theory is arguably one of the most systematic attempts at formulating a psychological approach to personality and psychotherapy. It is in many ways a difficult theory to penetrate because many of the terms used by Kelly are either totally new or used by him in a way that differs slightly from general usage. As with psychoanalytic theory, the very abundance of new concepts makes the theory vulnerable to a charge of lack of economy of assumptions: the fundamental postulates of the theory are simple, but their elaborations are probably overly complex. This complaint is the most likely reason for the relative unpopularity of the theory, especially in its place of origin, the United States. Nevertheless, in recent years with the emergence of a cognitive approach to clinical psychology which recognizes that cognitions (thoughts, constructs) may be causes of abnormal emotional responses and behaviour, Kelly's theory is beginning to receive increased attention. It is widely acknowledged as a forerunner of the cognitive approach and a model that is in many respects ahead of its time. It is perhaps notable that it was not until 1982 that Fransella, with the assistance of Bannister, set up the first Centre for Personal Construct Psychology in London.

Bannister and Fransella (1981) proposed that the theory's intuitive appeal was itself indicative of its validity. This, of course, cannot be considered as a scientific statement. The grid studies attempted to provide evidence in support of some of Kelly's simpler suggestions. Grid methodology has, however, come under critical scrutiny. Kline (1983) questions the scientific status of grid data but provides no evidence for his comments. Others (e.g. Goodge, 1979; Shaw, 1980) have reviewed the statistical problems involved when analysing grid data and concluded that the most serious problems arise with the most complex analyses. Grid data do not meet most of the assumptions of the statistical procedures which are commonly employed to analyse them. Despite the fact that Fransella (1981b) cites some respectable figures, most reliability estimates are low. Kelly's more elaborate constructs in any case remain unvalidated for the moment. The recent growth of interest in the field of personal construct theory has also produced new Kellian proposals which remain to be tested (e.g., Landfield, 1980; Leitner, 1981).

A major shortcoming of the approach is the inadequacy of the theory of emotion it proposes (Bruner, 1956). (This has been perhaps better tackled by current cognitive theorists: see Chapter 8.) The developmental aspects of the theory are also probably too vague to be useful. Moreover, personal construct psychologists fail to explain adequately the development of construct systems which lead people to psychological difficulties. A related severe criticism concerns the circularity of many aspects of Kelly's theory: to claim that obsessive-compulsive neurosis is the use of tightening as a defence against a construct system threatened by invalidation is to say little more than that a person's problem behaviour of thinking in a rigid way can be accounted for by his tendency to think in a rigid way.

Neither Rogers' nor Kelly's humanistic approaches have become as widely accepted or used as their proponents might have hoped. The popularity of the humanistic approach may have suffered from the competition of behavioural approaches with their greater scientific appeal and the fuller, more rigorous and in-depth approach of dynamic (i.e. psychoanalytic) psychology. The humanistic approach was also considerably handicapped by the diversity of practice encouraged by its emphasis on flexibility. The lack of a relatively rigid set of techniques may have hindered the process of formal training of new therapists (Marmor, 1980) and so resulted in the relative shortage of clinical psychologists espousing this orientation.

Although the popularity of the humanistic approaches has probably been declining since the late 1960s, many of the central tenets of the theory have been absorbed into the cognitive approaches to clinical psychology.

6

Multi-trait and narrow-trait theories of personality

Trait theories of personality assume that we all possess broad dispositions to respond to stimuli in particular ways: for example, a friendly person is likely to respond with helpfulness, warmth, interest, attentiveness and thoughtfulness to a variety of situations such as meeting a stranger, visiting family members or going out with a friend. This predisposition is called a *trait*. According to Allport (1937), traits are neuropsychological entities: in other words, they actually exist somewhere in the human brain. They are held to be responsible for the stability of a person's behaviour over time and across situations. This stability is achieved through many stimuli being perceived as equivalent and hence initiating similar behaviours. An example of this would be that individuals predisposed to aggression might be quicker than most to perceive slights and humiliations, to initiate provocative acts and to have problems in controlling their own behaviour.

Individuals differ from each other in the degree to which they display any particular trait. Thus traits are *dimensions* along which everyone may be placed. Being rated 'high' in a trait indicates a high likelihood of acting consistently with that trait across a wide range of situations. An example is trait anxiety, which Spielberger (1971) has distinguished from state anxiety. The *state of anxiety* is familiar to all of us, but a person high in *trait anxiety* is much more likely to experience a state of anxiety in a wider range of situations than someone low in that trait.

Trait theorists agree that traits are organized hierarchically. There are some relatively superficial traits, but underlying these are more basic, highly generalized dispositions. These broad tendencies are thought to determine a large proportion of all behaviour. Theorists have not yet agreed on which are the fundamental traits that go to make up human personality; they differ on how many there are and what to call them.

The measurement of personality by trait theorists

By obtaining information about an individual's behaviour the trait theorist hopes to be able to infer the underlying trait structure (the basis of individual differences). Three data sources are used, each with its own disadvantages. Firstly, observers may rate an individual along trait dimensions such as friendliness or aggression: a difficulty with this method is that the observer may be biased by particular expectancies, may have idiosyncratic subjective standards or may be provided with inadequate definitions of the dimensions, thus producing questionable results. A second way of collecting data is to look at the individual's answers to items of a questionnaire, for example, those asking for agreement or disagreement with statements like 'I would describe myself as a self-confident person.' Such questionnaire responses are bedevilled by 'nuisance factors' such as *the wish to appear a nice person*, *test-taking attitudes* (varying with time of day, sex of tester) and *response sets* (e.g. a tendency always to agree). Brown (1979) pointed to the false objectivity of questionnaires: testers all too frequently assume that standard questions and uniform instructions will make the questionnaire a standard stimulus for each subject. Nevertheless, subjects may interpret questions in quite different ways.

The third data source is the objective test. This consists of examining the individual's behaviour under laboratory conditions. The range of such tests is almost infinite. Witkin and his colleagues (1962) developed one in which subjects were shown a frame with a rod in it; the angle of the frame was manipulated independently from that of the rod. They noted that subjects were differentially affected by the presence of the field cue (the frame) when asked to judge if the rod was upright. Subjects relatively unaffected by the field were called *field-independent*, while those more reliant on context were labelled *field-dependent*. Unfortunately, this particular dimension of individual difference seems heavily confounded by intelligence. There is, however, probably less likelihood of bias in tests such as these since it is not obvious to subjects what the 'desirable' response might be. Kline (1983) warns against relying on objective tests for personality measurement as so little is known about what the scores obtained might mean.

The trait theorist thus collects vast numbers of test scores from all three sources. This mass of data has to be reduced to manageable proportions, and the technique employed is that of *factor analysis*. Factor analysis starts with a large number of test items which have been administered to a substantial sample of subjects. The degree of similarity (correlation coefficients) between scores on different test items is calculated. If the correlation coefficient between two scores is high, it indicates that the two items might be measuring the same underlying trait: for instance, items relating to helpfulness and attentiveness may correlate highly. Factor analysis identifies 'clusters' of such highly correlated test items: for instance, helpfulness, outgoingness, attentiveness, pleasantness, warmth, interest and thoughtfulness may all be items correlating highly. According to trait theory, this correlation is due to a common underlying trait that they all reflect. The statistical procedure of factor analysis only finds these associations; it is left to the researcher to give the factor a name, in this case, perhaps, 'friendliness'. Thus, as Eysenck (1982) points out, there is a good deal of subjectivity involved in factor analysis: not only do researchers provide the names for factors but they actually decide how many factors they need to elicit in order to explain the observed inter-correlations. Some statistical rules providing guidance do exist, yet researchers still need primarily to rely on the psychological meaningfulness of the factors they have discovered.

In view of the subjectivity just mentioned it is hardly surprising that different analyses have produced different results. Even the number of factors considered necessary for an adequate description of personality varies from study to study: Goldberg (1982) identified five dimensions, Mehrabian and O'Reilly (1980) found nine, and Wiggins (1982) offered sixteen. Kline (1983) suggests that if the technique is correctly applied such conflicting results will vanish. However, in the case of anxiety, for example, even highly similar, methodologically sound studies have yielded very different results and conclusions (e.g. Bernstein and Eveland, 1982). The reliability of the factors resulting from factor analysis thus remains questionable.

Factor analysis assumes that factors can only combine in an additive way; interactions of factors are not allowed for. The correlational procedure may fail to pick out related behaviours which do not *always* increase or decrease together. The fact that interactions do occur is demonstrated by considering the example of an aggressive man. Such a man would be much more to be feared if, in addition to his aggression, he were unable to imagine how his victims felt. Mischel (1968) was the first to criticize this aspect of the use of factor analysis. In response, Eysenck and Eysenck (1980) point out an analogy with chemistry: studying single elements is a starting-point, but we must also study their interrelations and combinations. However, it was the inability of factor analysis to deal with such complexities that was criticized in the first instance. In addition, the correlational procedure of factor analysis could produce mathematically pure factors that are psychologically meaningless.

The procedure of factor analysis is of course entirely dependent on the quality of the test items selected; if the items are inadequate and the data collection methods are poor, then factor analysis will produce misleading results. One of the major disputes in the area has been over the use of 'orthogonal' as opposed to 'oblique' methods of factor analysis. Orthogonal methods extract factors which by the very nature of the process are independent of each other. (Knowledge of a person's score on one factor will tell us nothing about his scores on the other factors.) Following an oblique procedure, the factors may be interrelated. The inter-correlations of these related factors can be submitted to further factor analysis which permits the researcher to identify so-called second-order factors (types). The differences between many multi-trait personality theories are attributable primarily to their respective choice of oblique and orthogonal methods. Finally, it should be noted that factors are only statistical abstractions: they have no psychological reality. All the above problems should be borne in mind when evaluating the theories that use factor analysis as their main source of data about personality. We shall use the work of the British psychologist Hans Eysenck as an example of this approach to personality.

Eysenck's multi-trait theory

Eysenck (1947) began his investigations by factor-analysing observers' ratings of individuals' behaviour and identified a few highly stable and replicable factors (Eysenck and Eysenck, 1969). On the basis of his analysis he conceptualized personality as hierarchical. At its broadest level, personality consists of a multitude of *specific responses* (numerous observable pieces of behaviour). *Habitual response patterns* describe the clustering together of specific responses, such as disliking parties and being reluctant to act on impulse. At the next level are *traits* (e.g. shyness and rigidity); and *types* (e.g. introversion) are found at the top of the hierarchy. Types are in fact *dimensions* rather than categories and, as the label might suggest, represent factors which Eysenck elicited statistically.

The three dimensions identified in this way were: firstly, *extraversion-introversion* (E-I); secondly, *neuroticism-stability* (N); and thirdly, *psychoticism-stability* (P). People high in *extraversion* are sociable and outgoing: they seek out exciting activities, are impulsive, restless, talkative, optimistic and cheerful. By contrast, *introverts* are orderly, restrained and serious. They are quiet, somewhat inhibited and withdrawn, and interested in solitary activities such as reading. The term 'introvert' was borrowed from Jung, who used it in a different way, to describe some of his patients in psychotherapy. Individuals who are high in *neuroticism* are described as anxious, worrying, moody, often depressed and overtly emotional. The dimension of *psychoticism* is the most recent addition to Eysenck's description of personality, and high scorers on this scale are solitary, often clash with authority and lack feeling. They are also insensitive, hostile and aggressive. Just as neuroticism is thought to reflect vulnerability to neurotic illness, high scorers on the P scale are regarded as vulnerable to psychosis when under stress. Whereas the distribution in the population of extraversion and neuroticism is normal (most people scoring in the middle range of these scales), that of psychoticism is highly skewed, with most people positioned at the stable end of the dimension.

Initially, these dimensions were assessed on rating scales (observer data). In 1956, Eysenck introduced the first questionnaire measure of these types. The questionnaire has undergone several revisions, the most recent of which is the Eysenck Personality Questionnaire (EPQ) (1975). Each new scale represents a refinement of the instrument and also subtle changes in the dimensions. Barrett and Kline (1982), in an independent replication, found that the EPQ factors emerged with 'remarkable clarity' on three different substantial samples of subjects.

On the whole, Eysenck's dimensions of personality have proved on further study to be remarkably robust (replicable in a wide range of study populations in different conditions). The P scale has emerged as the most controversial. Even in Barrett and Kline's (1982) replication, this particular scale was not very robust. Kline (1983) suggested that this had been the case because of the relative absence of high P scorers (psychotic individuals) in their samples. However, Bishop (1977) and Block (1977a) both found that those diagnosed as psychotic do not necessarily score highly on P. It has also been noted that the P score averaged across the whole population at the age of peak rate of psychotic breakdown was no higher than at other ages. Block concluded that the P score had little to do with the process of psychosis, suggesting instead that some psychotic patients tend to score highly on P merely as a result of answering the questions in a random fashion. Certainly, psychotics do tend to have a wider scatter of scores than other groups, which could be attributed to random answering; yet it is more probable that the P scale is sensitive to some forms of psychosis but not to others. A recent study by Launey and Slade (1981) found a high correlation between a questionnaire measure of auditory hallucinations and P score. It may therefore be that the P scale is sensitive to florid psychotic symptoms (delusions and hallucinations) but not to the withdrawn state and flattening of affect so commonly seen in cases of chronic psychosis (Crow, 1980).

Some studies report that psychopaths tend to obtain high P scores – a finding which needs explaining. Hare (1982) demonstrated a correlation between the EPQ's P scale and his own measure of psychopathy in 123 male prison inmates. Eysenck suggested that psychopaths are in fact at risk of developing psychosis, which he felt was sufficient explanation for their elevated P scores. It is more likely, however, that the obtained association can be accounted for by the questions on the P scale referring to aggressive, antisocial tendencies (Block, 1977a; Hare, 1982).

Overall there is much in favour of postulating a P dimension of personality despite such negative findings. Nevertheless, it may still be too early on in the development of this theory to determine whether P adds substantially to the description of personality.

The biological bases of Eysenck's dimensions of personality

Psychoticism has no firm biological foundation in Eysenck's theory. The more firmly established traits of extraversion and neuroticism, on the other hand, are held to have evolutionary significance in addition to being mediated by known neuro-physiological processes. The concept of *cortical arousal* underlies extraversion. Extraverts are seen as *less aroused* than introverts and to seek stimulation so as to increase their arousal to an optimal level. Introverts, on the other hand, are seen as continually *over-aroused* and so to develop strategies to avoid additional excessive sensory input. Cortical arousal is controlled by the *ascending reticular activating system* of the brain, which is too readily activated in introverts but is slower to respond and more inhibitory in extraverts. Eysenck sees neuroticism as mediated by the brain's *limbic system* (closely linked to the autonomic nervous system). The limbic system mediates emotional responses. In neurotics, the autonomic nervous system (controlling heart rate, respiratory rate, gut activity, etc.) is more labile and highly responsive to stimulation; autonomic (emotional) reactions therefore occur more frequently. Extremes of anxiety are thus readily aroused and may become associated with (conditioned to) previously neutral situations.

There are four types of evidence to support Eysenck's biological theory. Firstly, as Eysenck suggests that differences in cortical arousal and autonomic lability are inherited, genetic studies must be considered. Secondly, laboratory findings should be consistent with Eysenck's neurophysiological predictions. Thirdly, individuals' behaviour outside the laboratory should be in line with Eysenck's dimensions. Finally, clinical studies should provide evidence of the relevance of the dimensions to an understanding of psychopathology.

The *genetic* evidence in support of Eysenck's claims is quite strong. Shields (1976), for example, showed that identical twins (all genes the same) were substantially more similar in terms of extraversion and neuroticism than were non-identical twins. Although Eysenck's conclusion from such evidence that environmental influences are less important than heredity in personality development is unpalatable to many theorists, genetic influences are clearly not to be ignored.

Much *laboratory-based research* has been performed to test Eysenck's model, but not all of it has been supportive of his theory. Most important to Eysenck's theory are the studies of *conditionability*. Cortical excitation is known to facilitate conditioning, provided excitation does not exceed an optimal level. From Eysenck's contention that extraverts are less aroused than introverts it is predicted that introverts will on the whole condition more easily and resist extinction for longer. A study by Gattaz (1981) provides support for this by demonstrating that introverts do indeed condition more easily than extraverts unless the stimulus is of a high enough intensity to compensate for the extravert's relatively low arousal. Levey and Martin (1981) however, emphasized that although this effect is reliable, differences in conditionability will only be seen if conditions are such that the subject's habitual level of arousal is not altered. This makes extrapolation from the laboratory to the real world a problem (Kline, 1983). It can be said that given certain very special laboratory conditions – that is, a controlled intensity of UCS and specific schedules of reinforcement – an introvert conditions more readily. Outside the laboratory, however, such conditions are not definable or controllable, and so we cannot presume the results will be the same.

Direct study of the electrical activity of the brain (EEG) seems the most direct way of assessing cortical arousal, as subjects characterized as being highly aroused should display more cortical activity. Many studies have attempted to relate EEG activity to personality measures, and in his review Gale (1981) lists thirty. On balance, about half of them support Eysenck's hypothesis of greater cortical arousal in introverts with the more recent, better designed studies doing so more frequently. Gale, however, makes the important point that cortical activity greatly depends on the laboratory situation. Introverts are likely to be less affected by being alone and more affected by the presence of others than extroverts. Thus the experiments need to be remarkably well controlled if meaningful conclusions are to be drawn.

Clinical data support Eysenck's contention that the neuroticism dimension is associated with the functioning of the autonomic nervous system. Laboratory studies have established that in psychiatric samples individuals identified as neurotic (i.e. high N scorers) will show autonomic lability (i.e. show a wide variation in such measures as heart rate and palmar sweating). The resting levels of physiological measures of arousal in the autonomic nervous system are also higher in neurotics. Frequently they fail to habituate to external stimuli (stop responding after repeated presentations), which also implies that they may have an inadequately functioning autonomic nervous system (Lader, 1975). These findings apply to the patient population, but on the whole no evidence of an association between N scores and these measures has been found in normal subjects. Thus it seems that neuroticism is only necessarily associated with autonomic dysfunction in cases of extremely high levels of neuroticism or *very* high levels of state anxiety in non-neurotic individuals. Thus, Eysenck is perhaps premature in attributing such significance to the autonomic nervous system in accounting for this trait.

The EPQ has turned out to be a reasonably good predictor of behaviour outside the laboratory. Furnham (1981, 1982), for example, studied subjects' choices of leisure-time activity, preferred social situations and tendency to avoid stressful situations. He found that extraverts appeared to seek out stimulating social situations involving assertiveness, intimacy and competitiveness. He explained this on the basis of the extravert seeking to raise his arousal level. Neurotics tended to avoid situations involving competitiveness and social interaction. High P scorers chose unusual, inconsistent situations where they were able to manipulate people. Williams (1981) found that high N scorers, as predicted, reported lower mood levels over a three-month period than did low N scorers. These and other findings seem to validate Eysenck's ideas. However, Nicholls *et al.* (1982) warn us that often the correlation between the personality measure from the questionnaire and observed or self-reported behaviour results from overlapping item content; for example, in Furnham's study the behaviours looked at were very similar, if not identical, to some

EPQ questions such as 'Do you find it hard to enjoy yourself at a lively party?' This criticism could apply to many studies.

Clinical applications of Eysenck's theory

The clinical applications of Eysenck's theory have, on the whole, been disappointing. They generally consist of attempts at describing patient groups in terms of Eysenck's dimensions. His theory of criminality will serve as an example. Eysenck (1964) suggested that the poorer conditionability of extraverts would result in poorer socialization and that hence there would be more crime in that group. In addition, he suggested that high degrees of neuroticism would combine with this to produce a high drive level – reinforcing the extravert's tendency to antisocial conduct. In 1970, Eysenck and Eysenck also related criminality to high levels of P, although on less clear grounds. Empirical evidence is mixed. Edmunds and Kendrick (1980) and Farrington et al. (1982) found that delinquent boys had higher P scores than controls. Rushton and Chrisjohn (1981) found that E and P but not N were related to self-reported delinquency. Many studies (cf. Cochrane, 1974) produce evidence against Eysenck's theory. McEwan (1983) explains these mixed results by the fact that delinquent populations contain a mixture of personality types of which some fit Eysenck's theory but others do not (for example a group of delinquents with low E scores). Finally, Raine and Venables (1981) investigated 101 15-year-old schoolboys and found no correlation between self-report or teacher ratings of socialization and conditionability of skin conductance. Thus it seems that Eysenck's assumption about the nature of the association between E and criminality is not borne out by the evidence.

In many of the clinical areas upon which Eysenck has commented (including smoking, alcoholism and neurosis) the empirical evidence is too variable to give clear support to his personality theory. In response (1982) he claims that many of the experimental studies that apparently fail to back up his theory either do not actually test the theory or have methodological shortcomings. Moreover, he asserts that the fact that the theory is testable at all is in its favour in an area where systematic studies are in short supply. The biological basis for Eysenck's theory is an important move away from the meaningless circularity of so many accounts of personality; a person's aggressive behaviour is *not* 'accounted' for by a questionnaire finding of a high score on the trait of aggression.

Evaluation

Although Eysenck's theory has many positive aspects, there is much in it that is inadequate. We shall restrict ourselves to the main issues. Firstly, clinical applications of his theory have been narrow: the EPQ has not been sufficiently well validated on clinical samples to firmly establish its practical usefulness (Lanyon, 1984). Eysenck's emphasis on a learning theory approach to psychopathology during the 1950s and 1960s greatly strengthened the then budding behavioural approach to treatment. Yet his continued insistence on a conditioning theory approach to behavioural work is now felt by many clinicians to be a constraining rather than a productive influence. In addition, clinicians do not find that measurement of his three dimensions tells them more about the client than would a brief interview. In support of this impression, Kendrick (1981) reports that in the leading behaviour therapy journal *Behaviour Research and Therapy* only thirteen of 843 articles between 1963 and 1978 used Eysenck's dimensions, none of which gave any indication of having taken his theoretical predictions into account in treatment. Eysenck's scales may provide unambiguous answers, but clinicians, it seems, may not find the questions relevant.

The second issue is Eysenck's emphasis on the concept of arousal. Andrew (1974) pointed out that there are a large number of meanings of the word 'arousal' and that to some extent Eysenck himself is guilty of using it in slightly different ways at different times (cf. Kline, 1983). Current physiological evidence indicates that arousal is in any case not a unitary dimension: studies employing more than one arousal measure find little correlation between them (Fahrenberg *et al.*, 1982). Recent anatomical findings indicate that the ascending reticular activating system is not usefully viewed as a single structure (see Bindman and Lippold, 1981). Gray's (1972, 1981) work has placed Eysenck's theory on a sounder physiological basis by postulating two physiological systems in the brain mediated by two different neurotransmitters (chemical messengers between nerve cells in the central nervous system). The first of these is held to determine the level of anxiety (neurotic introvert) and the second the level of impulsiveness (neurotic extravert). Gray's ideas are based mostly on animal work, so their applicability to humans is as yet unknown. The current state of the arousal concept is thus questionable, and its extensive use as an explanatory construct must be considered unwise.

Eysenck's theory has given rise to more research than probably any other theory of personality. One reason for this is the simplicity of the theory and ease of application of the EPQ. Sadly, psychologists are sometimes drawn to areas of research not by the scientific value or practical implications of what they are doing but by the ease with which they are able to do it.

Narrow-trait approaches to personality: the Type A behaviour pattern

Narrow-trait theories of personality are concerned with the role played by *one particular* part of personality structure in the determination of behaviour, usually within rather specific contexts. In this chapter we shall consider one such approach: Type A behaviour in the context of coronary heart disease.

Coronary heart disease accounts for about 50 per cent of all deaths in the western world. The disease is caused by a narrowing or blockage occurring in one or more of the arteries providing the heart muscle with oxygen via the blood. An insufficient oxygen supply to the heart results in chest pain (angina), inefficient pumping of the heart (heart failure) or death of heart muscle (myocardial infarction or heart attack). This narrowing is usually the result of fat deposits accumulating in the walls of the arteries and blood clots forming on top.

Theory

Physicians treating patients with coronary heart disease have repeatedly reported them as displaying certain consistent characteristics. As far back as 1892, Sir William Osler attributed arterial degeneration to 'the high pressure at which men live and the habit of working the machine to its maximum capacity'. Von Dusch, twenty-four years earlier, had noted that individuals with loud speech and excessive work habits were predisposed to developing heart disease. Friedman and Rosenman (1959) attempted to sum up the features of the 'coronary-prone personality' in what they describe as the 'Type A behaviour pattern'. It included at least one, but often several, of the following features: extreme competitiveness, drive for success, impatience, restlessness, hyperalertness and a subjective sense of time urgency and pressure of commitments and responsibilities. People with this behaviour pattern were felt to be striving against impossible odds for indefinite goals. Type B personalities are those lacking these characteristics.

Several studies have found an association between the Type A behaviour pattern and coronary heart disease. In the Western Collaborative Group's prospective study (Friedman and Rosenman, 1974) initiated in San Francisco in 1960, over 3500 healthy men aged between thirty-nine and fifty-nine were interviewed. Type A personality was assessed by means of a structured interview administered by the physician. About twenty-five questions were asked aimed at eliciting from the individual his habitual ways of responding to situations that might be expected to produce impatience, hostility and competitiveness. Subjects were asked, for example, how they would react to working with a slow partner or waiting in a long queue. Other questions concerned their competitiveness: would their spouse or a close friend describe them as hard-driving; would they take work home at weekends? In addition to their actual answers being noted, their style of responding was closely observed. Some questions were asked in a deliberately slow and hesitant fashion such as would tempt a Type A person to interrupt. The questions asked in this interview have now become part of a standardized method for assessing Type A behaviour. About 50 per cent of the population are usually classified as extreme or mild Type A personalities when assessed in this way.

In Rosenman et al.'s (1975) report of the Western Collaborative Project, out of 257 men who developed coronary heart disease during the eight and a half year follow-up, 178 had been labelled as Type A at the outset. Thus more than twice as many Type As as Type Bs were diagnosed as having heart disease. This difference could not be explained simply in terms of the Type A group smoking more, having higher blood pressures or raised levels of fats in the blood (all well-recognized risk factors in this context). When these factors were taken into account statistically, the coronary heart disease risk in Type As was still 1.97 times higher than in the others.

The Jenkins Activity Survey (JAS) is a questionnaire containing twenty-one items aimed at measuring Type A behaviour (Jenkins *et al.*, 1978). The competitive aspect is tapped via items such as: 'It really bothers me when my team loses.' Also covered are the speed at which a person lives ('I've often been told I eat too fast') and a pressured style of working (e.g. holding more than one job simultaneously, not taking a holiday). This instrument was used to study 2750 healthy men who were followed up for four years. Over this period sixty-seven men suffered acute heart attacks, thirty others were found to have developed changes on their electrocardiographs (recording of the electrical activity of the heart) indicative of an unrecognized heart attack, and a further twenty-three had angina (chest pain). The men in all three of these groups tended to have Type A personalities, but they had a different pattern of Type A behaviour depending on which group they were in.

Angina sufferers tended to have been impatient with people doing things slowly, very conscious of time and to have problems in controlling their own irritability. Those with isolated electrocardiographic changes, on the other hand, differed especially in terms of their eating habits; they hurried themselves by using deadlines rather than by hurrying other people. This study illustrates that the Jenkins Activity Survey can not only identify coronary-prone individuals but also distinguish between subtypes of coronary disease. Haynes *et al.* (1980) found essentially the same results in a smaller sample of middle-aged men and women studied over an eight-year period.

Cross-sectional evidence also supports the link between Type A behaviour and coronary heart disease. In this case individuals already suffering from coronary heart disease are contrasted with people diagnosed differently. Such studies generally find that the Type A behaviour pattern is more common in the heart disease group, whether interviews or questionnaires are used (e.g. Williams *et al.*, 1980).

Type A behaviour is now accepted by many workers as an independent risk factor for coronary heart disease, that is, one that is totally separate from other factors such as smoking and high blood pressure.

The two instruments for assessing Type A behaviour have been shown to possess reasonable psychometric properties. Two independent raters using the structured interview assign individuals to the same group (Type A versus Type B) 75–90 per cent of the time (Rosenman, 1978), which demonstrates good inter-rater reliability. The Jenkins Activity Survey has a test-retest reliability of .7 over a four-year period (Jenkins, 1978), which is also reasonably high. The association between these two measures is, however, less impressive. Mathews *et al.* (1982), for example, found very low correlations between them. The two measures appear to have only a slight margin of overlap (both classifying subjects as Type A 15 per cent more often than would be predicted by chance).

Some authors criticize the tests used. The items in them seem not to measure a single dimension of 'Type A-ness' but rather a series of dimensions, such as ambition and activity, which correlate no more highly with each other than with other personality dimensions such as extraversion, achievement motivation and psychoticism (Ray and Brozek, 1980; Eysenck and Fulker, 1981). They suggest the abandonment of the psychological concept of Type A behaviour since it implies an entity but in fact consists of several relatively independent components.

The validity of the personality dimension itself has none the less received support from experimental studies. Mathews (1982) provides an exhaustive review. Individuals identified as Type A have been observed in the laboratory to speak quickly, loudly and explosively in situations which are difficult or moderately competitive. As is consistent with their striving for achievement, they seem superior in tasks requiring speed and persistence and perform less well on tasks requiring slow work in which impatience can interfere with the results. The laboratory behaviour of these individuals thus seems in line with their clinical description.

Possibly stronger evidence of the validity of the Type A concept is provided by studies of psychophysiological responding. Since Type A personality is claimed to be an independent risk factor for coronary heart disease, the personality type should have psychophysiological correlates which could mediate its effect on the heart. In a typical study, Glass *et al.* (1980) put Type A and Type B subjects into competitive situations. They had to play video games against a highly skilled confederate of the experimenter. In addition, they were subjected to harassment from their opponent in the form of taunts such as 'Can't you keep your eye on the ball?' or 'Come on, you're not trying!' Predictably, in the Type

As the hostile components in the competitive situation led to increases in heart rate, blood pressure and blood noradrenaline, whilst Type Bs were unaffected by the experimental situation. Both Houston (1983) and Mathews (1982) review these findings thoroughly. Individuals identified by either the structured interview or the JAS as Type As tend to exhibit markedly raised blood pressure and alterations in their blood chemistry (e.g. elevation of plasma noradrenaline) indicative of autonomic arousal when faced with frustrating, difficult and competitive situations; for the JAS the psychophysiological links are less strong than for the structured interview. Holmes (1983), who has also reviewed the literature in this area, claims that previous reviewers have failed to mention the numerous negative findings and questions whether the increased physiological responsivity of Type A subjects has been established unequivocally.

Some recent studies have even questioned the association between the Type A behaviour pattern and heart disease. Bass and Wade (1982) examined ninety-nine patients who underwent X-ray examination of their coronary arteries because of chest pain. Those patients who proved to have normal coronary arteries were the most psychiatrically disturbed and also scored highest on the measure of Type A behaviour. This runs contrary to the usual findings. A possible explanation is that their heart disease patients were in fact less severely affected than in other studies and that cases with very severe coronary heart disease are the ones who score most highly on Type A measures. Also, this is a study on British rather than American subjects, and the measure of Type A may be to some extent influenced by cultural factors.

A number of authors have questioned the relevance of the behaviour pattern for personality theory. After all, the association between the behaviour pattern and coronary heart disease can only be said to be clearly proven for a very narrow population (middle- and upper-class employed, middle-aged American males).

Defenders of the Type A behaviour pattern argue that it is a configuration of traits. The particular configuration is captured by the interview and the JAS. The fact that this combination of traits might be associated with heart disease does not, however, establish Type A behaviour as a dimension of personality in general. The components of the dimension are not correlated and therefore, despite the fact that they have been individually linked with cardio-vascular disorder, cannot be thought of as a single dimension of personality. Kline (1983) points out that many tests may succeed in distinguishing between groups by using a large number of randomly selected items but will contribute nothing to our understanding of the nature of these groups. However, the originators of the Type A personality pattern were seeking to establish it not as a general personality dimension, but merely as a specific combination of traits that happened to increase an individual's risk of coronary heart disease.

Implications for treatment

Finally, the validity of the Type A behaviour pattern might be enhanced if it could be demonstrated that altering the behaviour produced a reduction in the risk of heart disease. As modifying the known risk factors (smoking, cholesterol and blood pressure) is an expensive and only marginally effective procedure (Oliver, 1982), interest in the use of the Type A concept in treatment has increased. Studies have shown that the behaviour pattern can be modified using a wide range of behavioural methods (e.g. Razin, 1982). Most effective programmes tend to involve comprehensive behaviour modification (e.g. Fisher *et al.*, 1982) which integrates several behavioural and cognitive procedures. Typically, subjects are presented with an overview emphasizing the excessive, unnecessary and often poorly directed expenditure of energy associated with the Type A pattern. Subjects are also instructed to anticipate specific situations to which they typically respond with Type A behaviours (e.g. slow-moving traffic or waiting in a queue). Coping strategies are recommended, such as removing one's wrist-watch when unavoidably delayed, taking less work home in the evenings or adjusting personal schedules. Relaxation training may be taught and self-reinforcement programmes instituted, such as waiting in a lay-by for five minutes as a punishment for unnecessary overtaking or going to the back of the queue for impatiently looking at one's watch.

Studies examining the effectiveness of this form of intervention demonstrated that the frequency of Type A behaviours can be reduced successfully in this way (e.g. Levenkron *et al.*, 1983 and reviews by Johnston, 1982 and Suinn, 1982). Many of these studies demonstrated that serum lipids (e.g. cholesterol) decrease significantly more in treated than in control groups. The clinical significance of this mode of intervention is indicated by Thoresen *et al.*'s (1982) intermediate report of their five-year coronary prevention project in which 1,035 post-heart attack patients took part. Results showed that after three years the behaviour therapy group had had roughly half the recurrence rate for both fatal and non-fatal heart disease of the control group who received normal cardiological care, despite being equal on other physical factors (7.9 per cent as against 14.6 per cent).

Evaluation

The exploration of the Type A behaviour pattern has undoubtedly been the most exciting recent development within the area of trait theories. Some might disagree with our reference to Type A behaviour pattern as a trait, yet as the term is clearly used to refer to a broad disposition to respond to particular stimuli (such as competitive situations) in specific ways (by tense, hard driving to win) we feel this question to be more on the level of a semantic quibble than a scientific argument. Descriptions of Type A behaviour patterns appear to identify a dimension with substantial clinical significance; moreover, psychometric, laboratory and physiological evidence seem, on the whole, supportive. In reviewing the literature, however, we have seen that the clinical association between Type A behaviour and heart disease is somewhat controversial. The methods available to identify Type A individuals are not ideal, and the behavioural and physiological manifestations of the pattern are only loosely correlated with the psychometric indices. Thus perhaps at this stage it is most appropriate to record an 'open verdict' on the Type A behaviour pattern.

7

The controversy over the consistency of personality

Can we talk of personality traits?

Most of us would recognize that we have some friends who are shy and others who are outgoing. We know people who appear aggressive and yet others who seem excessively dependent on the people around them. The existence of underlying mental structures that affect behaviour in a general way to bring about these differences appears crucial to most personality theories. Whether we conceptualize the underlying structure as a motivating force (e.g. an aggressive drive), a hypothetical predisposition (e.g. an aggressivity trait) or as a tendency to apply constructs inappropriately (forcing someone to validate one's constructs), we expect to be able to observe general consistencies in the behaviour of an individual across many, if not most, situations. Mischel (1968, 1981) radically questioned this assumption, writing: 'With the possible exception of intelligence, highly generalized behavioural consistencies have not been demonstrated, and the concept of personality traits as broad dispositions is thus untenable' (1968, p. 146).

Thus Mischel refuses to accept the common assumption that

generalized consistencies in behaviour or predispositions such as dependency, shyness, aggression and so on exist. He argues instead that it is particular situations which may consistently elicit, for instance, an aggressive response from an individual. Consistencies in behaviours which are not attributable to intelligence must therefore be the result of similarities between situations in which individuals find themselves.

The critique of traditional personality theories

Mischel's criticism was aimed at both conceptual and empirical issues concerning traditional personality theories. At the conceptual level, all theories using the concept of trait are held by Mischel to have two major problems. Firstly, there is the problem of *reification*: the tendency to treat the hypothetical construct of trait as if it was a physical entity. It would be wrong to talk of an abstract concept such as a disposition as if it had a physical presence in the brain; trait theorists often appear to assume that a trait such as aggression has a neural representation. Secondly, the use of the trait concept in a *causal* framework is unacceptable. If we see a person acting honestly, we might rate him/her as high in the trait of honesty. This is a descriptive process. It makes nonsense to turn the description on its head by saying that the person's honest behaviour is in any way accounted for by his/her being 'high on the honesty trait' – this would be a completely circular argument.

On the *empirical* level, Mischel's criticisms included the following major issues: Firstly, there is a low correlation between personality dimensions derived from questionnaires and observed behaviours. This is rarely greater than 0.3, which means that the questionnaire scores account for only 9 per cent of the variance in observed behaviour. Mischel therefore felt that knowledge of personal characteristics obtained from questionnaires told us little about how a person will actually behave. Thus questionnaire responses indicating aggression are not effective predictors of an individual's aggressive behaviour on the athletic field, in conflicts with friends or in any of the other situations in which aggression might play a part. Correlations *between* questionnaires are high, but behavioural responses in different situations correlate poorly with them. Thus, Mischel concludes, the predictive power of traits is not great.

The second empirical issue, the one upon which most of the

criticisms of trait theory are focused, concerns the low consistency of behaviour across situations. Mischel terms this *behavioural specificity* (the dependence of behaviour on specific situations). Studies which used objective measures of behaviour (mainly direct observation) have tended to indicate that a given individual's actions are specific to the particular situation. It was found many years ago (Hartshorne and May, 1928) that children may be highly honest at home and much less so at school (and vice versa); thus the behaviour they displayed depended upon the situation. Mischel agrees that in similar situations behaviour may be stable over time but states that if the situations vary the behaviour will be expected to change also. He does not regard this continuity of behaviour over long periods of time as sufficient evidence for assuming the existence of relatively stable reaction tendencies or personality traits; he feels rather that the stability reflects an unchanging situation.

In addition, Mischel reiterates the criticisms of the factor analytic method which underlies so much of trait theory. These include the subjectivity of the procedure and its inability to generate models which include complex interactions between traits (see Chapter 6).

The situationist approach

The approach to personality proposed by Mischel puts such heavy emphasis on the importance of situations in determining behaviour that it is usually labelled the situationist approach. The learning-theory-based approaches considered earlier and to some extent the socio-cognitive approaches described in the next chapter may be considered as such situationist models.

Experimental research dramatically illustrating the powerful effect of the situation on behaviour was performed by Haney *et al.* (1973). These workers carefully selected a group of student volunteers with no known antisocial tendencies. All the students were kept round the clock in a mock prison. Some students were randomly allocated to be 'guards', while others were chosen to be 'prisoners'. After a few days the 'guards' started to display extreme antisocial behaviour and brutality towards the 'prisoners'. It is important to note that this was completely different from their usual behaviour.

The consistencies repeatedly found by trait personality theorists in their questionnaires or rating studies are attributed by situationists to the social stereotypes of raters. In a study by Passini and Norman (1966), subjects were asked to rate fellow college students on various personality dimensions. Since they had met for the first time only five minutes earlier, these must necessarily have been very superficial ratings. The item correlations were submitted to factor analysis, and interestingly enough produced a similar factor structure to that produced by Cattell's (1957) trained raters after prolonged observations. Mischel (1981) claims that such factors cannot be considered as real dimensions of behaviour but are best thought of as reflecting the way that raters think about people.

D'Andrade (1974) reported studies where subjects, rather than being asked to rate individuals, had to rate the scales themselves for similarity to one another. He found that scales which inter-related highly when used by people to rate themselves or others were also closely related semantically (in meaning). Thus, 'sincere' and 'kind' or 'aggressive' and 'masculine' may go together in personality ratings because they are related in meaning. Personality ratings, situationists claim, might therefore be telling us not which behaviours go together in the real world but which words go together in the rater's head.

Are we then to assume that our firm belief in the stability of character of people around us is no more than an illusion? There is a basic paradox here: though we cannot doubt that we experience ourselves and others as possessing predispositions to certain behaviours, situationists claim that our behaviour is not consistent across situations. Some situationists point to the human tendency to simplify things and suggest that we all have *implicit personality theories* which lead us to ignore or forget about many inconsistencies in behaviour we observe whilst concentrating on aspects which are consistent with our assumptions.

Mischel provides some evidence for this. Cantor and Mischel (1979) described an experiment in which character descriptions were read to subjects. Typical extravert or introvert characters were recalled more accurately than those with a mixture of traits. Also, subjects embellished what they recalled, making the original descriptions more homogeneous, i.e. typically extraverted or introverted. Such findings imply that we do indeed have preconceived person categories available to us which to some extent bias our perception of people around us.

It seems likely that these categories are identified by *prototypes*. Each person category is identified by a typical member. The category of extravert has the typical extravert at its centre: in other words, we judge people as belonging to particular categories to the extent that they resemble our idea of the most typical member of the category. They do not need to have *all* the characteristic features of the category; they only need to be consistent on one or two of its most typical features and we happily assign them to the category concerned.

Mischel and Peake (1982) claim that for us to judge someone as conscientious they do not need to behave conscientiously all the time. It is enough for them to be consistently conscientious in one or two situations which are regarded as highly typical for such people: for instance, invariably handing in work on time despite being sometimes late for appointments would get a person classified as conscientious. This model is consistent with current views of the nature of categorization of all other aspects of our world (see, for example, Hampton, 1979).

Criticisms of situationism

In the extreme situationist view of personality, all behaviour is seen as under the control of its antecedents, the environmental events that preceded it. Whereas the layman sees a person as honest, the situationist sees him/her as telling the truth under certain conditions. As Loevinger and Knoll (1983) pointed out, if there were no cross-situational consistency in behaviour then the field of personality would disappear and be replaced by social psychology. That this has not occurred is largely attributable to the weakness of the extreme situationist position.

One of the main shortcomings of a purely environmentalist account is its failure to consider human beings as self-determining, in other words responsible for their own actions. As Bowers (1973) put it, situationism is inattentive to the importance of the person; the focus of interest in the experiments performed by situationists is the effect of environmental manipulations upon behaviour. Bowers feels that this approach is inherently biased towards finding inconsistencies. If the environmental changes are found not to affect behaviour, i.e. if stability is demonstrated, the experimenter is likely to try different manipulations until he/she achieves a 'significant' result. Furthermore, all experiments find variability between subjects – a fact which none the less tends to be ignored.

It seems that situationists probably exaggerate the objectivity of their approach. Rorer and Widiger (1983) cite the example of the observation of a hand coming into contact with an arm. In a direct observation study this event might be coded as a greeting, a blow, a seduction, an accident or a signal. The behaviour itself tells the observers nothing. Their concern in reality is with the behavioural intent. This they cannot observe but need to infer from numerous unspecified (probably unspecifiable) features of the interaction. In their emphasis on objective direct observational methods many situationists choose not to acknowledge the many automatic, unverifiable, unobservable assumptions that are implicit in their frequency counts of behaviour. This makes the situationist account no more objective or open to scientific evaluation than accounts which make use of the hypothetical construct of trait.

The purely situationist account is, in a way, a straw man. Few psychologists, with the exception of some neo-behaviourists, would currently subscribe to this position. Nevertheless, it stimulated personality theorists to re-examine their assumptions in the light of the situationist critiques.

The defence of the trait approach

More traditional personality theorists have attempted to defend the concept of trait against the conceptual criticisms of reification and circularity. One especially eloquent attempt was made by Eysenck and Eysenck (1980). They pointed out that the physical reality of traits such as extraversion receive considerable independent validation from genetic studies. They claim, moreover, that since extraversion can be understood in terms of cortical arousal the trait can no longer be said to amount to 'no more than a redescription' of the behaviour; it may be considered to *cause* the behaviour since it links genetic and physiological factors to behavioural observations.

However, this attempt at justifying trait descriptions is, for the moment at least, inadequate. As Mischel (1981) stated, the genetic and physiological evidence is still weak and controversial. Until the biological bases of traits are firmly established, the concept of trait will always be at risk of circularity. The criticism is nevertheless not a devastating one. The trait construct is capable of explaining the diverse effects of several independent variables: extraversion, for example, accounts for an individual's response to social situations as well as for his/her perceptual sensitivity. In that sense, it remains a useful summary term even in the absence of physical correlates.

The Eysencks (1980) also replied to Mischel's criticisms about the low correlation between test scores and overt behaviours, the so-called 'personality coefficient'. Eysenck argued that the size of such correlations is only one way of assessing the adequacy of the theory. He claimed that it was equally valid to look at how wide a range of behaviours was associated with a personality measure. Thus, questionnaire measures of extraversion may not correlate very highly with behaviour but do predict performance in a theoretically consistent manner across a very wide range of situations indeed. These include pain threshold, time estimation, sensory deprivation, sleep-wakefulness patterns, conditioning, patterns of speech, etc.

There is much wrong with the Eysencks' argument. A wide range of weak correlations in itself provides no validatory evidence for a construct. One could imagine a series of reasons why a variable such as height might correlate weakly with a broad range of performance measures; yet this would not establish height as of psychological importance.

A better defence of low personality coefficients may be formulated in terms of the nature of associations found. Certain specific correlations may be of great practical importance despite their low level. Finding personality variables correlating with coronary heart disease, for instance, may allow behavioural intervention which may save lives even if the association is small. Thus it is the nature of the association between test scores and behaviour rather than its strength which should determine the importance we ascribe to it. From a theoretical point of view, however, trait theorists are still faced with having to explain the small proportion of variance in behaviour predicted by the tests.

Hogan *et al.* (1977) also speak up for personality tests in spite of their overall poor prediction of behaviour. They point out that poor research can be mixed in with research of better quality to yield a low mean personality coefficient. Gough (1965), in a 'good' study of over 10,000 youths, demonstrated that the sociability scale of his inventory was correlated very highly with delinquent behaviour ($r = .73$). Hogan *et al.* and also Eysenck and Eysenck

(1980) argue in addition that the sheer number of personality measures taken may serve to reduce the personality coefficient. Many measures used would not be predicted to have associations with the behavioural criterion. Whilst this is possibly true, it should be recalled that Mischel was in fact talking of maximal correlations, not averages: that is, even the highest correlations of tests with behaviour seldom exceed .3.

The issue of the consistency of behaviour

Undoubtedly the central question of the person-situation debate is this: 'Is behaviour consistent?' Over the past decade evidence has accumulated to indicate that behaviour is highly consistent over time. Perhaps the most impressive demonstration of this has come from a major longitudinal study carried out by the Institute of Human Development at the University of California, Berkeley, (Block, 1971, 1977b). Subjects were rated by observers in junior high school, senior high school and then at between thirty and forty years of age. These studies were carried out very carefully, involving 114 measures and several different observers at each stage. There was 60 per cent consistency in behaviour from junior to senior high school and 30 per cent from high school to the mid-thirties. Items remaining consistent included 'Is a genuinely dependable and responsible person' and 'Rebellious and non-conforming'. There is thus an impressive indication of personality consistency over a substantial proportion of the life span.

Similar conclusions may be drawn from Olweus' (1980) review of the stability of aggressive behaviour patterns over periods ranging from six months to twenty-one years. Consistencies in aggressive tendencies as high as 64 per cent have been reported over a three-year period. Some consistency across measurement settings as well as over time has also been observed for aggression: for example, Farrington (1978) reports significant associations between teachers' ratings of aggressive behaviour and future convictions for violent crime. The chances of becoming a violent delinquent were roughly five times as high for boys rated 'aggressive' at the age of thirteen as for their non-aggressive counterparts. Similar substantial longitudinal consistencies are found for introversion, extraversion and neuroticism (Hindley and Giuganino, 1982; Giuganino and Hindley, 1982).

Mischel (1981) disputes that these longitudinal studies provide evidence for global predispositions in personality; rather they support the *temporal* (longitudinal) consistency of behaviour. This indicates that similar responses are being seen to similar situations even over prolonged periods of time. He disputes that people will respond in a similar way to substantially different situations (*cross-situational* consistency). However, the situation in which a three-year-old finds itself is likely to be substantially different from that it will encounter seven years later. The longitudinal studies do seem to provide some support for the notion of stable dispositions (Rutter and Garmezy, 1983). Mischel and Peake (1983) suggest that both the approach which involves aggregating behaviours across occasions and situations and that favouring the examination of specific behavioural events have much to recommend them and should be pursued vigorously.

Three approaches have been taken in attempts to directly tackle the issue of *cross-situational consistency*. Epstein (1979, 1980, 1983) suggested that measures of traits would predict behaviour much more accurately if 'multiple act criteria' were used. He recommended an *'aggregation strategy'*, which involves averaging measures of the behaviour under observation over a large number of situations and occasions. He demonstrated (1979) that if behavioural scores over fourteen-day periods were compared with test measures, correlations of .80–.90 were obtained. (These included self-ratings, observer ratings, questionnaires and physiological measures.)

Mischel and Peake (1982), however, challenge Epstein's conclusions. They claimed that averaging measures cross-situationally as in his study bypassed the issue of the importance of situational determinants. Epstein did indeed manage to enhance the apparent stability of behaviours, but they felt he had achieved this at the cost of eliminating any influence of situational variables.

Mischel and Peake's (1982) own study of sixty-three students at Carleton College was designed to see if more reliable estimates of behaviour would provide evidence for the existence of traits. The students were assessed by their parents, close friends and unknown observers in several situations for evidence of conscientiousness. Measures of such things as class attendance, neatness of work, punctuality, tidyness of rooms and personal appearance were obtained on repeated occasions. (All of these were supposed to be measures of the trait of conscientiousness across situations, should it in fact exist.) The relationship between all these different measures proved to be very weak when based on single measures (mean correlation .08). Epstein had previously suggested that this could be due to single measures/observations being unreliable, but when Mischel and Peake averaged all the repeated measures (of a single behaviour) the correlation between the various behaviours scarcely increased (mean correlation .13). Thus, each separate measure was found to show stability over time but the correlations between measures (across situations) remained small. It seems that Epstein achieved the enhanced correlations only by eliminating situational effects by averaging across situations; he failed to provide evidence that behaviour is consistent across situations.

Bem and Funder (1978) proposed the second solution to the question of consistency: the *template-matching procedure*. They suggested that it was possible to classify situations in terms of the personality best suited to them. Situations apparently differing only slightly might be dealt with most efficiently by totally different types of individual; thus one person might behave very differently in two closely similar situations because he/she was well suited to one and not to the other. This would give the appearance of non-consistency of behaviour across situations, when really it was stable personality variables which determined that the individual would be able to deal effectively with one situation but not with another. Mischel and Peake (1982) point out that this is very speculative: all Bem and Funder in fact demonstrated experimentally was that all children good at performing a particular task were described by their parents as having similar personalities. In addition, Mischel and Peake were unable to replicate Bem and Funder's findings of a particular personality pattern being relevant to a particular task. This study, however, raises the question of just how we may assess or classify situations and what considerations would make us state that one situation was like another.

Finally, Bem and Allen (1974) proposed a third approach to the problem: the *person-centred approach*. They suggested that each individual has his/her own characteristic traits and that only these characteristic traits would be expected to be consistent across situations. They found that students who saw themselves as consistently friendly (i.e. possessing the trait of friendliness) did indeed act in a friendly fashion in a variety of situations, evidenced by ratings from parents and peers and direct observation. On the other hand, students who rated themselves as inconsistently friendly were found to be friendly in some situations and not in others. Thus the trait of friendliness may not be characteristic of all individuals; only those for whom it is characteristic can be expected to behave in a consistently friendly fashion across all situations.

Since people seem able to predict their own consistent (characteristic) traits, the approach seems a promising one. Kenrick and Stringfield (1980) asked subjects to identify dimensions from Cattell's (1957) sixteen dimensions of personality on which they felt themselves to be consistent. These workers went on to show that the aforementioned subjects did indeed have higher correlations between trait ratings and behaviour on their consistent dimensions, which backs up Bem and Allen's proposals.

In both these studies, however, cross-situational consistency was assessed using general ratings rather than the more objective behavioural measures used in Mischel and Peake's Carleton study (1982). This most recent study agreed with Bem and Allen that raters assessed as similar subjects who felt themselves to be consistent on the trait in question: in this case, conscientiousness. Yet the careful observational records showed that both groups of subjects had a similar variability in their degree of conscientiousness from one situation to another. It seems therefore from this more rigorous study that individuals possessing a particular trait are in fact as likely to behave inconsistently from one situation to another as are subjects without that trait.

Conclusion

Thus, we have seen that approaches which assume the existence of stable underlying predispositions are in serious conceptual and empirical difficulty: with our present physiological knowledge, the trait approach appears to be a circular one. It has been pointed out that the relationship of general dispositions to behaviour is on the whole poor, despite suggestions that have been made relating to possible moderating variables. Finally, the lack of consistency of behaviour in different situations cannot be explained by trait approaches to personality.

The interactionist approach

Trait theorists have increasingly been forced to recognize that traits cannot be studied adequately unless an allowance is made for the situation in which they are examined. The *interactionist approach* is to some extent a compromise between the pure trait and pure situationist positions (Magnusson and Endler, 1977). In addition to considering person variables and situation variables, interactionist theory must take into account the process by which the one affects the other (Pervin and Lewis, 1978). As a result of differences in general dispositions (traits) people will be attuned to different aspects of the same situation. Thus at a formal dinner Fred, a boisterous extravert, would merely find the formality restricting, while Cedric, who is anxious about status and concerned about being accepted by others, would worry considerably about the meaning of the seating arrangements and the amount of attention he received.

Interaction has been considered from several viewpoints. In the complex *transactional approach*, interactionism is seen as a reciprocal sequence of actions which takes place between the person and situation (Endler and Magnusson, 1976; cf. Chapter 8). Thus in considering a child with his/her classmates we need to study not only the way he/she may be affected by them but also the effect he/she has on their behaviour; their reactions will, of course, influence him/her as well, and so on. These complex sequences of behaviours have been described on the basis of naturalistic observations of children (e.g. Raush, 1965) and also of interactions between married couples (e.g. Raush *et al.*, 1974). The transactional approach is thus couched in terms of the dynamic interaction of both situational and trait variables. It has not been employed extensively in empirical research however.

On the whole, a more limited meaning of the term 'interaction' has been applied to the trait-situation issue. In the *statistical sense*, interaction refers to the differential effects of situations on people with different predispositions. For example, McCord and Wakefield (1981) hypothesized that extraverts would achieve more than introverts in those classes in which rewards predominate; introverts, on the other hand, would do better when punishment predominated. The authors found this to be the case when looking at the performance on arithmetical tasks. The interaction illustrated indicates that personality (extraversion-introversion) interacts with type of situation (punishment-reward). Perform-ance is enhanced for extraverts in the reward class, whilst intro-verts do better in the punishment class.

It can be seen that this interaction is 'one-way' (the situation affecting the person, and not vice versa). This is by no means a dynamic model, but it has been the basis of a great deal of experimental work. Researchers have endeavoured to estimate the extent of the influence of person factors, situation factors and their interaction on behaviour. A study by Moos (1969) is a good example. He studied various behaviours of psychiatric patients (e.g. smoking, talking) in different situations (such as occupational therapy, on the ward, in the hospital chapel). He found that person factors accounted for 12 per cent of the observed differences, situation factors for 10 per cent and their interaction for 21 per cent. Thus the interaction comes out as having a greater effect than either the person or the situation considered alone.

Endler (1975) has examined the problem of anxiety from the interactionist perspective. He views anxiety as a multidimensional personality trait with several components (e.g. physical harm anxiety and ego threat anxiety). A person scoring highly on one component will only be anxious in a congruent situation. Thus, only if there is an ego threatening situation (e.g. fear of failure) will a person scoring highly on ego-threat anxiety be anxious. Sarason *et al.* (1975), after reviewing many studies of this type, concluded that neither person nor situation factors nor their interaction adequately explained the observed differences in behaviour, which largely remain unaccounted for.

This kind of interactionist research has been heavily criticized. Firstly, there are two types of interaction which have been observed between person and situation variables. A so-called *cross-over interaction* is said to exist if a person who is highly anxious in aeroplanes is not at all anxious on the underground, whereas his friend panics on the tube but is not at all afraid of flying. A *scalar interaction*, on the other hand, would describe the difference noted between two people of whom neither is anxious in supermarkets but one is extremely anxious in lifts.

Furnham and Jaspers (1983) have provided a near-exhaustive review of the literature on the nature of interactions between person and situation, although not everyone accepts the use of this kind of statistical technique to study person-situation interaction. They found that most of the observed interactions are of the latter (scalar) type. This implies that all that situations can do is amplify individual differences which already exist; they do not seem to be able to modify them radically. Thus, the difference between the anxious and the non-anxious person will be more obvious under certain conditions; the non-anxious person, will, however, *always* be less anxious than his nervous counterpart whatever the situation. As Olweus (1979) pointed out, this approach to interactionism is not substantially different from a traditional trait approach. He also (1977) remarked that estimates of the relative importance of persons, situations and their interaction depends entirely on the range of persons sampled and the situations to which they were exposed. Furthermore, a significant interaction tells us nothing about the process underlying that interaction; it also tells us precious little about why people behave the way they do. Nobody disputes the importance of studying the way personality may interact with situations, but such study can progress only within the context of a firm theory of personality dispositions. From the situationist's viewpoint, Mischel (1981) pointed out that it is necessary to analyse the psychological bases for 'interaction'; without such an analysis, an emphasis on interaction is in danger of being little more than the announcement of the obvious. Cronbach and Snow (1977) stress that the potential number of interactions which could be systematically studied in this fashion is practically infinite. The only way of limiting this would be to use a unifying theory within psychology capable of incorporating each additional finding of an interaction. Since no such theory exists as yet, demonstrating new interactions adds little to psychological knowledge. Interaction is thus not currently a useful paradigm.

Finally, the interactionists' approach faces a major problem in defining what is meant by 'situation'. Psychologists have tried to create classifications (or taxonomies) for different types of situation but have run into enormous difficulties. It is not clear, for example, whether situations are definable objectively or whether we must always take the perception of the situation as the basis of the classification. If we take the latter course, the model is totally confounded since perceiving situations in particular ways could be a trait variable not independent of personality. The word 'situation' is currently often used in a vague sense to refer to nothing in particular yet to explain potentially all differences.

Interactionism is a useful reminder that we should not study the person in isolation from his/her situation. Pervin (1980) cites

Eysenck, who pointed out correctly that the influence of person and situation on behaviour can never be separated as *the person is studied in the situation*. Physicists studying the properties of molten metals would not ask: 'Is the quality of the heat (situation) more or less important than the substance being melted (person)?' It is self-evident that it is the interaction of the two that he is examining. Nevertheless, he feels able to put forward hypotheses concerning the properties of the metal regardless of the source of the heat. Interactionism may be a useful conceptual framework, but it is an empty one until it can be filled with an adequate theory of the person.

8

Socio-cognitive models

The socio-cognitive approach arose from the work of psychologists studying the social aspects of the learning process (i.e. social learning theorists) and clinical psychologists who regard maladaptive thinking patterns as the primary cause of abnormality (i.e. cognitive therapists). The social learning theorists (e.g. Bandura, 1977; Mischel, 1973, 1980) provide a framework for looking at personality, whilst cognitive therapists (e.g. Mahoney, 1980; Meichenbaum, 1977a; Ellis and Whitely, 1979; Beck *et al.*, 1979) have developed treatment approaches within this framework.

A major impetus to the development of the socio-cognitive approach was the behaviour therapists' growing dissatisfaction with classical learning theory. This we will consider in three points. In the first place, laboratory studies showed that learning was more complex than was allowed for by traditional learning theory (see Walker, 1984). A clear example is provided by Brewer (1974). He showed that when subjects performing in classical conditioning experiments were *told* that the unconditioned stimulus was no longer going to follow the conditioned stimulus the conditioned response did not extinguish gradually but disappeared at once (i.e. when told a puff of air to the eye would no longer follow the tone, subjects immediately ceased to blink on hearing the tone). This implies that something other than classical conditioning principles must play a part, since Pavlovian theory would have predicted a gradual loss of the response. In the second place, traditional learning theory fails to explain adequately how neurotic behaviours arise and persist. (This is discussed in Chapter 4.) Thirdly, learning theory does not provide entirely adequate explanations as to why behavioural treatments work. As Wilson (1982) suggested, the developments in the techniques of behaviour modification seem to have outstripped the progress of theoretical accounts.

Besides this dissatisfaction of behaviour therapists with learning theory, a further accompaniment to the development of the socio-cognitive approach has been the emergence of increasingly complex cognitive models in general psychology. Schwartz (1982) has listed the following four groups of concepts currently in general use in psychology which have fostered the development of the socio-cognitive model:

1 Information processing, which covers the acquisition, storage and use of information.
2 Beliefs and belief systems, including ideas, attitudes and expectations about oneself and others.
3 Self-statements which are described as internal monologues influencing behaviour and emotions.
4 Problem-solving and coping, which are conceptual and symbolic processes involved in producing effective responses to difficult situations.

Finally, developments in social psychology, particularly the emergence of *attribution theory*, have had a marked impact on clinical psychology. Attribution theory (Heider, 1958) concerns the way a person's behaviour is influenced by his/her perception of causation. An example is the classical study by Nisbett and Schachter (1966), in which subjects were warned they would receive electric shocks; they were also given some totally inactive pills (placebos). Half the subjects were told the pills had side-effects such as increased heart rate and sweating (i.e. symptoms of fear) and half that the major side effect would be itching. All subjects then received shocks of increasing intensity. Those subjects who could *attribute* their pain-induced autonomic arousal to the pills were able to tolerate a much greater strength of shock. This experiment shows how the process of attribution may profoundly influence emotional experiences.

The socio-cognitive model encompasses the social learning theory perspective. Unlike traditional learning theory approaches, however, it focuses on the acquisition of complex behaviour patterns and on the person's ability to learn to discriminate between increasingly subtle social situations. The socio-cognitive approach is the 'marriage' of cognitive psychology and social learning theory perspectives (Bower, 1979). Below we list nine important characteristics of the socio-cognitive approach:

1 Workers in this area assume that there is a two-way interaction between the person and his/her environment. Mahoney (1980) emphasized that people can actively change situations as well as be affected by their environment.

2 Social learning theorists generally favour *situationalism* (see Chapter 7). This involves a rejection of the use of traits (i.e. generalized dispositions) in accounting for people's behaviour (Mischel, 1981). Thus a man who displays aggressive behaviour with his peers but not with his boss or his father would be seen as displaying different response patterns in different situations. A trait theorist, on the other hand, might say that he was a fundamentally aggressive man mastering his aggression in the presence of authority figures. To the extent that enduring cognitive structures are postulated by the socio-cognitive model, its bias may be regarded as one towards interactionism rather than situationalism.

3 The socio-cognitive model is seen as *mediational.* Thus, it emphasizes that stimuli impinging on the person are acted upon by a series of symbolic and cognitive processes which affect the response emitted.

4 Learning is still seen as the central process, but conditioning and reinforcement are felt to play only a minor role. Behaviours are largely acquired via *observation, instruction and the learning of rules.* It is well established that children can rapidly learn long, complex sequences of behaviours merely via observation and in the absence of rehearsal or reinforcement. Yarrow *et al.* (1973), for example, showed that children will learn to perform altruistic behaviours by watching a model behave in that way to others;

a kindly, live model was more effective than the scene enacted by dolls in producing the altruistic behaviour in the children. Instructions and rules also facilitate learning (probably by helping in the organization of information and by providing internalized modes of regulating and controlling behaviour during its emission).

5 The likelihood of a person performing a particular behaviour once it has been learned is thought to depend largely upon what he/she expects to result from it (Mischel, 1981). To predict behaviour we need to be able to estimate the strength of an individual's belief (expectancy) that it will lead to a positive outcome. Mischel (1981) also described expectancies activated by stimuli. Thus stimuli are seen as indicating the probability that other events will occur rather than as eliciting behaviours directly. Carr (1979) considered phobias in this light. Phobic objects or situations are stimuli that lead us to anticipate harm. An individual may be afraid of speaking in public because of feeling that his/her mouth will go dry, and the resultant squeaky voice will cause the audience to laugh. Avoidance behaviour persists because it reduces the probability of the harmful outcome. A refusal ever to speak in public will ensure the audience can never laugh at one.

6 An individual's response to stimuli is largely a function of their meaning (i.e. how he/she *appraises* them). Appraising a stimulus as non-threatening (the ticking box as an alarm clock rather than a bomb) can markedly reduce the induced anxiety (Lazarus, 1981). Research suggests that people with depression consistently interpret events in the worst possible light (e.g. Coyne *et al.*, 1981) – an example of negative appraisal.

7 The concept of appraisal implies that stimuli do not necessarily have a direct effect on behaviour. Bandura (1977) and Mischel (1981) suggest that stimulus control may be overcome by self-control (for example, by selecting the environments to which we expose ourselves, by rearranging the environment to suit ourselves or by cognitively transforming it by paying attention to one aspect rather than another). Mischel and Baker (1975) showed that although young children are usually unable to delay taking sweets put in front of them, they can resist for significantly longer if taught a cognitive transformation to employ, i.e. to imagine that marshmallows are little balls of cotton wool. In a similar way, surgical patients were helped to

reconstrue their threatening ordeal (Langer *et al.*, 1975). Instead of dwelling on the surgery, they were encouraged to focus on the hospital admission as an escape from work pressures and a chance to relax. This group coped much better with their admission and needed significantly less medication for pain relief. People in general seem to adopt similar strategies in attempting to cope with stressful situations.

8 Bandura (1977) suggests that the initiation and persistence of behaviour is governed by its consequences, which consist of three forms:

(a) The first is the direct feedback received by the individual from the environment consequent upon the behaviour. This is in line with the concept of reinforcement within the operant learning theory approach but must also allow for the role of appraisal (how the feedback is evaluated by the person), as mentioned above. Feedback acts by changing people's expectancies about the consequences of their actions.

(b) The observed (i.e. vicarious) consequences of someone else's behaviour can also have a major influence upon our expectancies. A model's behaviour is far more likely to be imitated if he/she is seen to have been rewarded.

(c) Self-produced consequences may also determine whether or not a behaviour is performed. People learn internalized standards by which they judge their own performance and then control their behaviour using self-praise and self-criticism. Bandura's important and novel concept of *self-efficacy* explains how such self-produced consequences can affect behaviour. This term refers to people's expectation that they will carry out successfully an action required of them. Success is judged on the basis of internalized standards: if an individual's self-efficacy (expectation of success) is high, he/she will initiate or attempt tasks required of him/her, while if he/she expects to fail, anxiety and avoidance behaviour can result.

9 The final point we shall consider here is Bandura's (1978, 1982) belief that the effectiveness of all psychological procedures can be attributed to their effectiveness in strengthening an individual's self-efficacy expectations (to encourage his/her conviction that he/she can successfully execute the behaviour required to produce the desired outcome). With an increase in self-efficacy, a wider range of behaviours will be attempted.

Experimental work with various diagnostic groups in treatment, including phobics (Bandura *et al.*, 1977) and those having suffered heart attacks (Bandura, 1982), has shown that the best predictor of outcome is the subject's self-efficacy rating (self-rated prediction of success). Thus it is the individual's expectations that determine how well he/she will deal with a phobic object, rather than previous responses during pre-treatment or treatment periods. Lee (1983), however, points to methodological shortcomings in Bandura's demonstrations which cast some doubt on the concept of self-efficacy. Others, including Wolpe (1978), have suggested that it is not the changes in self-efficacy expectations that produce behavioural improvements but rather the other way round. Thus evidence cautions against the uncritical acceptance of self-efficacy as an explanation for all psychotherapeutic effects.

Learned helplessness: an example of a cognitive elaboration of learning theory

The theoretical development from traditional learning theory to the socio-cognitive models occurred gradually from the late 1960s. Learning theory observations were expanded, and theoretical accounts for them came to include more and more concepts to do with appraisal, reasoning and thinking. These concepts are considered to mediate between the stimulus and the response and were felt by theorists to be essential assumptions if an adequate account of behaviour, both in the laboratory and in the clinical context, were to be provided. A good example of how this development occurred is provided by an account of learned helplessness, a concept put forward by Seligman to provide an explanation for neurotic depressions.

Seligman (1975) proposed the concept of learned helplessness to explain the effects produced in an animal by uncontrollable aversive events. His original experiment involved two groups of dogs, one able to avoid electric shocks by learning to make a particular voluntary response and the other having no control whatsoever over the shock. The total number of shocks received by each group was the same. Subsequently, both groups of dogs were placed in identical aversive situations from which escape was possible. Only the first group was able to learn how to escape. The second group, which had had no control over the original shocks, was described as having developed learned *helplessness*; they seemed to 'give up' and just wait to be shocked again, making no attempt at all to escape. These helpless animals appeared apathetic and despondent and were very slow to learn that they could actually control what would happen to them. It was also suggested that helplessness produced lowered mood and increased anxiety.

These debilitating consequences of uncontrollable aversive stimulation have been repeatedly demonstrated in work with animals (see Maier and Seligman, 1976) and have also been seen in human volunteers who have been subjected to uncontrollable aversive events such as failure at tasks, mild shocks, etc. (Hiroto and Seligman, 1975). Miller and Seligman (1982) report depression, dysphoria, passivity, physical stress reactions (including the development of ulcers), a wide range of behavioural disorders and an increased mortality rate as probable results of learned helplessness.

The clinical relevance of this model lies in the link made by Seligman between learned helplessness and reactive depression (depression which seems to result from external events). In many ways they seem to be similar states: in both conditions there is a reduction in voluntary activity, a loss of appetite and libido plus a strong feeling of being powerless to alter the situation. Helplessness has been noted as being associated with lowered aggression (an aspect of depression noted by Freud in 1917). Seligman's suggestion is that reactive depression is equivalent to learned helplessness (the uncontrollable aversive event being some life stress, such as bereavement).

Whilst learned helplessness is in many ways a promising model, it has not gone uncriticized. Costello (1978) has pointed out that the vast bulk of the evidence supporting this model of *human* depression comes from work with *animals* and what human work there is is by no means totally supportive. Furthermore, the negative view of oneself which is so characteristic of depression is not accounted for by the model. Beck *et al.* (1979), whose own theory will be discussed later in this chapter, noted that another typical feature of depression, blaming oneself for all that seems to have gone wrong, is hardly consistent with the feeling of having no control over events. Perhaps the most significant criticism is that Seligman's theory has no way of accounting for the wide variation in susceptibility to learned helplessness noted in reviews of the area (see, for example, Zuroff, 1980); in other words, it does not predict when the effects of uncontrolled aversive stimulation will lead to depression and when they will not.

Attribution theory reformulation of learned helplessness

Abramson *et al.* (1978) have provided a substantial reformulation of Seligman's original theory which goes some way towards answering the above criticisms. It also illustrates the increasing cognitive influences on the theory which was in any case more cognitive than other learning theory formulations. They suggest that the debilitation of learned helplessness is dependent not only on an expectation of uncontrollability but also on the causal attributions the individual makes to explain the failures that have already occurred. The attributions of individuals responding to uncontrollable aversive events by learned helplessness are characterized by three features. The attributions tend to be *internal*, which means that the person holds him/herself responsible for failing to reach the desired goal whereas *external* attributions would locate the blame elsewhere. They tend also to be *global* attributions referring to a wide range of situations. In addition, the state of learned helplessness might well be expected to be particularly negative and persistent when the person believes that it reflects a *stable* feature of him/herself: for example, after the breakup of a relationship the conclusion 'I'll never be attractive to women' is likely to produce a much greater loss of self-esteem than the stable, less global and more external attribution 'That person finds me unattractive'. The state of depression was held by Abramson *et al.* (1978) to be associated with global, internal and stable attributions for personal failure and specific, external and unstable attributions for personal successes.

Evidence for the reformulation was summarized by Miller and Seligman (1982). Raps *et al.* (1982) found that a clinical sample of depressed subjects were more likely than non-depressed individuals to attribute hypothetical failure to internal, global and stable causes. When depressed subjects are made to fail in laboratory tasks they are more likely to attribute their failure to some shortcoming in themselves (internal causes) but show no differences in other aspects of attributional style such as globality or stability (e.g. Zuroff, 1981). A more stringent test of the theory in terms of the attributions made by depressed individuals about actual negative life events has yielded less convincing results

(Coyne and Gotlib, 1983). For example, Feather and Davenport (1981) found that depressed, unemployed young people tended to make more external attributions (i.e. blamed the government or the political climate) and fewer internal attributions (e.g. their lack of skill or training). Thus the reformulation model of learned helplessness is poorly supported by those studies approximating most closely to the naturalistic setting.

The attributions people make for success or failure might, however, provide a promising area for therapeutic cognitive intervention. Dweck (1975) showed that children's motivation to persist in the face of failure could be manipulated in this way. One group of children was trained to ascribe failure to lack of effort rather than lack of ability; effort, unlike ability, is under volitional control and so can be increased. This group showed improved persistence and performance compared with the others not given such *attributional retraining*. This technique has also been applied in the psychological management of physical pain. In the latter case, clients are encouraged to relabel their painful sensations as something under their control and less distressing to them. Levendusky and Pankratz (1975) reported the case of a 65-year-old man with abdominal pain of two and a half years' duration. He was taught to visualize the sensations as tight steel bands which he could loosen and as electrical impulses under his control. (He had been an engineer by profession.) The treatment proved to be highly effective, and the man was withdrawn from his medication after six weeks. Pearce (1983) reviewed a number of similar studies and concluded that such techniques appear promising, although firm empirical evidence remains scarce.

The reformulation of learned helplessness has thus provided a context for the development of methods for helping people with both psychological and medical problems via the manipulation of their attributions (Kopel and Arkowitz, 1975). Despite its poor empirical basis, the learned helplessness model has undoubtedly been one of the most productive formulations in clinical psychology. It continues to stimulate research and has greatly influenced contemporary views of depression.

The clinical application of the socio-cognitive model

A wide range of techniques have arisen out of various aspects of the socio-cognitive model. Many of these are markedly similar to behavioural procedures, whilst others are radically different. Perhaps more than in most other therapeutic approaches, cognitive therapists are inclined to use more than one technique with a particular client. However, for the sake of convenience, we will separate the methods.

Techniques of self-control

All cognitive therapies make use of the client's ability to modify his/her own behaviour. The techniques taught to clients to help them achieve greater self-control fall into three groups. All these have been used on their own but are more frequently applied as part of more elaborate cognitive packages.

Stimulus control is a technique based on the assumption that certain features of the environment act to 'cue' behaviours, i.e. to set them in motion. Thus strictly controlling the situations in which certain behaviours are likely to occur may serve to alter their frequency. Borkovec *et al.* (1983) successfully treated 111 subjects who complained of excessive worrying by allotting them half-hour 'worry periods' in which they had to concentrate on worrying at the same time and in the same location each day. It is claimed that the worrying comes only to be associated with these periods. Similar techniques of manipulating the cueing function of the environment have been of value in obesity, alcoholism and work problems. Overeating may sometimes be reduced by instructing clients not to eat in any situation except at a well-laid table. The technique seems only to be successful, however, if used as part of a treatment package which includes other interventions.

The act of closely monitoring one's own actions has been noted to result in a reduction of the frequency of the spontaneous performance of the behaviour being monitored. It is this aspect of *self-monitoring*, known as reactivity, which makes it suitable to form part of many treatment programmes aimed at reducing the frequency of behaviours. It normally entails the subject keeping a check on how often a behaviour is performed. For example, Nelson *et al.* (1982) found that the frequency of face-touching was significantly reduced if each occurrence had to be recorded. The effect lasted for nine weeks but disappeared as soon as the self-monitoring ceased. This lack of long-term effectiveness is reported in many studies, and in addition the problem of inaccuracies in people's self-monitoring has not been solved. Self-monitoring is a necessary part of many cognitive interventions, but on its own it is unlikely to lead to lasting improvements.

Laboratory evidence from Bandura (1971b) suggested *self-reward* as a possible technique for altering behaviours. Self-reward is the evaluation of one's own behaviour followed by the self-administration of reinforcement. If deserved, self-praise may be as effective a motivator of behaviour as more concrete self-rewards such as money (Mahoney, 1981). Self-reward appears more effective than self-punishment. In interviewing subjects who had attempted to give up smoking, Perri *et al.* (1977) found that those who spontaneously used self-reward were more successful than those attempting to control their own behaviour through self-punishment.

Unlike self-monitoring, self-reward has been observed to have long-term effects. Kendall (1982) followed up children with behavioural problems who had been treated by being taught to reward themselves for good behaviour: after a year there still seemed to be beneficial effects. Self-reward has been found to be helpful in dealing with a wide range of conditions, and it forms an integral part of a number of cognitive programmes to be reviewed later in this chapter (see Meichenbaum's self-instructional training, 1977a).

Cognitive restructuring therapies

The three treatments we shall consider in this category have as their primary aim the modification of the clients' habitual ways of thinking about themselves and the world. The three approaches agree in identifying maladaptive cognitions as the basis of neurotic behaviour but differ in the techniques they recommend for modifying them.

Ellis, whose training was in psychoanalysis, turned to cognitive therapy in the 1960s, developing what he termed *rational-emotive therapy*. He proposed that irrational thoughts were the main cause of emotional distress of all types. Irrational thinking, he suggested, is an inherent human characteristic, a biological predisposition encouraged by childhood experiences. The following are examples of what he regarded as common irrationalities: 'I *can't* live without love', 'I *must* be perfectly competent to be a valued person', 'One *cannot help* feeling certain things', etc.

The notion that specific irrational thoughts cause abnormal

behaviour of different kinds is well illustrated by Ellis's (1977) suggestions about phobias. Ellis views phobias as linked to 'catastrophizing self-statements'. Simply stated, this means that the individual says to him/herself that something terrible will happen in a certain situation; as a result he/she will experience fear and avoidance of that situation. It is the person's catastrophic pattern of thinking about the situation that is the real cause of the phobia. An agoraphobic, for example, might fear above all else the 'disaster' of being overcome by anxiety and fainting in a public place. Such a person could be so worried about this happening that he/she avoids leaving the house altogether. The anticipation of disaster leads to avoidance.

Ellis's treatment suggestions are simple. They involve first of all identifying the irrational ideas and then replacing them with more constructive, rational thoughts. For example, a depressed client might perceive that no one loves him/her and conclude, irrationally, from this that he/she is worthless. Ellis would emphasize to the client that although he/she may indeed have no friends at present this need not last; that in any case not having friends no more implies that a person is worthless than having lots of them would prove its opposite, and so on. Thus the client's irrational thinking is challenged.

Furthermore, the client would be encouraged to verbalize the more rational alternative thought, 'There's nothing terrible about no one loving me'. Alternatively, the client might be discouraged from over-generalizing and putting too much emphasis on trivial events. Antidotes to irrational thoughts may be used. Thus instead of the thought, 'I can't cope with too much anxiety', the client will state: 'Anxiety may be a cue for coping. I know that the anticipation is always worse than the event.'

The evidence backing up Ellis's theory is by no means unanimous. The question as to whether neurotics have more irrational ideas than do normal people has been widely studied. The results are none the less mixed. Favouring Ellis, some studies show that questionnaire measures of emotional distress on the whole correlate with admission to irrational beliefs on other questionnaires. Goldfried and Sobucinski (1975), for example, found that anxiety problems were associated with irrational beliefs about the need for others' approval, unrealistically high self-expectations and anxious over-concern about potential catastrophes (Alden and Safran, 1978). This association has been found in a wide range of disorders including depression (Nelson, 1977), Type A behaviour pattern (Smith and Brehm, 1981) and lack of assertiveness (Alden and Safran, 1978). Such correlations as are found nevertheless tend to be quite weak (0.25–0.50). Furthermore, not all individuals with emotional difficulties appear to have an excessive number of irrational ideas. Rimm *et al.* (1977) found that only 26 per cent of phobic patients admitted to irrational ideas and many of these claimed the ideas did not cause but followed the disorder. A further problem for Ellis's theory is that if irrational thoughts *cause* neurotic symptoms we might well expect phobias, excessive timidity and depression to be associated with their own particular idiosyncratic patterns of thinking. Yet this does not appear to be the case: generally emotionally disturbed individuals do have more irrational thoughts, this is not a specific association (Harrell *et al.*, 1981).

Evidence in support of the effectiveness of rational-emotive therapy (RET) has been sparse. Some studies have found RET to be effective: for instance, Wise and Haynes (1983) found that this form of therapy helped people with test anxiety more than did a placebo treatment. Smith (1982) in a review of almost thirty studies concluded that it was an effective form of therapy. Unfortunately, as Rachman and Wilson (1980) point out, most of these are poor-quality studies with inadequate follow-up. Perhaps the most crucial point is that it is rare for such studies to report a change in beliefs associated with the therapeutic success. For example, Glogower *et al.* (1978) reported that the successful treatment of speech anxiety was not related to an awareness of the role of irrational beliefs. This type of finding casts a long shadow of doubt over Ellis's formulations. Eschenroeder's (1982) severe critique of Ellis also focused on the weaknesses inherent in his theory, feeling that the theoretical principles underlying RET were far too loosely formulated. Ellis, for example, never explained fully what he meant by rationality, which after all very much depends on one's point of view. Mahoney (1977) also expressed concern that Ellis's approach had in recent years become so general that it was in great danger of losing its uniqueness.

In sum, despite some promising findings a number of doubts have been expressed concerning the adequacy of empirical evidence in support of Ellis's theory and therapy.

Meichenbaum (1977b) regards neurotic behaviour as due, at

least in part, to what he calls 'faulty internal dialogues' in stressful situations. Whereas Ellis stresses the importance of the individual's irrational beliefs, Meichenbaum attributes a central role to *internal speech*. He was strongly influenced in this by the Russian psychologist Luria (1961), who believed that 'self-talk' (private monologues) controlled the individual's behaviour. According to Luria, the behaviour of children is at first regulated by the instructions of other people, such as their parents; subsequently they learn to control their own behaviour via a kind of running commentary which they ultimately internalize as covert (hidden) *self-instructions*. Meichenbaum suggests that in individuals with neurotic problems the self-instructions are faulty. Faulty internal dialogues, unlike irrational thinking patterns, are not assumed to be stable characteristics of a person. Some faulty self-instructions sound similar to Ellis's descriptions, as in the case of a train phobic telling himself 'If the train stops in the tunnel I shall go mad!' Another type of faulty internal dialogue might contain self-fulfilling prophecies such as those of the agoraphobic thinking, 'When I get into that crowded room I shall get into a panic worrying that I might faint and so I shall have to leave at once.' Other self-statements are thought to be faulty because they include self-defeating messages such as a socially anxious person saying to herself at a party, 'I don't think I have much of a chance of talking to anyone interesting here.'

Meichenbaum's approach to treatment (*self-instructional training*) is more influenced by behavioural methods than is Ellis's, and the term 'cognitive behaviour modification' is frequently linked with it. Meichenbaum feels that the first step in therapy must be the demonstration to the client of the primary role of cognitions. Following this, he/she is trained to identify and become aware of the maladaptive nature of his/her self-statements. A client might have numerous negativistic thoughts such as 'It's no good, I'll never get it finished. My work is no good anyway.' The therapist could say to this client: 'It seems to me that these thoughts may prevent you from trying as hard as you can. It must be difficult to put a lot into your work if you've convinced yourself you'll fail anyway.' Following the identification of the faulty internal dialogue the emphasis shifts to the development of coping skills. These could include the production of coping self-statements, the learning of relaxation techniques and the creation of plans for behavioural change. The coping self-statements originate with the therapist and are gradually adopted by the client. Examples would be: 'Look for the positive aspects. Don't jump to conclusions!' or 'I know this will upset me, but I know how to deal with it. I'll just take it step by step. I'm not going to let myself down by losing control.' A clear plan of action needs to be formulated and adopted as part of the process of developing coping skills. Thus a person with interpersonal anxieties might propose the following strategies: 'Think out clearly what to say', 'Remember to look at the other person', 'Speak clearly, slowly, firmly and without hesitation', etc. Practising these coping skills is an integral part of Meichenbaum's approach. The client could start by writing out his strategy and then role-play it with a continuous commentary on his self-statements before trying it all out in the feared situation for which it was intended.

One way of developing coping skills rapidly for specific stressful situations is described in Meichenbaum's (1977a) *stress inoculation programme*. Here the client is intentionally exposed to mild stress (such as electric shock) in the laboratory. This would be at a level with which he/she could cope. Together with the therapist he/she analyses the coping strategies just used so successfully, and an attempt is then made to transfer them to the problem situations.

There is some evidence linking maladaptive internal dialogues to abnormal behaviour. Studies of patterns of self-referent speech have found quite strong associations between negative self-referent thoughts such as 'My work is no good anyway' and psychological problems such as social anxiety and low self-esteem (e.g. Cacioppo *et al.* 1979). The problem facing Meichenbaum's theory concerns the feasibility of the concept of internal speech. He assumes that internal language (self-statements) has a central role in the organization of behaviour. This view has been hotly disputed by some eminent cognitive psychologists (see Piaget, 1963). Moreover, current evidence from developmental psychology indicates that highly organized complex behaviours may be identified in infants long before the development of language (Bower, 1982). Thus, internal speech might be neither a necessary nor a sufficient condition for the regulation of complex behaviour.

Evidence about the effectiveness of this form of treatment is also mixed. Meichenbaum and his colleagues (1971) showed in an early study that training clients with public-speaking anxiety to identify and alter maladaptive self-talk patterns resulted in significant reductions in anxiety levels compared with placebo and no treatment controls. More recent studies which compared self-instructional training (SIT) with traditional behavioural methods found it to be neither more nor less effective than behaviour therapy: for example, Emmelkamp and Mersch (1982) found flooding alone no *less* effective than flooding plus SIT and *more* effective than SIT alone in highly anxious subjects. In all, there have been approximately fifty outcome studies, few of which, however, include a long-term follow-up of clients treated in this way. Furthermore, in many of these studies volunteers were used; they were as a result probably less severely affected by their symptoms than were clients in certain other experiments. Thus, as with RET, the clinical effectiveness of the SIT procedure remains to be demonstrated.

Like Ellis and Meichenbaum, Beck (1976) asserted that a causal relationship existed between cognitions (thoughts, beliefs and expectations) and emotions. He claimed that behaviour patterns characteristic of a depressed person were a direct result of specific, maladaptive thought processes. These cognitions would represent a sufficient if not a necessary cause for depression. Beck and his colleagues (1979) described depressive cognitions (or *silent assumptions*) as negative attitudes concerning current experience, the world, the self and the future. An example of the negative view of current experiences would be viewing small deprivations as major losses (e.g. travelling alone is seen as missing out on companionship). Further examples of distorted thinking are a tendency towards deprecation (e.g. ambiguities in conversation are seen as implied criticisms) and a tendency to accept defeat overreadily (e.g. regarding a small obstacle to progress as a sign of failure).

The depressed individual not only views the world as bad but regards him/herself in a like manner. There is a tendency to generalize from a single example of behaviour to a disposition so that one small problem is regarded as a major shortcoming. Beck (1976) described a depressed female client with the poor self-image and feelings of being unlovable so often to be found in depression. When she kept a diary as her therapist requested, she found to her great surprise that the majority of her experience was in fact positive: her memory had selectively retrieved the negative incidents because her perceptual set had concentrated exclusively on confirming her expectations of being unlovable. There is also a marked tendency for depressed individuals to blame themselves for the defeats and deprivations they feel. The negative expectations about the future are natural extensions of how the individual sees the present. They are convinced that both in the long and the short term their personal efforts will not bring about change.

The theory holds that depressive cognitions come about because of faulty aspects of the thought processes of the depressed person. It is held that such a person has a greater tendency to make arbitrary inferences (draw conclusions on subjective impressions alone), to overgeneralize and to pay selective attention to particular aspects of the situation. In addition, depressed people show gross inaccuracies in estimating the significance of events; they view life in extreme terms and have a marked tendency towards personalization (incorrectly referring all external events to themselves).

There is some evidence supporting Beck's descriptions of depressive cognitions. Gotlib (1981) has shown that depressed people underestimate the amount of positive reinforcement they receive even when they administer this themselves. Similarly, Finkel *et al.* (1982) found that depressives reading a list of statements see fewer statements as positive than do normal subjects. Both these studies indicate that depressed people do selectively ignore positive events. The cognitive abnormalities associated with depression could, however, as easily be the result of the depression as its cause. Beck argues that since altering the cognitions in therapy appears to improve mood, cognitions must come first. As we shall see, this view is highly controversial.

In Beck's cognitive therapy, all clients are taught the theory behind the therapy (the association between thinking and emotion) and are initially trained to focus on their automatic thoughts, to identify them and ultimately replace them with less maladaptive cognitions. They are trained to distance themselves from the events around them and to try to be more objective. They learn to evaluate the evidence upon which their subjective appraisal was made – to distinguish fact from opinion. Between sessions they are encouraged to monitor automatic thoughts and to generate appropriate alternatives. In the process of making clients try out alternative views of the world, various traditional behavioural techniques may be used. Individuals may be asked, for instance, to test out the view that they are unable to enjoy spending time with their children by carrying out a homework programme of 'graded exposure assignments', in other words, by gradually spending more time with them. Tasks are designed that are likely to lead to experiences of success which may break their negative expectations concerning themselves.

On the whole, studies of the effectiveness of Beck's therapy have shown it to be as good as or even better than the most widely used treatment for depression, namely antidepressant drugs. In two major studies, Rush *et al.* (1977, 1982) found Beck's therapy to be initially more effective than drugs, although this difference disappeared at six-month follow-up. More recently, the initial difference in effectiveness has not been observed, but both types of therapy have independently been found superior to control treatments (Murphy *et al.*, 1984). Most studies also fail to show that Beck's therapy is superior to traditional behaviour therapy (Rachman and Wilson, 1980).

In conclusion, Beck's approach seems promising, but like the other two approaches to cognitive restructuring it is not without its problems. The causes of the cognitive abnormalities in depression are not clear. Studies of therapeutic outcome are few and open to much criticism. There are, for example, doubts as to the adequacy of the drug dosage in Rush *et al.*'s studies; in other poorly controlled studies, the number of hours of patient-therapist contact was much greater for cognitive therapy than for drug treatments. Thus Beck's therapy may have been shown to be superior only to inadequate drug therapy with very little therapist contact. Nevertheless, it is undoubtedly a significant contribution to the field. As yet it is impossible to determine whether the effectiveness of cognitive therapy is due to its use of behavioural techniques, its non-specific features (placebo effects) or whether the outcome studies constitute a genuine demonstration that the elimination and replacement of certain maladaptive modes of cognition can have a lasting and clinically substantial effect on mood.

Evaluation

Currently, the socio-cognitive approach is probably the most popular theoretical framework in clinical psychology. The socio-cognitive model of personality perhaps does not really merit being termed a theory. It is a collection of diverse and sometimes contradictory ideas and techniques, not closely unified but rather considered together because of certain shared assumptions. The common bases include an appealing view of humans as active, conscious and problem-oriented (Mischel, 1977). The approach incorporates developments in psychology in areas outside the clinical field such as social, developmental and experimental psychology. In addition, it maintains scientific rigour whilst broadening the range of behaviours encompassed.

It needs to be considered whether the popularity of the socio-cognitive model represents a substantial and permanent change of psychological orientation or merely reflects the current fashion. In order to answer this question some of the most fundamental assumptions of the model will be re-examined in some detail.

What is cognition?

Should cognition be considered as a new concept, or did it always play a major role in behaviour therapy? Marzillier (1980) suggested that the term is used in three different ways. The first meaning refers to internal thoughts and images. In this sense, behaviour therapists have always accepted cognitions as covert (hidden) behaviours. (For example, systematic desensitization involves the use of imaginal processes.) The second sense describes a process by which external stimuli are transformed (e.g. attention and recall). This position is intermediate between the one used in traditional behaviour modification and that used in cognitive therapy. It enables the therapist to consider the meaning of a stimulus for a particular client and so adjust the programme accordingly. For example, a subject who presents as anxious about going into pubs may dislike the experience because any laughter he hears there seems to be directed at him; the programme would therefore need to expose the subject to laughter rather than to the smell of beer or large crowds.

Finally, the word 'cognition' is used in the sense of cognitive structure (a framework of attitudes and beliefs similar to George Kelly's personal constructs). The assumption of the existence of such structures is implicit, for example, in Ellis's notion of irrational belief systems, Meichenbaum's concept of covert self-instructions and Beck's idea of negatively biased perceptions. It is this final use of the term (cognition as an internal structure) that produces disagreement between cognitive therapists and other

153

psychologists. Behaviour therapists especially find the notion of mental schemas troublesome, for the following reasons.

Firstly, cognitive structures are unobservable, and to some behaviourists (e.g. Williams, 1977) this means the concept is inherently unscientific. Secondly, how do we know what, for example, depressed clients really think? Structures, such as Beck's dysfunctional schemas may be elicited from such individuals, but how do we know that these people actually use them in their thinking? Available evidence indicates that in real life people tend to do and react to things without reflecting and without being aware of why they did them. Thus they are inherently unlikely to be at all affected by a permanent bias of their cognitive system (Nisbett and Wilson, 1977; Wortman and Dintzer, 1978). Thirdly, both Ellis and Beck assume that the cognitive structures of individuals with psychological problems are in some sense 'in error', are 'irrational' or 'bias reality'. This, of course, raises serious questions about what objective reality is. Even if we decide to side-step this particular problem, the evidence is still not on the side of the cognitive theorists. Lewinsohn *et al.* (1980) found depressed subjects to be quite accurate in assessing their ability in social situations; it was normal subjects who exhibited an 'illusory glow', seeing themselves as better than others saw them.

Does cognition have primacy over emotion?

Some psychologists dispute the assumption, made by all cognitive therapists, that cognitions determine emotions (e.g. unhappiness may result from certain maladaptive ideas). One way in which the causal role of maladaptive cognitions (such as overgeneralization or selective perception of negative experiences) may be established would be by showing that maladaptive cognitions predict future emotional disturbance. The cognitions could then be assumed to make the individual *vulnerable* to future emotional disturbance. Golin *et al.* (1981), for example, found that stable and global attributions reported by students to hypothetical negative events predicted depressed mood one month later. Studies with clinical samples rarely show this effect (Lewinsohn *et al.*, 1981), and most attempts at replicating the results of Golin and his colleagues have also failed (Coyne and Gotlib, 1983). Thus we cannot assume that cognitions are enduring factors making the individual forever vulnerable to emotional upset.

An alternative is that changes in patterns of cognition cause the concurrent onset of emotional disturbances: in other words, cognitive changes represent the underlying dysfunction in emotional disturbance. In support of such a causal role, writers have cited studies where manipulating thought content in a negative manner leads to apparent deterioration in mood. In these so-called 'Velten-type' studies, subjects are asked to read statements referring to them which can be of depressed (e.g. 'I'm useless'), elated (e.g. 'I feel I could conquer the world') or netural content. Reading the negative self-statements is shown to result in increased self-report of negative affect. (See, for example, Blackburn and Bonham, 1980.) The cognitive interpretation usually suggested is that the negative thoughts induced lead to a negative mood, thus demonstrating the primacy of the former over the latter.

Other interpretations have nevertheless been offered. Buchwald *et al.* (1981) felt that there was a strong pressure from the experimenter on the subject to report feeling miserable which might be hard to resist. Further evidence is provided by Simons *et al.* (1984). In their study, clinically depressed subjects were assigned to either Beck's cognitive therapy or to drug treatment. Surprisingly, changes in patterns of cognition were as marked in the group receiving drugs as in the group whose treatment focused upon altering their cognitive processes. This indicates that improvements in emotional state may at times be the cause rather than the result of changed cognitions. Coyne and Gotlib (1983) point out that since manipulating the emotional state leads to cognitive changes perhaps causality cannot be demonstrated in this way. Taking all these points into account, it seems that no clear conclusions concerning the status of cognitions can be drawn from the mood induction studies.

According to some models of the relationship between cognition and emotion, cognitions are unlikely to lead to emotional changes because the two phenomena are not related. In two influential papers, Zajonc (1980, 1984) proposed that affect and cognition were separate and partially independent systems and that, although they ordinarily functioned conjointly, affect could be generated without a prior cognitive process. The independence of emotional responses and cognitions, in Zajonc's view, is supported by the existence of separate neuro-anatomical structures for mediating the two types of response (Izard, 1984). He also cited evidence to show that affective reactions could be established without the participation of cognition, as stimuli never reaching consciousness are capable of eliciting emotional responses (Watts, 1983). Zajonc claimed that emotions are immediate, effortless and inescapable. In this view, since emotions and cognitions are independent of each other it is very difficult for thoughts ever to modify feelings. Zajonc believes that this is why verbal persuasion so rarely produces genuine attitude change (Petty and Cacioppo, 1981). This view is, of course, totally opposed to that of the socio-cognitive theorists.

In a paper reviewing the implications of Zajonc's work for clinical psychology, Rachman (1981) found many well-known clinical phenomena to be consistent with that author's views: for example, the independence of cognitions and emotions explains the persistence of much abnormal behaviour despite its irrationality (e.g. a pigeon phobia persisting despite the bird being harmless). The same paper points out that Zajonc's views are incompatible with Seligman's theory of learned helplessness: the latter depends upon the individual's perception that his/her actions cannot affect outcome, while the former cannot allow for such cognitive intermediaries leading to the emotion. Zajonc receives further support from Eysenck (1982), who also considers neurotic behaviours as relatively primitive and mediated by structures separate from the neo-cortex (and hence inaccessible to rational control).

Other psychologists however are more impressed by experimental demonstrations of the *interdependence* of the cognitive and emotional systems than by Zajonc's (1980) theoretical arguments. Bower (1981) reported a number of studies showing that people in sad moods are more likely to recall the sad words from a mixed list and happy people to recall the happy words. Such findings support the concept of an integrated matrix of emotion and cognition. Teasdale and Taylor (1981) and Fogarty and Hemsley (1983) both found that depressed individuals recalled more unhappy memories than did control subjects and that as their depression lifted so the tendency to report negative experiences decreased. This suggests that a circular relationship exists between depressed mood and sad thoughts or memories: depressed mood leads to the recall of further sad thoughts, which in turn lead to further negative mood change. It seems therefore that this issue of the relationship between affect and cognition has not yet been settled. The likely conclusion is probably, as suggested by Lazarus (1984) in his response to Zajonc, that at this stage of theorization and research it can no more be proven that cognition is not present in any emotion than that it is present.

Do changes in cognitions lead to behaviour changes?

There would be little point in carrying out cognitive therapies aimed at altering cognitions if it were not proven that behaviour could change as a result; there is in fact little evidence to demonstrate clearly that altering cognitive structures does lead to behavioural change. Finding a simple correlation between changes in thinking patterns and behavioural changes would of course prove little, as it might well be that the cognitive alterations *follow* the behavioural changes. Furthermore, several studies have shown that behaviour can alter even in the absence of changes in cognition. Berkowitz (1978), for example, reported effects on behaviour in the absence of conscious cognitions. Subjects taking part in a pedalling competition and losing at the last moment administered stronger electric shocks to their competitors than did winning subjects, yet they were totally unaware of feeling angry. Such studies (reviewed by Nisbett and Wilson, 1977) are not well explained by cognitive theory.

A further criticism of cognitive accounts of behaviour change concerns the problem of circularity: a person may avoid a social situation because of fearing that 'something awful might happen'. It is unclear if this is an explanation or just a description of the problem behaviour. Introducing cognitive variables such as anticipation of harm does not lead to clarification. The root of the problem may well be the absence of a comprehensive model of causality to account not only for the way in which maladaptive cognitions lead to abnormal behaviour but also to provide an explanation for why and how the maladaptive cognitions come about. In the absence of such independent predictors, the problem of circular arguments will probably continue to haunt cognitive accounts.

What is the role of cognitions in cognitive therapy?

The argument here, not surprisingly, runs both ways. Cognitive therapists (e.g. Locke, 1979) tend to argue that the effectiveness of traditional behaviour therapy in fact depends upon cognitive changes. Thus they would explain the effectiveness of systematic desensitization by a change in the person's expectation of mastering the feared situation. The positive results of contingency management (altering reinforcement schedules) could be a consequence of changes in internal dialogues (Meichenbaum, 1978). Mahoney and Kazdin (1979) go so far as to suggest that behavioural techniques may be the best way of causing permanent changes in cognition which would then lead to long-term and stable behaviour change. Wilson (1982) argues forcefully that a socio-cognitive model provides a more comprehensive and integrative account of the facts of behaviour change than any other account at present available.

The reverse argument comes from the traditional behaviour therapists (e.g. Ledwidge, 1979). He suggested that the effectiveness of cognitive therapies is purely and simply a function of how great a use is made of behavioural methods during their application. The charge is not unreasonable, since most cognitive therapists make extensive use of traditional behavioural methods. The critique is answered by Miller and Berman's (1983) review of studies which used cognitive restructuring as a therapeutic tool. Studies which made extensive use of behavioural procedures appeared to yield no greater effects than did those relying entirely on cognitive restructuring. Dush *et al.* (1983) reviewed studies which evaluated the somewhat under-researched technique of self-instruction modification and found that the probability of effectiveness increased with the addition of other socio-cognitive techniques (such as cognitive restructuring, modelling, etc.) but not traditional behavioural interventions. Thus review studies indicate that the effectiveness of cognitive intervention is, on the whole, specific to its procedures and does not rely on a behavioural component for its effects. It should, however, be remembered, as we saw throughout our review, that cognitive therapies were rarely superior to behavioural approaches when the two were compared.

The socio-cognitive models of normal personality, abnormality and therapy are very popular, but such enthusiasm seems somewhat in advance of its receiving substantial empirical support. The model has, nonetheless, come the closest to achieving general acceptance in clinical psychology. It is interesting to note a study by Mahoney (1979) in which he reported that, irrespective of clinical psychologists' positions on the cognitive versus behaviour therapy debate, they all were agreed as to the role of awareness, expectancy and relationship factors in therapy. The conclusion to be drawn is thus perhaps that the gulf between cognitive and behavioural therapists is not so wide as might be imagined, but there is as yet no general agreement about how such undoubtedly important elements may be put together into a cohesive and empirically sound model of personality.

9

The integration of theories and future developments

In the previous chapters, we considered several quite separate theoretical approaches to the study of personality and noted their suggestions concerning clinical interventions. We may well wonder why so many different viewpoints exist; would it not be possible to bring these approaches together and combine them to form one single personality theory?

The arguments for integration

There are many good reasons, especially in clinical work, for abandoning the ideological posturing associated with rigid adherence to particular theoretical orientations. Perhaps most important is the inability of the existing orientations to provide a full account.

The language of psychodynamic theories has emerged as confusing. All attempts at clarification have by and large failed, probably because of the lack of a full understanding of the psychological processes underlying its data base (dreams, slips of the tongue, free association, etc.). Behavioural formulations also have their problems, both in explaining the persistence of neurotic symptoms and in understanding the mechanisms involved in improvements following behaviour therapy. Cognitive theories provide us with at least as many new problems as they deal with old ones, especially in the area of affect.

None of the approaches we have considered is free of major difficulties. It is therefore not surprising that workers are increasingly reaching the conclusion that no single existing orientation can ever hope to deal with the complexity of human behaviour (Marmor and Woods, 1980). This is perhaps most obvious to practising clinicians who are acutely aware that their understanding of their clients' behaviour is less than adequate. Mahoney (1979), a leading proponent of cognitive therapy, conducted a survey of eminent cognitive and non-cognitive behaviour therapists and discovered that both groups expressed equal dissatisfaction with their current understanding of human behaviour (the average satisfaction rating on a seven-point scale was less than 2). As Goldfried (1980) and Murray (1983) commented, there is a ground-swell movement of dissatisfaction with theory amongst practising clinical psychologists. This general feeling has encouraged attempts to link such diverse orientations as learning theory and psychoanalysis to form a single approach.

The need for an integrated approach to clinical psychology (or a '*rapprochement*' of major orientations as Goldfried, 1980, termed it) is highlighted by the fragmentation and multiplication of therapies. This mushrooming of theories can be taken as an indication of dissatisfaction with existing approaches. Garfield (1982) reported on the increase from sixty schools of psychotherapy, which he had distinguished in a survey in the 1960s, to 130 by 1975 and 200 by 1980. The existence of so many distinct orientations to therapy is itself an indication of the need for integration.

Recent developments in both the behavioural and the traditional psychotherapeutic camps have tended towards the middle ground between the two approaches. Many behaviour therapists have, for instance, accepted the importance of cognitive factors, and the role of environmental factors in the causation of mental disorders is being increasingly accepted by psychodynamic therapists. These signs of bridging the gap are regarded by some as symptomatic of a trend towards a single, integrated theory.

Empirical research into the outcome and process of psychotherapy is also encouraging to the integrationist. The early claims about the superior effectiveness of behaviour therapy as compared with other methods were probably exaggerated (Barlow and Wolfe, 1981). The initial figures of a 75 per cent success rate in the behavioural treatment of phobias drop to 49 per cent if individuals refusing to participate in the studies or terminating prematurely are included. Outcomes from other treatment methods with similar clients would be expected to be in a similar range. It should not, therefore, be surprising that in some recent carefully controlled studies systematic desensitization turned out to be neither more nor less effective than supportive psychotherapy (dynamically oriented and non-directive; see Klein *et al.*, 1983). Large-scale reviews of studies comparing two or more forms of treatment for similar patient groups frequently report no differences. In their review of the area, Bergin and Lambert (1978) borrowed the Dodo's verdict from *Alice's Adventures in Wonderland* to describe such results: '*Everybody* has won, and all must have prizes' (Carroll, 1865). The verdict is not, however, unanimous. Many (e.g. Giles, 1983) maintain that reviewers have been biased in their interpretations of results and that there are in fact very real differences in outcome in favour of behaviour therapy. Although there is as yet no general agreement on this issue, few clinical psychologists would doubt that dynamic, behavioural, humanistic and cognitive approaches can all be effective. This being the case, a unitary theory would provide the simplest explanation.

A further impetus towards integration is contained in the practicalities of clinical work. Many experienced clinicians agree that there is a kind of unofficial consensus amongst therapists of differing theoretical orientations over the nature of mental disorder and its treatment. Only rarely is such agreement publicly acknowledged.

Attempts at integration

Attempts have been made to combine the use of different therapies with particular clients, and in some cases these have had what are apparently very fruitful results. Wachtel (1975, 1982), for example, suggests that dynamic therapy should be introduced to help understand the nature of insurmountable resistances (barriers to progress) in certain behavioural treatments. Along similar lines, Seagraves and Smith (1976) presented a case report of a profusely perspiring, anxious clergyman with religious doubts which he wished to hide from his congregation. These authors, with the assistance of two therapists, provided a combination of behavioural and psychodynamic therapy which seemed to benefit the client. Probably the best worked-out example of such combinations is that of Lazarus (1977), the developer of *multimodal therapy*. His view of 'technical eclecticism' held that techniques from different systems could be used without a need to accept their theoretical underpinnings. He suggests systematically taking into account the behaviours, affects, sensations, images, cognitions, interpersonal relationships and physiological states of each client and devising intervention strategies appropriate for each.

The number of clinical psychologists openly admitting that they choose what appear to them to be the best techniques from very diverse approaches has shown a marked increase. Garfield (1982) suggested that the proportion of so-called eclectic therapists has increased from 40 per cent in 1961 to 65 per cent in 1980. This increased willingness to mix orientations as far as techniques go suggests that the majority of clinicians no longer adhere to any single theoretical approach in its pure form. Such clinical practice would undoubtedly be assisted by an integration of theories to match the integrated therapeutic techniques.

Probably the simplest level at which such an integration may be attempted is by identifying the *features in common* between the methods used. Many authors have been able to recognize features which they felt were shared by all modes of psychological intervention. Most clients, for example, see their therapist as caring, accepting and trustworthy (Torrey, 1972; Egan, 1980; Strupp, 1980). It is important that a good relationship is established between the client and the therapist (e.g. Marmor, 1971). The client's expectation of getting better is regarded as an essential feature of all treatments (Sloane, 1969). Some writers see the release of emotional tension as running across all approaches (Frank, 1971); others the presence of rewards and punishments (Locke, 1971). It has also been suggested that all therapies must succeed in correcting the client's unrealistic perceptions about him/herself or the environment (Goldfried and Padawer, 1982). Yet others feel that raising the client's self-esteem is the crucial element (Brady, 1980). Thus the procedures and actions of different forms of treatment may be described in the same terms. However, the mere fact that a feature may be common to several therapies by no means implies that it accounts for therapeutic effectiveness or that such therapies could be combined; just because history and mathematics are both taught using a blackboard does not mean that these lessons could be combined in the same hour.

It has also been claimed that the differences between therapies are much smaller in practice than theory would predict. *Observational studies* of leading traditional psychotherapists have noted the use of reinforcement strategies for certain verbalizations (i.e. self-disclosure) more in line with a behavioural approach (Truax, 1966). In a similar vein, the observation of the work of eminent behaviour therapists revealed a surprising use of suggestion, manipulation of clients' expectations and a reliance on the therapeutic relationship as would be expected in analytic therapy (Klein *et al.*, 1969). On the whole, however, studies observing the process of psychotherapies have found that the differences between them far outweigh their similarities (Yates, 1983); though whether studies counting the frequencies of 'advisements', disclosures and questions (which is the focus of most such studies) actually tell us a great deal about the therapeutic process must remain in doubt. The variables examined seem somehow to miss the essence of psychotherapy.

A number of *theoretical frameworks* have been proposed in attempts at integration, but in general they have not proved entirely adequate. Perhaps the earliest of these were endeavours to reduce psychodynamic theory to learning theory principles. More than fifty years ago, French (1933) linked psychoanalysis and Pavlovian conditioning at a theoretical level. He considered, for example, that Pavlov's ideas of extinction and inhibition were equivalent to the psychoanalytic concept of repression. More recently, Wolpe (1981) and Eysenck (1980) have suggested that *all* psychotherapies are based on the principles of learning. Such attempts are, however, hardly likely to provide an acceptable account of personality and clinical approaches when we consider that for the past decade most behaviourists have declared existing learning theory principles to be inadequate.

Other workers have proposed models whereby the results of behaviour therapy may be accounted for in terms of dynamic principles. One obstacle to the dynamic explanations of behaviour therapy effects is that clients apparently get better without any attempt being made to deal with the underlying problem which psychoanalysts assume exists. Wachtel (1977) suggested that removal of the symptom does modify aspects of the unconscious conflict, although Yates (1983) claimed that there is absolutely no evidence of any such shift. Messer and Winokur (1980) also pointed out that although some superficial similarities between behaviour therapy and psychoanalysis do exist, the two are in fact intrinsically different. They see behaviour therapy as having a realistic, objective and non-introspective world-view as opposed to that of psychoanalysis, which is idealistic, subjective and introspective.

More recently it has been suggested that the cognitive mechanisms underlying change, whatever method of therapy is used, could provide a focus for attempts at integration. In this view, changes in the way people interpret their environment (appraisal) or alter the mental structures used to organize their perceptions and actions (schemata) could explain all psychotherapeutic effects. Goldfried (1980) described a method he called problem-solving therapy whereby clients are taught various coping skills which can include cognitive restructuring and the more behavioural skill of relaxation. They also have to be taught when to use these skills, which necessitates their becoming aware of the emotional upset felt when facing problems. Such awareness can be developed via traditional psychotherapeutic methods. Goldfried's therapy (see previous chapter) thus integrates techniques from various therapies as seems appropriate within a cognitive framework. Ryle (1978) also made a valiant attempt to fit the major tenets of psychoanalytic theory into a cognitive framework. He suggested that the defence mechanisms of repression and denial may with benefit be viewed as examples of selective perception and the selective accommodation of perceptions into an individual's construct system using Kellian ideas.

Most serious attempts at translating both behavioural and dynamic approaches into a cognitive framework may be considered to be quite successful. Unfortunately, as we have seen in the evaluation section of the last chapter, the cognitive approach is burdened with great, and as yet unresolved, problems. It has not yet, for instance, been able to demonstrate that cognitions are indeed primary to affect, rather than the other way around (i.e. seeing oneself as a failure being the cause of depression rather than its consequence). Moreover, the term 'cognition' and much of the rest of the vocabulary of the cognitive approach is frequently used to disguise our ignorance of the psychological processes underlying the clinical phenomena being described. The renaming of defence mechanisms as 'examples of selective perception' adds little in the way of clarity: the new expression turns out to be no more precise than the language of psychoanalysis it is designed to replace.

Thus, however desirable theoretical integration might be, no attempt yet made within existing theoretical frameworks can be considered a success. Each succeeds at the expense of omitting vital aspects of the person as a whole and faces both formal theoretical and empirical problems.

The future of personality theory and clinical practice

In this book we have tried to illustrate how the solutions offered to clinical problems are largely determined by the ideas clinicians hold concerning the structure and functioning of normal personality. Perhaps just as we found no one good theory, there is also no one good method of psychological intervention. Most reviews of investigations of psychotherapy outcome present a confused picture. Sampling, design and measurement characteristics of the studies seem far better predictors of therapeutic effectiveness than the theoretical orientation of the therapists.

It may be tempting to conclude – as, indeed, many have – that theories are without importance; that in reality benefits, if any, are derived from general features of these interventions (such as a boost to morale, the opportunity for a friendly relationship or the expectancy of improvement). This conclusion, however tempting it may be, is likely to be incorrect for a number of reasons. Firstly, numerous studies exist which have demonstrated that the effects of psychological intervention (behavioural, cognitive or dynamic) are quite specific to the theories on which they are based. Thus, Malan (1976) demonstrated that the amount of improvement observed in psychotherapy was predicted by the number of transference interpretations. Similarly, Mathews and Shaw (1973) demonstrated that exposure duration was associated with improvement rate in behaviour therapy. In fact, Bandura (1978) also showed specific effects when he found self-efficacy expectations to be crucial predictors.

Secondly, studies of psychotherapy outcome, confused as they are, seem to have running through them several important threads which are inconsistent with an argument for an atheoretical approach. For example, comparative studies tend to show that focused approaches (whether behavioural or dynamic) are more effective than those relying on more diffuse changes to produce benefit (see, for example, Smith *et al.*, 1980). In addition, groups receiving placebo treatments which maximize general factors (such as expectancy and attention) appear to do no better than control groups for whom such general factors are substantially reduced (Shapiro and Shapiro, 1982).

A more probable solution to the puzzle is that there is a very broad range of possible effective intervention procedures which can be applied in clinical practice. The reason for this is very likely to be that there are a large number of psychological processes at work in the achievement of therapeutic improvements: some therapies are effective because they intervene at the level of one such process; others achieve success by intervention at a totally different level. This implies that clinicians are wrong to claim that their treatment is effective because it is based on operant conditioning, psychodynamics or the modification of particular cognitive structures. Too much evidence inconsistent with such claims exists to justify continuing to uphold them. It may, however, be accurate to claim that a particular treatment works for reasons that are specific to it and that are independent of the effectiveness of other treatment methodologies. It is simply that the complexity of the human organism spans several theoretical approaches.

It would be wrong to take this conclusion as encouraging of sterile eclecticism (a view that maintains that all theories and all approaches are of equal value). What it highlights is the need for further research in order to find out more about all the mechanisms and processes which mediate individual differences and which interact with psychological treatments to foster psychological well-being. We should avoid 'premature closure' and rejecting ideas inconsistent with our own. This open-minded attitude should not lead to complacency as far as current theory goes, but stimulate us to further research in the hope of it providing us with even more effective approaches to understanding personality and alleviating psychological distress.

Suggestions for further reading

Chapter 1

Anastasi, A. (1968) *Psychological Testing*, 3rd edn, New York, Macmillan.
Clare, A. (1980) *Psychiatry in Dissent*, 2nd edn, London, Tavistock.
Davison, G.C. and Neale, J.M. (1982) *Abnormal Psychology*, 3rd edn, Chichester, Wiley.

Chapter 2

Dixon, N.F. (1981) *Preconscious Processing*, Chichester, Wiley.
Kline, P. (1981) *Fact and Fantasy in Freudian Theory*, 2nd edn, London, Methuen.
Wolheim, R. (1971) *Freud*, London, Fontana.

Chapter 3

Sandler, J., Dare, C. and Holder, A. (1973) *The Patient and the Analyst: The Basis of the Psychoanalytic Process*, London, George Allen & Unwin.
Greenberg, J.R. and Mitchell, S.A. (1983) *Object Relations in Psychoanalytic Theory*, Cambridge, Mass., Harvard University Press.

Chapter 4

Walker, S. (1984) *Learning Theory and Behaviour Modification*, London, Methuen.

Boulougouris, J.C. (ed.) (1982) *Learning Theory Approaches to Psychiatry*, Chichester, Wiley.

Rachman, S. and Wilson, G. (1980) *The Effects of Psychological Therapy*, Oxford, Pergamon. (Chapters on behaviour therapy)

Chapter 5

Bannister, D. and Fransella, F. (1981) *Inquiring Man: The Psychology of Personal Constructs*, 2nd edn, London, Penguin.

Rogers, C.R. (1980) 'Client-centered Psychotherapy' in Freedman, A.M., Kaplan, H.T. and Saddock, B.J. (eds.) *Comprehensive Textbook of Psychiatry*, 2nd edn, Baltimore, Maryland, Williams and Wiggins.

Chapter 6

Kline, P. (1983) *Personality: Measurement and Theory*, London, Hutchinson.

Mathews, K.A. (1982) Psychological perspectives on the Type A behaviour pattern, *Psychological Bulletin*, 91, 293–323.

Gibson, H.B. (ed) (1981) *Hans Eysenck, the Man and his Work*, London, Peter Owen.

Chapter 7

Eysenck, M.W. and Eysenck, H.J. (1980) 'Mischel and the concept of personality', *British Journal of Psychology*, 71, 71–83.

Mischel, W. and Peake, P.K. (1982) 'Beyond déjà vu in the search for cross-situational consistency', *Psychological Review*, 89, 730–55.

Funder, D.C. (1983) 'Three issues in predicting more of the people: a reply to Mischel and Peake', *Psychological Review*, 90, 283–9.

Bem, D.J. (1983) 'Further déjà vu in the search for cross-situational consistency: a response to Mischel and Peake', *Psychological Review*, 90, 390–3.

Epstein, S. (1983) 'The stability of confusion: a reply to Mischel and Peake', *Psychological Review*, 90, 179–84.

Mischel, W. and Peake, P.K. (1983) 'Some facets of consistency: replies to Epstein, Funder and Bem', *Psychological Review*, 90, 394–402.

Chapter 8

Bandura, A. (1977) *Social Learning Theory*, Englewood Cliffs, New Jersey, Prentice-Hall.

Zajonc, R.B. (1984) 'On the primacy of affect', *American Psychologist*, 39, 117–23.

Lazarus, R.S. (1984) 'On the primacy of cognition', *American Psychologist*, 39, 124–9.

Rachman, S. and Wilson, G. (1980) *The Effects of Psychological Therapy*, Oxford, Pergamon. (Chapters on cognitive therapy)

Chapter 9

Marmor, J. and Woods, S. M. (1980) 'Preface' in Marmor, J. and Woods, S.M. (eds) *The Interface Between the Psychodynamic and Behavioural Therapies*, New York, Plenum Medical.

Goldfried, M.R. (ed.) (1982) *Converging Themes in Psychotherapy: Trends in Psychodynamic, Humanistic and Behavioural Practice*, New York, Springer.

Yates, A.J. (1983) 'Behaviour therapy and psychodynamic psychotherapy: basic conflict or reconciliation and integration', *British Journal of Clinical Psychology*, 22, 107–25.

References and name index

The numbers in italics following each entry refer to page numbers in this book.

Abraham, K. (1927) 'The influence of oral eroticism on character formation', in *Selected Papers*, London, Hogarth Press. *28*

Abramson, L.Y., Seligman, M.E.P. and Teasdale, J.D. (1978) 'Learned helplessness in humans: critique and reformulation', *Journal of Abnormal Psychology*, 87, 49–74. *142*

Achenbach, T.M. and Edelbrock, C.S. (1984) 'Psychopathology of childhood', *Annual Review of Psychology*, 35, 227–56. *19*

Ainsworth, M.D.S. (1973) 'The development of infant-mother attachment', in Caldwell, B.M. and Ricciuti, H.N. (eds) *Review of Child Development Research*, 3, Chicago, University of Chicago Press. *48*

Ainsworth, M.D.S., Blehar, M.C., Waters, E. and Wall, S. (1978) *Patterns of Attachment*, Hillsdale, New Jersey, Lawrence Erlbaum. *49*

Akhtar, S., Thomson, J. and Anderson, T. (1982) 'Overview: narcissistic personality disorder', *American Journal of Psychiatry*, 139, 12–19. *50*

Alden, L. and Safran, J. (1978) 'Irrational beliefs and nonassertive behaviour', *Cognitive Therapy and Research*, 2, 357–65. *146, 147*

Alexander, F. and French, T.M. (1946) *Psychoanalytic Therapy*, New York, Ronald Press. *52*

Allport, G.W. (1937) *Personality: A psychological interpretation*, New York, Holt, Rinehart & Winston. *102*

Anastasi, A. (1982) *Psychological Testing*, New York, Macmillan. *18*

Andrew, R.J. (1974) 'Arousal and the causation of behaviour', *Behaviour*, 51, 135–65. *112*

Appelbaum, S.A. (1970) Review of Maher, B. (ed.) *Clinical Psychology and Personality: Selected Papers of George Kelly*. (New York, Wiley, 1969), *Psychiatric Social Science Review*, 3, 20–5. *93*

Ashworth, C.M., Blackburn, I.M. and McPherson, F.M. (1982) 'The performance of depressed and manic patients on some repertory grid measures: a cross-sectional study', *British Journal of Medical Psychology*, 55, 247–55. *98*

Atkinson, J.R. (1981) 'Studying personality in the context of an advanced motivational psychology', *American Psychologist*, 36, 117–28. *51*

Ayllon, T. and Azrin, N.H. (1968) *The Token Economy: A Motivational System for Therapy Rehabilitation*, New York, Appleton-Century-Crofts. *80*

Bandura, A. (1971a) *Social Learning Theory*, Morristown, New Jersey, General Learning Press. *76*

Bandura, A. (1971b) 'Vicarious and self-reinforcement processes', in Glaser, R. (ed.) *The Nature of Reinforcement*, New York, Academic Press. *145*

Bandura, A. (1977) *Social Learning Theory*, Englewood Cliffs, New Jersey, Prentice-Hall. *78, 83, 135, 138, 139*

Bandura, A. (1978) 'Reflections on self-efficacy', in Rachman, S. (ed.) *Advances in Behaviour Research and Therapy*, 1, Oxford, Pergamon Press. *83, 139, 166.*

Bandura, A. (1982) 'Self-efficacy mechanisms in human agency', *American Psychologist*, 37, 122–48. *139, 140*

Bandura, A., Adams, N.E. and Beyer, J. (1977) 'Cognitive processes mediating behavioural change', *Journal of Personality and Social Psychology*, 35, 125–39. *140*

Bannister, D. (1963) 'The genesis of schizophrenic thought disorder: a serial invalidation hypothesis', *British Journal of Psychiatry*, 109, 680–8. *96*

Bannister, D. (1965) 'The genesis of schizophrenic thought disorder: a retest of the serial invalidation hypothesis', *British Journal of Psychiatry*, 111, 377–82. *96*

Bannister, D. (1982) 'Personal construct psychotherapy', in Pilgrim, D. (ed.) *Psychology and Psychotherapy–Current Trends and Issues*, London, Routledge & Kegan Paul. *98, 99*

Bannister, D. (1983) 'Personal construct psychotherapy', *British Journal of Hospital Medicine*, 30, 72–4. *98*

Bannister, D. and Fransella, F. (1981) *Inquiring Man: The Psychology of Personal Constructs*, 2nd edn, London, Penguin. *95, 100*

Barker, C. (1983) 'The psychotherapist', in Singleton, W.T. (ed.) *The Study of Real Skills*, 4, Boston, Massachussetts Institute of Technology Press. *89, 90*

Barlow, D.H. and Wolfe, B.E. (1981) 'Behavioral approaches to anxiety disorders: a report on the NIMH-SUNY, Albany, research conference', *Journal of Consulting and Clinical Psychology*, 49, 448–54. *162*

Barrett, P.T. and Kline, P. (1982) 'The Itemetric Properties of the Eysenck personality questionnaire: a reply to Helmes', *Personality and Individual Differences*, 3, 73–80. *107*

Bass, C. and Wade, C. (1982) 'Type A behaviour: not specifically pathogenic', *The Lancet*, 20 November 1980, ii, 1147–50. *117*

Baucom, D.H. (1982) 'A comparison of behavioural contracting and problem-solving/communications training in behavioural marital therapy', *Behaviour Therapy*, 13, 162–74. *81*

Bebbington, P., Hurry, J., Tennant, C., Sturt, E. and Wing, J.K. (1981) 'Epidemiology of mental disorders in Camberwell', *Psychological Medicine*, 11, 561–79. *8*

Beck, A.T. (1976) *Cognitive Therapy and the Emotional Disorders*, New York, International Universities Press. *150*

Beck, A.T., Rush, A.J., Shaw, B.F. and Emery, G. (1979) *Cognitive Therapy of Depression*, New York, Guilford Press. *135, 141*

Bem, D.J. and Allen, A. (1974) 'On predicting some of the people some of the time: the search for cross-situational consistencies in behaviour', *Psychological Review*, 81, 506–20. *129*

Bem, D.J. and Funder, D.C. (1978) 'Predicting more of the people more of the time: assessing the personality of situations', *Psychological Review*, 85, 485–501. *78*

Bennett-Levy, J. and Marteau, T. (1984) 'Fear of animals: What is prepared', *British Journal of Psychology*, 75, 37–42. *59*

Berger, R.J. (1963) 'Experimental modification of dream content by meaningful verbal stimuli', *British Journal of Psychiatry*, 109, 722–40. *26*

Bergin, A.E. and Lambert, M.J. (1978) 'The evaluation of therapeutic outcomes', in Garfield, S.L. and Bergin, A.E. (eds) *Handbook of Psychotherapy and Behaviour Change*, 2nd edn, New York, Wiley. *162*

Bergin, A.E. and Strupp, H.H. (1972) *Changing Frontiers in the Science of Psychotherapy*, New York, Aldine-Atherton. *93*

Berkowitz, L. (1978) 'External determinants of impulsive aggression', in Hartup, W.W. and de Wit, J. (eds) *Origins of Aggression*, The Hague, Mouton, *157*

Bernstein, G.S. (1982) 'Training behaviour change agents: a conceptual review', *Behaviour Therapy*, 13, 1–23. *81*

Bernstein, I.H. and Eveland, D.C. (1982) 'State vs trait anxiety: a case study in confirmatory factor analysis', *Personality and Individual Differences*, 3, 361–72. *105*

Bersh, P.J. (1980) 'Eysenck's theory of incubation: a critical analysis', *Behaviour Research and Therapy*, 11–17, 18. *62*

Bijou, S.W. and Baer, D.M. (1966) 'Operant methods in child behaviour and development', in Honig, W.K. (ed.) *Operant Behaviour: Areas of Research and Application*, New York, Appleton-Century-Crofts. *82*

Bindman, L. and Lippold, O. (1981) *The Neurophysiology of the Cerebral Cortex*, Gateshead, Tyne and Wear, Spottiswoode Ballantyne. *112*

Bishop, D.V.M. (1977) 'The P scale and psychosis', *Journal of Abnormal Psychology*, 86, 127–34. *107*

Blackburn, I.M. and Bonham, K.G. (1980) 'Experimental effects of a cognitive therapy technique in depressed patients', *British Journal of Social and Clinical Psychology*, 19, 353–63. *155*

Blackman, D. (1981) 'The experimental analysis of behaviour and its relevance to applied psychology', in Davey, G. (ed) *Applications of Conditioning Theory*, London, Methuen. *63*

Blatt, S.J. and Lerner, H. (1983) 'Investigations in the psychoanalytic theory of object relations and object representations', in Masling, J. (ed.) *Empirical Studies of Psychoanalytic Theory*, Hillsdale, New Jersey, Analytic Press. *47*

Block, J. (1971) *Lives Through Time*, Berkeley, California, Bancroft. *127*

Block, J. (1977a) 'P scale and psychosis: continued concerns', *Journal of Abnormal Psychology*, 86, 431–4. *107, 108*

Block, J. (1977b) 'Advancing the psychology of personality: paradigmatic shifts or improving the quality of research', in Magnusson, D. and Endler, N.S. (eds) *Personality at the Crossroads: Current Issues in Interactional Psychology*, Hillsdale, New Jersey, Lawrence Erlbaum. *127*

Block, J. (1981) 'Some enduring and consequential structures of person-ality', in Rabin, R.A., Aronoff, J., Barclay, A.M. and Zucker, R.A. (eds) *Further Explorations of Personality*, New York, Wiley. *41*

Bonarius, J.C.J. (1970) 'Fixed role therapy: a double paradox', *British Journal of Medical Psychology*, 43, 213–19. *100*

Borkovec, T.D., Wilkinson, L., Folensbee, R. and Lerman, C. (1983) 'Stimulus control applications to the treatment of worry', *Behaviour Research and Therapy*, 21, 247–51. *144*

Bower, G. (1978) 'Contacts of cognitive psychology with social learning theory', *Cognitive Therapy and Research*, 2, 2–3. *83*

Bower, G.H. (1981) 'Mood and memory', *American Psychologist*, 36, 129–48. *156*

Bower, T.G.R. (1982) *Development in Infancy*, 2nd edn, San Francisco, Freeman. *149*

Bowers, K. (1973) 'Situationism in psychology: an analysis and critique', *Psychological Review*, 80, 307–36. *124*

Bowlby, J. (1969) *Attachment and Loss*, 1, *Attachment*, London, Hogarth Press. *48*

Boyd, T.L. and Levis, D.J. (1983) 'Exposure is a necessary condition for fear reduction: a reply to de Silva and Rachman', *Behaviour Research and Therapy*, 21, 143–50. *78*

Brady, J.P. (1980) 'Contribution to "Some views on effective principles of psychotherapy" ', *Cognitive Therapy and Research*, 4, 271–306. *164*

Breuer, J. and Freud, S. (1895) 'Studies on hysteria', in *Standard Edition of the Complete Psychological Works of Sigmund Freud*, 2, London, Hogarth Press. *25*

Brewer, W.F. (1974) 'There is no convincing evidence for operant or classical conditioning in adult humans', in Weimer, W.B. and Palermo, D.S. (eds) *Cognition and the Symbolic Processes*, Hillsdale, New Jersey, Lawrence Erlbaum. *135*

Broadhurst, P. (1972) 'Abnormal animal behaviour', in Eysenck, H.J. (ed.) *Handbook of Abnormal Psychology*, 2nd edn, London, Pitman. *58*

Brown (1979) 'The social aetiology of depression–London studies', in Depue, R.A. (ed) *The Psychobiology of Depressive Disorders*, London, Academic Press. *103*

Brown, G.W. and Prudo, R. (1981) 'Psychiatric disorder in a rural and an urban population: 1 Aetiology of depression', *Psychological Medicine*, 11, 581–99. *9*

Bruner, J.S. (1956) 'You are your constructs', *Contemporary Psychology*, 1, 355–6. *101*

Buchwald, A.M., Strack, S. and Coyne, J.C. (1981) 'Demand characteristics and the Velten mood inducation procedure', *Journal of Consulting and Clinical Psychology*, 49, 478–9. *155*

Burgio, L.D., Whitman, T.I. and Reid, D.H. (1983) 'A participative management approach for improving direct-care staff performance in an institutional setting', *Journal of Applied Behaviour Analysis*, 16, 37–52. *79, 81*

Button, E. (1983) 'Personal construct theory and psychological well-being', *British Journal of Medical Psychology*, 56, 313–21. *95, 97*

Cacioppo, J., Glass, C. and Merluzzi, T. (1979) 'Self-statements and self-evaluations: a cognitive response analysis of heterosocial anxiety', *Cognitive Therapy and Research*, 3, 249–62. *149*

Cannell, C.F. and Kahn, R.L. (1969) 'Interviewing', in Lindzey, G. and Aronson, E. (eds) *The Handbook of Social Psychology*, 3, 2nd edn, Cambridge, Mass., Addison-Wesley. *19*

Cantor, N. and Mischel, W. (1979) 'Prototypes in person perception', in Berkowitz, L. (ed) *Advances in Experimental Social Psychology*, 12, New York, Academic Press. *123*

Cantor, N., Smith, E.E., French, R. and Mezzich, J. (1980) 'Psychiatric diagnosis as prototype categorization', *Journal of Abnormal Psychology*, 89, 181–93. *12*

Carr, A.T. (1979) 'The psychopathology of fear', in Sluckin, W. (ed.) *Fear in Animals and Man*, New York, Reinhold. *138*

Carroll, L. (1865) *Alice's Adventures in Wonderland*, rep. 1929, London, Dent, 20. *162*

Cattell, R.B. (1957) *Personality and Motivation Structure and Measurement*, Yonkers, New York, New World. *35*

Clare, A. (1980) *Psychiatry in Dissent*, 2nd edn, London, Tavistock. *16*

Claridge, G.S., Donald, J.R. and Birchall, P.M. (1981) 'Drug tolerance and personality: some implications for Eysenck's theory', *Personality and Individual Differences*, 2, 153–66. *109*

Cochrane, R. (1974) 'Crime and personality: theory and evidence', *Bulletin of the British Psychological Society*, 27, 19–22. *111*

Cohen, S.D., Monteiro, W. and Marks, I.M. (1984) 'Two-year follow-up of agoraphobics after exposure and imipramine', *British Journal of Psychiatry*, 144, 276–81. *76*

Cone, J.D. (1978) 'The behavioural assessment grid (BAG): a conceptual framework and a taxonomy', *Behaviour Therapy*, 9, 882–8. *72*

Cooper, J.E., Kendell, R.E., Gurland, B.J., Sharpe, L., Copeland, J.R.M. and Simon, R. (1972) *Psychiatric Diagnosis in New York and London*, Maudsley Monograph No. 20, London, Oxford University Press. *12*

Costello, C. (1978) 'Learned helplessness and depression: critical review of recent experiments', *Journal of Abnormal Psychology*, 87, 21–31. *141*

Costello, C.G. (1982) 'Fears and phobias in women: a community study', *Journal of Abnormal Psychology*, 91, 280–6. *7*

Coyne, J.C., Aldwin, C. and Lazarus, R.S. (1981) 'Depression and coping in stressful episodes', *Journal of Abnormal Psychology*, 90, 439–47. *138*

Coyne, J.C. and Gotlib, I.H. (1983) 'The role of cognition in depression: a critical appraisal', *Psychological Bulletin*, 94, 472–505. *143, 154, 155*

Critelli, J.W. and Neuman, K.R. (1984) 'The placebo: conceptual analysis of a construct in transition', *American Psychologist*, 39, 32–9. *79*

Cronbach, L.J. and Meehl, P.E. (1955) 'Construct validity in psychological tests', *Psychological Bulletin*, 52, 177–94. *21*

Cronbach, L.J. and Snow, R.E. (1977) *Aptitudes and Instructional Methods: A Handbook for Research on Interactions*, New York, Irvinton. *133*

Crow, T.J. (1980) 'Molecular pathology of schizophrenia: more than one disease process', *British Medical Journal*, 12 January 1980, 66–8. *107*

Crow, T.J. (1983) 'Is schizophrenia an infectious disease', *The Lancet*, 22 January 1983, 173–5. *6*

Cullen, C., Hattersley, J. and Tennant, L. (1981) 'Establishing behaviour: the constructional approach', in Davey, G. (ed.) *Applications of Conditioning Theory*, London, Methuen. *79*

D'Andrade, R.G. (1974) 'Memory and the assessment of behavior.' in Blalock, H. (ed.) *Measurement in the Social Sciences*, Chicago, Aldine. *123*

Davey, G. (1981) 'Behaviour modification in organisations', in Davey, G. (ed.) *Applications of Conditioning Theory*, London, Methuen. *64, 70*

De Silva, P. and Rachman, S. (1981) 'Is exposure a necessary component for fear reduction', *Behaviour Research and Therapy*, 19, 227–32. *78*

De Silva, P. and Rachman, S. (1983) 'Exposure and fear reduction', *Behaviour Research and Therapy*, 21, 151–2. *78*

De Silva, P. and Rachman, S. (1984) 'Does escape strengthen agoraphobic avoidance: a preliminary study', *Behaviour Research and Therapy*, 22, 87–91. *79*

De Silva, P., Rachman, S. and Seligman, M.E.P. (1977) 'Prepared phobias and obsessions: therapeutic outcome', *Behaviour Research and Therapy*, 15, 65–77. *61*

Department of Health and Social Security (1983) *Mental Health Act 1983*, London, HMSO. *10*

Dixon, N.F. (1981) *Preconscious Processing*, Chichester, Wiley. *27*

Dush, D.M., Hirt, M.L. and Schroeder, H. (1983) 'Self-statement modification with adults: a meta-analysis', *Psychological Bulletin*, 94, 408–22. *158*

Dweck, C.S. (1975) 'The role of expectation and attribution in the alleviation of learned helplessness', *Journal of Personality and Social Psychology*, 31, 674–85. *143*

Eagle, M. (1983) 'Interests as object relations', in Masling, J. (ed.) *Empirical Studies of Psychoanalytic Theory*, Hillsdale, New Jersey, Analytic Press. *47*

Eastman, C. (1976) 'Behavioural formulations of depression', *Psychological Review*, 83, 277–91. *65*

Edmunds, G. and Kendrick, D.C. (1980) *The Measurement of Human Aggressiveness*, Chichester, Ellis Horwood. *111*

Eelen, P. (1982) 'Conditioning and attribution', in Boulougouris, J.C. (ed.) *Learning Theory Approaches to Psychiatry*, Chichester, Wiley. *62*

Egan, G. (1980) 'Contribution to "Some views on effective principles of psychotherapy" ', *Cognitive Therapy and Research*, 4, 271–306. *163*

Egan, G. (1982) *The Skilled Helper: Model, Skills and Methods for Effective Helping*, 2nd edn, Monterey, California, Brooks/Cole. *90*

Ellis, A. (1977) 'Can we change thoughts by reinforcement? A reply to Howard Rachlin', *Behaviour Therapy*, 8, 666–72. *146*

Ellis, A. and Grieger, R. (1977) *Handbook of Rational-Emotive Therapy*, New York, Springer. *146*

Ellis, A. and Whitely, J. (1979) *Theoretical and Empirical Foundations of Rational-Emotive Therapy*, Belmont, California, Wadsworth. *135*

Emerson, E. and Lucas, H. (1981) ' "Preparedness" and the development of aversive associations', *British Journal of Clinical Psychology*, 20, 293–4. *61*

Emmelkamp, P. (1982) *Phobic and Obsessive-Compulsive Disorders*, New York, Plenum Press. *75*

Emmelkamp, P.M.G. and Mersch, P.P. (1982) 'Cognition and exposure in vivo in the treatment of agoraphobia: short-term and delayed effects', *Cognitive Therapy and Research*, 6, 77–88. *150*

Emmelkamp, P.M.G. and Wessels, H. (1975) 'Flooding in imagination vs flooding in vivo: a comparison with agoraphobics', *Behaviour Research and Therapy*, 13, 7–15. *76*

Endicott, J. and Spitzer, R.L. (1978) 'A diagnostic interview: the schedule for affective disorders and schizophrenia', *Archives of General Psychiatry*, 35, 837–44. *12*

Endler, N.S. (1975) 'A person-situation interaction model for anxiety', in Speilberger, C.D. and Sarason, I.G. (eds) *Stress and Anxiety*, 1, Washington DC, Hemisphere. *132*

Endler, N.S. and Magnusson, D. (1976) *Interactional Psychology and Personality*, Washington DC, Hemisphere. *131*

Epstein, S. (1979) 'The stability of behaviour: I On predicting most of the people much of the time', *Journal of Personality and Social Psychology*, 37, 1097–126. *128*

Epstein, S. (1980) 'The stability of behaviour: II Implications for psychological research', *American Psychologist*, 35, 790–806. *128*

Epstein, S.C. (1983) 'Aggregation and beyond: some basic issues on the prediction of behaviour', *Journal of Personality*, 51, 360–92. *128*

Epting (1982) *Personal Construct Psychotherapy*, London, Wiley. *99*

Erikson, E.H. (1959) 'Identity and the life cycle: selected papers', *Psychological Issues, Monograph 1*. *41*

Erwin, E. (1978) *Behaviour Therapy: Scientific, Philosophical and Moral Foundations*, London, Cambridge University Press. *83*

Eschenroeder, C. (1982) 'How rational is rational-emotive therapy a critical appraisal of its theoretical foundations and therapeutic methods.', *Cognitive Therapy and Research*, 6, 381–92. *147*

Exner, J.E. and Weiner, I.B. (1982) *The Rorschach: A Comprehensive System*, 3, *Assessment of Children and Adolescents*, New York, Wiley. *19*

Eysenck, H.J. (1947) *Dimensions of Personality*, London, Routledge & Kegan Paul. *106*

Eysenck, H.J. (1956) 'The questionnaire measurement of neuroticism and extraversion', *Revista di Psicologica*, 50, 113–40. *107*

Eysenck, H.J. (1959) *Manual of the Maudsley Personality Inventory*, London, University of London Press. *51*

Eysenck, H.J. (1964) *Crime and Personality*, London, Routledge & Kegan Paul. *111*

Eysenck, H.J. (1976) 'The lerning theory model of neurosis – a new approach', *Behaviour Research and Therapy*, 14, 251–67. *66*.

Eysenck, H.J. (1979) 'The conditioning model of neurosis', *The Behavioural and Brain Sciences*, 2, 155–99. *61*

Eysenck, H.J. (1980) 'A unified theory of psychotherapy, behaviour therapy and spontaneous remission', *Zeitschrift fur Psychologie*, 188, 43–56. *164*

Eysenck, H.J. (1981) 'The neo-behaviourist (S-R) theory of behaviour therapy', in Wilson, G.T. and Franks, C.M. (eds) *Handbook of Behaviour Therapy*, New York, Guilford Press. *67*

Eysenck, H.J. (1982) 'Present and future', in Eysenck, H.J. (ed.) *Personality, Genetics and Behaviour: Selected Papers*, New York, Praeger. *104, 156*

Eysenck, H.J. and Eysenck, S.B.G. (1969) *Personality Structure and Measurement*, London, Routledge & Kegan Paul. *106*

Eysenck, H.J. and Eysenck, S.B.G. (1975) *The EPQ*, London, University of London Press. *107*

Eysenck, H.J. and Fulker, D. (1982) 'The components of Type A behaviour and its genetic determinants', in Horvath, M. and Frantik, E. (eds) *Psychophysiological Risk Factors of Cardiovascular Diseases*, Basle, Karger. *116*

Eysenck H.J. and Rachman, S. (1965) *The Causes and Cures of Neurosis*, London, Routledge & Kegan Paul. *58*

Eysenck, H.J., Wakefield, J.A. Jr. and Friedman, A.F. (1983) 'Diagnosis and clinical assessment: the DSM-III', *Annual Review of Psychology*, 34, 167–93. *12*

Eysenck, M.W. and Eysenck, H.J. (1980) 'Mischel and the concept of personality', *British Journal of Psychology*, 71, 71–83. *105, 125*

Eysenck, S.B.G. and Eysenck, H.J. (1970) 'Crime and personality: an empirical test of the three factor theory', *British Journal of Criminology*, 10, 225–39. *111*

Fahrenberg, J., Walschburger, P., Foerster, F., Myrteck, M. and Muller, W. (1982) 'Psychophysiologische Aktivierungsforschung, ein beitrag zu den grundlagen der multivariaten emotions–und stresse–theorie', *Personality and Individual Differences*, 3, 349

Fairbairn, R. (1952) *Object Relations Theory of the Personality*, New York, Basic Books. *45*

Fairbairn, R. (1963) 'Synopsis of an Object-Relations Theory of the personality', *International Journal of Psychoanalysis*, 44, 224–5. *45*

Farina, A., Holland, C.H. and Ring, K. (1966) 'The role of stigma and set in interpersonal interaction', *Journal of Abnormal Psychology*, 71, 421–8. *16*

Farrington, D.P., Biron, L, and Le Blanc, M. (1982) 'Personality and delinquency in London and Montreal', in Gunn, J.C. and Farrington, D.P. (eds) *Advances in Forensic Psychiatry and Psychology*, Chichester, Wiley. *111*

Feather, N.T. and Davenport, P.R. (1981) 'Unemployment and depressive effect: a motivational and attributional analysis', *Journal of Personality and Social Psychology*, 41, 422–36. *143*

Feighner, J.P., Robins, E., Guze, S.B., Woodruff, R.A., Winokur, G. and Munosz, R. (1978) 'Diagnostic criteria for use in psychiatric research', *Archives of General Psychiatry*, 26, 57–63. *11*

Finkel, C.B., Glass, C.R. and Merluzzi, T.V. (1982) 'Differential discrimination of self-referent statement by depressives and nondepressives', *Cognitive Therapy and Research*, 6, 173–83. *151*

Fisher, E.B. Jr., Levenkron, J.C., Lowe, M.R., Loro, A. Jr. and Green, I. (1982) 'Self-initiated self-control in risk reduction', in Stuart, R.B. (ed.) *Adherence, Compliance and Generalisation in Behavioural Medicine*, New York, Brunner/Mazel. *118*

Fisher, S. (1973) *The Female Orgasm*, New York, Basic Books. *31*

Fisher, S. and Greenberg, R. (1977) *The Scientific Credibility of Freud's Theories and Therapy*, Brighton, Harvester Press. *29, 30*

Fogarty, P. and Hemsley, D. (1983) 'Depression and the accessibility of memories', *British Journal of Psychiatry*, 142, 232–7. *156*

Fonagy, P. (1981) 'Experimental research in psychoanalytic theory', in Fransella, F. (ed.) *Personality*, London, Methuen. *54*

Fonagy, P. (1982) 'The integration of psychoanalysis and experimental science: a review', *International Review of Psychoanalysis*, 9, 125–45. *55*

Fonagy, P. and Higgitt, A. (1984) 'Hemispheric asymmetry and sleep', *Sleep Topics*, 4, 3–4. *55*

Ford, J.D. and Kendall, P.C. (1979) 'Behaviour therapists' professional behaviours: converging evidence of a gap between theory and practice', *The Behaviour Therapist*, 2, 37–8. *72*

Fowler, H.W. and Fowler, F.R. (eds) (1956) *Shorter Oxford English Dictionary*, Oxford, Oxford University Press. *1*

Frank, J.D. (1971) 'Therapeutic factors in psychotherapy', *American Journal of Psychotherapy*, 25, 350–61. *163*

Fransella, F. (1972) *Personal Change and Reconstruction: Research on a Treatment of Stuttering*, London, Academic Press. *97*

Fransella, F. (1981a) 'Nature babbling to herself: the self characterisation as a therapeutic tool', in Bonarius, H., Holland, R. and Rosenberg, S. (eds) *Recent Advances in the Theory and Practice of Personal Construct Psychology*, London, Macmillan. *95, 98*

Fransella, F. (1981b) 'Personal construct psychology', in Fransella, F. (ed.) *Personality: Theory, Measurement and Research*, London, Methuen. *101*

Fransella, F. and Bannister, D. (1977) *A Manual for Repertory Grid Technique*, London, Academic Press. *97*

French, T.M. (1933) 'Interrelations between psychoanalysis and the experimental work of Pavlov', *American Journal of Psychiatry*, 89, 1165–203. *164*

Freud, A. (1937) *The Ego and the Mechanisms of Defence*, London, Hogarth Press. *35*

Freud, A. and Dann, S. (1951) 'An experiment in group upbringing', *Psychoanalytic Study of the Child*, 6, 127–68. *59*

Freud, S. (1905) 'Three essays on the theory of sexuality', in *Standard Edition of the Complete Psychological Works of Sigmund Freud*, 7, London, Hogarth Press. *28*

Freud, S. (1908) 'Character and anal eroticism', in *Standard Edition of the Complete Psychological Works of Sigmund Freud*, 9, London, Hogarth Press. *29*

Freud, S. (1913) 'Totem and taboo', in *Standard Edition of the Complete Works of Sigmund Freud*, 13, London, Hogarth Press. *31*

Freud, S. (1915) 'Instincts and their Vicissitudes', in *Standard Edition of the Complete Psychological Works of Sigmund Freud*, 14, London, Hogarth Press. *33*

Freud, S. (1923) 'The ego and the id', in *Standard Edition of the Complete Psychological Works of Sigmund Freud*, 19, London, Hogarth Press. *33*

Freud, S. (1926) 'Inhibitions, symptoms and anxiety', *Standard Edition of the Complete Psychological Works of Sigmund Freud*, 20, London, Hogarth Press. *65*

Friedman, M. and Rosenman, R.H. (1959) 'Association of specific overt behavior pattern with blood and cardiovascular findings', *Journal of the American Medical Association*, 169, 1286–96. *113*

Friedman, M. and Rosenman, R.H. (1974) *Type A Behavior and Your Heart*, New York, Knopf. *114*

Furnham, A. (1981) 'Personality and activity preference', *British Journal of Social Psychology*, 20, 57–68. *110*

Furnham, A. (1982) 'Psychoticism, social desirability and situation selection', *Personality and Individual Differences*, 3, 43–51. *110*

Furnham, A. and Jaspars, J. (1983) 'The evidence for interactionism in psychology: a critical analysis of the situation-response inventories', *Personality and Individual Differences*, 4, 627–44. *132*

Gale, A. (1981) 'EEG studies of extraversion-introversion: what's the next step', in Gibson, H.B. (ed.) *Hans Eysenck, the Man and his Work*, London, Peter Owen. *109*

Garcia, J. (1981) 'Tilting at the paper mills of academe', *American Psychologist*, 36, 149–58. *58*

Garfield, S.L. (1982) 'Eclecticism and integration in psychotherapy', *Behavior Therapy*, 13, 610–23. *161, 163*

Gattaz, W.F. (1981) 'HLA-B27 as a possible genetic marker of psychoticism', *Personality and Individual Differences*, 2, 57–60. *109*

Gelder, M. (1982) 'Is exposure a necessary and sufficient condition for the treatment of agoraphobia', in Boulougouris, J.C. (ed.) *Learning Theory Approaches to Psychiatry*, Chichester, Wiley. *82*

Giles, T.R. (1983) 'Probable superiority of behavioural interventions 1: Traditional comparative outcome', *Journal of Behaviour Therapy and Experimental Psychiatry*, 14, 29–32. *162*

Gillan, P. and Rachman, S. (1974) 'An experimental investigation of desensitization in phobic patients', *British Journal of Psychiatry*, 124, 392–401. *75*

Giuganino B.M. and Hindley, C.B. (1982) 'Stability of individual differences in personality characteristics from 3 to 15 years', *Personality and Individual Differences*, 3, 287–301. *127*

Glass, D.C., Krakoff, I.R., Contrada, R., Hilton, W.F., Kehoe, K., Nammucci, E.G., Collins, C., Snow, B. and Elting, E. (1980) 'Effect of harrassment and competition upon cardiovascular and plasma catecholamine response in Type A and Type B individuals', *Psychophysiology*, 17, 453–63. *116*

Glogower, F., Fremouw, W. and McCroskey, J. (1978) 'A component analysis of cognitive restructuring', *Cognitive Therapy and Research*, 2, 209–23. *147*

Glover, E. (1924/1956) 'Notes on oral character formation', in Glover, E. *On the Oral Development of the Mind*, London, Mayo. *28*

Goffman, E. (1961) *Asylums: Essays on the Social Situations of Mental Patients and Other Inmates*, Chicago, Aldine. *16*

Goldberg, D.P., Kay, C. and Thompson, L. (1976) 'Psychiatric morbidity in general practice and the community', *Psychological Medicine*, 6, 565–9. *18*

Goldberg, L.R. (1982) 'From ace to zombie: some explorations in the language of personality', in Spielberger, C.D. and Butcher, J.N. (eds) *Advances in Personality Assessment*, Hillsdale, New Jersey, Lawrence Erlbaum. *104*

Goldberger, A. (1972) 'Follow-up notes on the children from bulldog bank', (unpublished manuscript). *59*

Golderberger, L., Reuben, R. and Silberschatz, G. (1976) 'Symptom removal in psychotherapy: a review of the literature', *Psychoanalysis and Contemporary Science*, 5, 513–36. *53*

Goldfried, M. and Sobucinski, D. (1975) 'Effect of irrational beliefs on emotional arousal', *Journal of Consulting and Clinical Psychology*, 43, 504–10. *146*

Goldfried, M.R. (1980) 'Toward the delineation of therapeutic change principles', *American Psychologist*, 35, 991–9. *161, 165*

Goldfried, M.R. and Padawer, W. (1982) 'Current status and future directions in psychotherapy', in Goldfried, M.R. (ed.) *Converging Themes in Psychotherapy: Trends in Psychodynamic, Humanistic and Behavioural Practice*, New York, Springer. *163*

Golin, S., Sweeney, P.D. and Schaeffer, D.E. (1981) 'The causality of causal attributions in depression: a cross-lagged panel correlational analysis', *Journal of Abnormal Psychology*, 90, 14–22. *154*

Goodge, P. (1979) 'Problems of repertory grid analysis and a cluster analysis solution', *British Journal of Psychiatry*, 134, 516–21. *100*

Gorenstein, E.E. (1984) 'Debating mental illness', *American Psychologist*, 39, 50–6. *14*

Gotlib, I.H. (1981) 'Self-reinforcement and recall: differential deficits in depressed and nondepressed psychiatric patients', *Journal of Abnormal Psychology*, 90, 521–30. *151*

Gough, H.G. (1965) 'Conceptual analysis of psychological test scores and other diagnostic variables', *Journal of Abnormal Psychology*, 70, 294–302. *126*

Gray, J. (1971) *The Psychology of Fear and Stress*, London, Weidenfeld & Nicolson. *68*

Gray, J.A. (1972) 'The psychophysiological nature of introversion-extraversion: a modification of Eysenck's theory', in Neblitsyn, V.D. and Gray, J.A. (eds) *Biological Bases of Individual Behaviour*, New York, Academic Press. *112*

Gray, J.A. (1981) 'The psychophysiology of anxiety', in Gibson, H.B. (ed.) *Hans Eysenck, the Man and his Work*, London, Peter Owen. *112*

Greenberg, R.P. and Fisher, S. (1983) 'Freud and the female reproductive process: tests and issues', in Masling, J. (ed.) *Empirical Studies of Psychoanalytic Theory*, Hillsdale, New Jersey, Analytic Press. *31*

Hadley, J.L. (1983) 'The representational system: a bridging concept for psychoanalysis and neurophysiology', *International Review of Psycho-analysis*, 10, 13–30. *35*

Hafner, J. and Marks, I.M. (1976) 'Exposure *in vivo* in agoraphobics: the contributions of diazepam, group exposure and anxiety evocation', *Psychological Medicine*, 6, 71–88. *76*

Hall, C.S. and Lindzey, G. (1978) *Theories of Personality*, 3rd edn, New York, Wiley. *3*

Hallam, R.S. (1978) 'Agoraphobia', *British Journal of Psychiatry*, 133, 314–19. *69*

Hampton, J. (1979) 'Polymorphous concepts in semantic memory', *Journal of Verbal Learning and Verbal Behaviour*, 18, 441–61. *124*

Haney, C., Banks, C. and Zimbardo, P. (1973) 'Interpersonal dynamics in a simulated prison', *International Journal of Criminology and Penology*, 1, 69–97. *122*

Hare, R.D. (1982) 'Psychopathy and the personality dimensions of psychoticism, extraversion and neuroticism', *Personality and Individual Differences*, 3, 35–42. *107, 108*

Harrell, T.H., Chambless, D.L. and Clahoun, J.F. (1981) 'Correlational relationships between self-statements and affective states', *Cognitive Therapy and Research*, 5, 159–73. *147*

Harris, F.C. and Lahey, B.B. (1982a) 'Subject reactivity in direct observational assessment: a review and critical analysis', *Clinical Psychology Review*, 2, 523–38. *72*

Harris, F.C. and Lahey, B.B. (1982b) 'Recording system bias in direct observational methodology: a review and critical analysis of factors causing inaccurate coding behaviour', *Clinical Psychology Review*, 2, 539–56. *72*

Harris, S.L. and Ferrari, M. (1983) 'Developmental factors in child behaviour therapy', *Behaviour Therapy*, 14, 54–72. *79*

Harris, S.L. and Milch, R.E. (1981) 'Training parents as behaviour therapists for their autistic children', *Clinical Psychology Review*, 1, 49–63. *80*

Hartmann, H. (1939/1958) *Ego Psychology and the Problem of Adaptation*, New York, International Universities Press. *40, 41, 42, 43*

Hartshorne, H. and May, M.A. (1928) *Studies in Deceit*, New York, Macmillan. *122*

Haynes, S.G., Feinlieb, M. and Kannel, W.B. (1980) 'The relationship of psychosocial factors to coronary heart disease in the Framingham study: III. Eight-year incidence of coronary heart disease', *Journal of Epidemiology*, 111, 37–58. *115*

Heide, F.J. and Borkovec, T.D. (1984) 'Relaxation-induced anxiety: mechanisms and theoretical implications', *Behaviour Research and Therapy*, 22, 1–12. *75*

Heider, F. (1958) *The Psychology of Interpersonal Relations*, New York, Wiley. *136*

Higgins, K. and Schwarz, J.C. (1976) 'Use of reinforcement to produce loose construing', *Psychological Reports*, 38, 799–806. *97*

Higgitt, A.C. and Murray, R.M. (1983) 'A psychotic episode following Erhard Seminars Training', *Acta Psychiatrica Scandinavica*, 67, 436–9. *92*

Hindley, C.B. and Giuganino B.M. (1982) 'Continuity of personality patterning from 3 to 15 years in a longitudinal sample', *Journal of Personality and Individual Differences*, 3, 127–44. *128*

Hiroto, D.S. and Seligman, M.E.P. (1975) 'Generality of learned helplessness in man', *Journal of Personality and Social Psychology*, 31, 311–27. *141*

Hogan, R., DeSoto, C.B. and Solano, C. (1977) 'Traits, tests and personality research', *American Psychologist*, 32, 255–64. *126*

Holmes, D.S. (1974) 'Investigations of repression: differential recall of material experimentally or naturally associated with ego threat', *Psychological Bulletin*, 81, 632–53. *36, 51*

Holmes, D.S. (1983) 'An alternative perspective concerning the differential psychobiological responsivity of persons with the Type A and Type B behavior patterns', *Journal of Research in Personality*, 17, 40–7. *117*

Holt, R.R. (1976) 'Drive or wish: a reconsideration of the psychoanalytic theory of motivation', *Psychological Issues, Monograph 36*, 158–97. *42*

Houston, B.K. (1983) 'Psychophysiological responsivity and the Type A behaviour patterns', *Journal of Research in Personality*, 17, 22–39. *117*

Howarth, E. (1980) 'A test of some old concepts by means of some new scales', *Psychological Reports*, 47, 1039–42. *29*

Howarth, E. (1982) 'Factor analytic examination of Kline's scales for psychoanalytic concepts', *Personality and Individual Differences*, 3, 89–92. *29, 30*

Howlin, P.A. (1981) 'The effectiveness of operant language training with autistic children', *Journal of Autism and Developmental Disorders*, 11, 89–106. *80*

Iscoe, I. and Harris, L.C. (1984) 'Social and community interventions', *Annual Review of Psychology*, 35, 333–60. *17*

Israel, A.C., Pravder, M.D. and Knights, S.A. (1980) 'A peer-administered program for changing the classroom behaviour of disruptive children', *Behaviour Analysis and Modification*, 4, 224–38. *79*

Izard, C.E. (1984) 'Emotion-cognition relationships and human development', in Izard, C.E., Kagan, J. and Zajonc, R.B. (eds) *Emotions, Cognition and Behaviour*, New York, Cambridge University Press. *156*

Jahoda, M. (1972) 'Social psychology and psychoanalysis: a mutual challenge', *Bulletin of British Psychological Society*, 25, 269–74. *24*

Jemmott, J.B. III and Locke, S.E. (1984) 'Psychosocial factors, immunologic mediation and human susceptibility to infectious diseases: how much do we know', *Psychological Bulletin*, 95, 78–108. *9*

Jenkins, C.D. (1978) 'A comparative review of the interview and questionnaire methods in the assessment of the coronary-prone behavior pattern', in Dembroski, T.M., Weiss, S.M. and Shields, J.L. (eds) *Coronary-Prone Behavior*, New York, Springer. *116*

Jenkins, C.D., Zyzanski, S.J. and Rosenman, R.H. (1978) 'Coronary-prone behavior: one pattern or several', *Psychosomatic Medicine*, 40, 25–43. *115*

Johnson, S.B. and Melamed, B.C. (1979) 'The assessment and treatment of children's fears', in Lahey, B.B. and Kazdin, A.E. (eds) *Advances in Clinical Child Psychology*, 2, New York, Plenum Press. *72*

Johnston, D.W. (1982) 'Behavioural treatment in the reduction of coronary risk factors: Type A behaviour and blood pressure', British Journal of Clinical Psychology, 21, 281–94. *118*

Jones, E. (1923) 'Anal erotic character traits', in Jones, E. (ed.) *Papers on Psychoanalysis*, London, Baillière Tindall. *29*

Kadushin, C. (1969) *Why People Go to Psychiatrists*, New York, Atherton. *53*

Kagan, J. and Lemkin, J. (1960) 'The child's differential perception of parental attributes', *Journal of Abnormal and Social Psychology*, 61, 440–7. *31*

Kazdin, A.E. (1977) *The Token Economy: A Review and Explanation*, New York, Plenum Press. *80*

Kelly, G.A. (1955) *The Psychology of Personal Constructs*, 1 and 2, New York, Norton. *93, 96*

Kelly, G.A. (1969) 'Behaviour is an experiment', in Maher, B. (ed.) *Clinical Psychology and Personality: The Selected Papers of George Kelly*, New York, Wiley. *94*

Kendall, P.C. (1982) 'Individual versus group cognitive-behavioural self-control training: 1-year follow-up', *Behaviour Therapy*, 13, 241–7. *145*

Kendrick, D.C. (1981) 'Neuroticism and extraversion as explanatory concepts in clinical psychology', in Gibson, H.B. (ed.) *Hans Eysenck, the Man and his Work*, London, Peter Owen. *112*

Kenrick, D.T. and Stringfield, D.O. (1980) 'Personality traits and the eye of the beholder: crossing some traditional philosophical boundaries in the search for consistency in all of the people', *Psychological Review*, 87, 88–104. *130*

Kernberg, O.F. (1976) *Object Relations Theory and Clinical Psychoanalysis*, New York, Jason Aronson. *50*

Kety, S.S., Rosenthal, D., Schulsinger, F. and Jacobsen, B. (1978) 'The biologic and adoptive families of adopted individuals who became schizophrenic', in Wynne, L.C., Cromwell, R.L. and Matthysse, S. (eds) *The Nature of Schizophrenia*, New York, Wiley. *6*

Klein, D.F., Zitrin, C.M., Woerner, M.G. and Ross, D.C. (1983) 'Treatment of phobias II: behavior therapy and supportive psychotherapy: are there any specific ingredients', *Archives of General Psychiatry*, 40, 139–44. *162*

Klein, G.S. (1970) *Perception, Motives and Personality*, New York, Knopf.

Klein, G.S. (1976) 'Freud's two theories of sexuality', *Psychological Issues*, Monograph 36, 14–70. *42*

Klein, M. (1932) *The Psycho-Analysis of Children*, London, Hogarth Press. *43*

Klein, M. (1984) *Contributions to Psycho-Analysis, 1921–1945* London, Hogarth Press *43*

Klein, M.H., Dittman, A.T., Parloff, M.B. and Gill, M.M. (1969) 'Behavior therapy: observations and reflections', *Journal of Consulting and Clinical Psychology*, 33, 259–66. *164*

Klerman, G.L., Endicott, J., Spitzer, R. and Hirschfield, R.M.A. (1979) 'Neurotic depressions: a systematic analysis of multiple criteria and meanings', *American Journal of Psychiatry*, 136, 57–61. *11*

Kline, P. (1979) 'Psychosexual personality traits, fixation and neuroticism', *British Journal of Medical Psychology*, 52, 393–5. *33*

Kline, P. (1981) *Fact and Fantasy in Freudian Theory*, 2nd edn, London, Methuen. *30, 36, 54*

Kline, P. (1938) *Personality: Measurement and Theory*, London, Hutchinson. *22, 51, 100, 104, 105, 107, 109, 112, 118*

Kline, P. and Storey, R. (1978) 'The dynamic personality: what does it measure?', *British Journal of Psychology*, 68, 375–83. *29*

Kline, P. and Storey, R. (1980) 'The aetiology of the oral character', *Journal of Genetic Psychology*, 136, 85–94. *29*

Kohut, H. (1972) 'Thoughts on narcissism and narcissistic rage', *Psychoanalytic Study of the Child*, 27, 360–400. *50*

Kohut, H. (1977) *The Restoration of the Self*, New York, International Universities Press. *50*

Kopel, S. and Arkowitz, H. (1975) 'The role of attribution and self-perception in behaviour change: implications for behaviour therapy', *Genetic Psychology Monographs*, 92, 175–212. *143*

Korchin, S.J. (1976) *Modern Clinical Psychology: Principles of Intervention in the Clinic and Community*, New York, Basic Books. *17*

Kuhn, T.S. (1973) *The Structure of Scientific Resolutions*, 3rd edn, Chicago, University of Chicago Press. *3, 4*

Lader, M. (1975) *The Psychophysiology of Mental Illness*, London, Routledge & Kegan Paul. *110*

Lader, M.H. and Mathews, A.M.A. (1968) 'A physiological model of phobic anxiety and desensitization', *Behaviour Research and Therapy*, 6, 411–21. *78*

Landfield, A.W. (1980) 'The person as perspectivist, literalist and chaotic fragmentalist', in Landfield, A.W. and Leitner, L.M. (eds) *Personal Construct Psychology: Psychotherapy and Personality*, New York, Wiley. *101*

Landfield, A.W. and Leitner, L.M. (1980) *Personal Construct Psychology: Psychotherapy and Personality*, New York, Wiley. *96*

Landman, J.T. and Dawes, R.M. (1982) 'Psychotherapy outcome: Smith and Glass's conclusions stand up under strutiny', *American Psychologist*, 37, 504–16. *23*

Lang, P. (1970) 'Stimulus control, response control and desensitization of fear', in Levis, D. (ed.) *Learning Approaches to Behaviour Change*, Chicago, Aldine. *71*

Langer, E., Janis, I. and Wilfer, J. (1975) 'Reduction of psychological stress in surgical patients', *Journal of Experimental Social Psychology*, 1, 155–66. *139*

Lanyon, R.I. (1984) 'Personality assessment', *Annual Review of Psychology*, 35, 667–701. *19, 112*

Lasch, C. (1978) *The Culture of Narcissism: American Life in an Age of Diminishing Expectations*, New York, Norton. *50*

Launey, G. and Slade, P.D. (1981) 'The measurement of hallucinatory predisposition in male and female prisoners', *Personality and Individual Differences*, 1, 159–68. *107*

Lawlor, M. and Cochran, L. (1981) 'Does invalidation produce loose construing', *British Journal of Medical Psychology*, 54, 41–50. *97*

Lazarus, A.A. (1971) *Behaviour Therapy and Beyond*, New York, McGraw-Hill. *59, 63*

Lazarus, A.A. (1976) *Multimodal Behaviour Therapy*, New York, Springer. *71*

Lazarus, A.A. (1977) 'Has behaviour therapy outlived its usefulness?', *American Psychologist*, 32, 550–4. *163*

Lazarus, R.S. (1981) 'The stress and coping paradigm', in Eisdorfer, C., Cohen, D., Kleinman, A. and Maxim, P. (eds) *Theoretical Bases for Psychopathology*, New York, Spectrum. *138*

Lazarus, R.S. (1984) 'On the primacy of cognition', *American Psychologist*, 39, 124–9. *157*

Ledwidge, B. (1979) 'Cognitive behaviour modification: a step in the wrong direction', *Psychological Bulletin*, 85, 353–73. *158*

Ledwidge, B. (1979) 'Cognitive behaviour modification: a rejoinder to Locke and to Meichenbaum', *Cognitive Therapy Research*, 3, 133–9. *158*

Lee, C. (1983) 'Self-efficacy and behaviour as predictors of subsequent behaviour in an assertiveness training programme', *Behaviour Research and Therapy*, 21, 225–32. *140*

Leitner, L.M. (1981) 'Psychopathology and the differentiation of values, emotions and behaviours: a repertory grid study', *British Journal of Psychiatry*, 138, 147–53. *101*

Levendusky, P. and Pankratz, L. (1975) 'Self-control techniques as an alternative to pain medication', *Journal of Abnormal Psychology*, 84, 165–9. *143*

Levenkron, J.C., Cohen, J.D., Mueller, H.S. and Fisher, E.B. Jr. (1983) 'Modifying the Type A coronary-prone behaviour pattern', *Journal of Consulting and Clinical Psychology*, 51, 192–204. *118*

Levey, A.B. and Martin, I. (1981) 'Personality and conditioning', in Eysenck, H.J. (ed.) *A Model for Personality*, Heidelberg, Springer. *109*

Levinger, G. and Clark, J. (1961) 'Emotional factors in the forgetting of word associations', *Journal of Abnormal and Social Psychology*, 62, 99–105. *36*

Lewinsohn, P.M. (1974) 'Clinical and theoretical aspects of depression', in Calhoun, K.S., Adams, H.E. and Mitchell, K.M. (eds) *Innovative Methods in Psychopathology*, New York, Wiley. *65*

Lewinsohn, P.M. and Graf, M. (1973) 'Pleasant activities and depression', *Journal of Consulting and Clinical Psychology*, 41, 261–8. *65*

Lewinsohn, P.M., Mischel, W., Chaplin, W. and Barton, R. (1980) 'Social competence and depression: the role of illusory self-perceptions', *Journal of Abnormal Psychology*, 90, 213–19. *154*

Lewinsohn, P.M., Steinmetz, J.L., Larsen, D.W. and Franklin, J. (1981) 'Depression-related cognitions: antecedent or consequence', *Journal of Abnormal Psychology*, 90, 213–19. *154*

Lewis, N. and Engle, B. (1954) *Wartime Psychiatry*, New York, Oxford University Press. *58*

Lichtenberg, J.D. (1981) 'Implications for psychoanalytic theory of research on the neonate', *International Review of Psychoanalysis*, 8, 35–52. *41*

Likierman, H. and Rachman, S. (1982) 'Obsessions: an experimental investigation of thought stopping and habituation training', *Behavioural Psychotherapy*, 10, 324–38. *78*

Linden, W. (1981) 'Exposure treatment for focal phobias', *Archives of General Psychiatry*, 38, 760–75. *75*

Locke, A.E. (1971) 'Is behaviour therapy behaviouristic (An analysis of Wolpe's psychotherapeutic methods)', *Psychological Bulletin*, 76, 318–27. *163*

Locke, E.A. (1979) 'Behaviour modification is not cognitive – and other myths: a reply to Ledwidge', *Cognitive Therapy and Research*, 3, 119–25. *158*

Loevinger, J. and Knoll, E. (1983) 'Personality: stages, traits and the self', *Annual Review of Psychology*, 34, 195–222. *124*

Logue, A.W. (1979) 'Taste aversion and the generality of the laws of learning', *Psychological Bulletin*, 86, 276–96. *58*

Luria, A. (1961) *The Role of Speech in the Regulation of Normal and Abnormal Behaviour*, New York, Liveright. *148*

MacKay, A.V.P. (1983) 'Neurotransmitters in psychiatry', *Medicine International*, 1, 1531–5. *6*

Mackintosh, N.J. (1978) 'Cognitive or associative theories of conditioning: implications of an analysis of blocking', in Hulse, S.H., Fowler, M. and Honig, W.K. (eds) *Cognitive Processes in Animal Behaviour*, Hillsdale, New Jersey, Lawrence Erlbaum. *62*

Macoby, M. (1977) *The Gamesman: The New Corporate Leaders*, New York, Simon and Schuster. *50*

Magnusson, D. and Endler, N.S. (1977) 'Interactional psychology: present status and future prospects', in Magnusson, D. and Endler, N.S. (eds) *Personality at the Crossroads: Current Issues in Interactional*

Psychology, Hillsdale, New Jersey, Lawrence Erlbaum. *131*

Mahoney, M.J. (1977) 'A critical analysis of rational-emotive theory and therapy', *Counseling Psychologist*, 7, 44–6. *135, 147*

Mahoney, M.J. (1979) 'Cognitive and non-cognitive views in behavior modification', in Sjoden, P.O. and Bates, S. (eds) *Trends in Behavior Therapy*, New York, Plenum Press. *158, 161*

Mahoney, M.J. (1980) *Psychotherapy Process: Current Issues and Future Directions*, New York, Plenum Press. *135, 137*

Mahoney, M.J. (1981) 'Reflections on the cognitive-learning trend in psychotherapy', *American Psychologist*, 32, 5–13. *145*

Mahoney, M.J. and Kazdin, A.E. (1979) 'Cognitive behavior modification: misconceptions and premature evacuation', *Psychological Bulletin*, 86, 1044–9. *158*

Maier, S.F. and Seligman, M.E.P. (1976) 'Learned helplessness: theory and evidence', *Journal of Experimental Psychology*, 105, 3–46. *141*

Makhlouf-Norris, F., Jones, G. and Norris, H. (1970) 'Articulation of the conceptual structure in obsessional neurosis', *British Journal of Social and Clinical Psychology*, 9, 264–74. *98*

Malan, D. (1976) *Toward the Validation of Dynamic Psychotherapy*, New York, Plenum Press. *53, 166*

Malerstein, A.J. and Ahern, M. (1982) *A Piagetian Model of Character Structure*, New York, Human Sciences Press. *41*

Manchanda, R., Sethi, B.B. and Gupta, S.C. (1979) 'Hostility and guilt in obsessional neuroses', *British Journal of Psychiatry*, 135, 52–4. *37*

Mandler, G. (1975) *Mind and Emotion*, New York, Wiley and Sons. *34, 93*

Marcia, J.E., Rubin, B.M. and Efran, J.S. (1969) 'Systematic desensitization: expectancy change or counter-conditioning', *Journal of Abnormal Psychology*, 74, 382–7. *78*

Marks, I.M. (1978) 'Exposure treatments: conceptual issues', in Agras, W.S. (ed.) *Behaviour Modification*, Boston, Little, Brown. *77*

Marks, I.M. (1981a) *Cure and Care of Neurosis*, New York, Wiley. *76, 81*

Marks, I.M. (1981b) 'Review of behavioural psychotherapy, I: Obsessive-Compulsive disorders', *American Journal of Psychiatry*, 138, 584–92. *77*

Marks, I.M. (1982) 'Is conditioning relevant to behaviour therapy', in Boulougouris, J.C. (ed.) *Learning Theory Approaches to Psychiatry*, Chichester, Wiley. *78, 82*

Markus, H. (1977) 'Self-schemata and processing information about the self', *Journal of Personality and Social Psychology*, 35, 63–78. *92*

Marmor, J. (1971) 'Dynamic psychotherapy and behaviour therapy: are they irreconcilable?', *Archives of General Psychiatry*, 24, 22–8. *163*

Marmor, J. (1980) 'Recent trends in psychotherapy', *The American Journal of Psychiatry*, 137, 409–16. *161*

Marmor, J. and Woods, S.M. (1980) 'Preface', in Marmor, J. and Woods, S.M. (eds) *The Interface Between the Psychodynamic and Behavioural Therapies*, New York, Plenum Medical. *161*

Marzillier, J.S. (1980) 'Cognitive therapy and behavioural practice', *Behavioural Research and Therapy*, 18, 249–58. *153*

Mathews, A.M., Gelder, M.G. and Johnston, D.W. (1981) *Agoraphobia: Nature and Treatment*, New York, Guilford Press. *76*

Mathews, A.M. and Shaw, P.M. (1973) 'Emotional arousal and persuasion effects in flooding', *Behaviour Research and Therapy*, 11, 587–98. *76, 166*

Mathews, K.A. (1982) 'Psychological Perspectives on the Type A behaviour pattern', *Psychological Bulletin*, 91, 293–323. *116*

Mathews, K.R., Krantz, D.S., Dembroski, T.M. and MacDougall, J.M. (1982) 'Unique and common variance in structured interview and Jenkins Activity Survey measures of the Type A behavior pattern', *Journal of Personality and Social Psychology*, 42, 303–13. *116*

Matson, J.L., Ollendick, T.H. and Adkins, J. (1980) 'A comprehensive dining program for mentally retarded adults', *Behaviour Research and Therapy*, 18, 107–12. *79*

McCord, R.R. and Wakefield, J.A. Jr. (1981) 'Arithmetic achievement as a function of introversion-extraversion and teacher-presented reward and punishment', *Personality and Individual Differences*, 2, 142–52. *131*

McEwan, A.W. (1983) 'Eysenck's theory of criminality and the personality types and offences of young delinquents', *Personality and Individual Differences*, 4, 201–4. *111*

McGlynn, F.D., Mealiea, W.L. Jr. and Landau, D.L. (1981) 'The current status of systematic desensitization', *Clinical Psychology Review*, 1, 149–79. *75*

McNally, R.J. and Reiss, S. (1982) 'The preparedness theory of phobias and human safety-signal conditioning', *Behaviour Research and Therapy*, 20, 153–9. *61*

Mehlman, S.K., Baucom, D.H. and Anderson, D. (1983) 'Effectiveness of cotherapists versus single therapists and immediate versus delayed treatment in behavioural marital therapy', *Journal of Consulting and Clinical Psychology*, 51, 258–66. *81*

Mehrabian, A. and O'Reilly, E. (1980) 'Analysis of personality measures in terms of basic dimensions of temperament', *Journal of Personality and Social Psychology*, 38, 492–503. *104*

Meichenbaum, D. (1977a) *Cognitive-Behaviour Modification: An Integrative Approach*, New York, Plenum Press. *135, 149*

Meichenbaum, D. (1977b) 'Dr. Ellis, please stand up', *Counseling Psychologist*, 7, 43–4. *148*

Meichenbaum, D. (1978) 'Toward a cognitive theory of self control', in

Schwartz, G.E. and Shapiro, D. (eds) *Consciousness and Self-Regulation*, New York, Academic Press. *158*

Meichenbaum, D., Fogarty, S.J. and Hemsley, D.R. (1983) 'Depression and the accessibility of memories: a longitudinal study', *British Journal of Psychiatry*, 142, 232–7. *135*

Meichenbaum, D., Gilmore, J.B. and Fedoravicius, A. (1971) 'Group insight versus group desensitization in treating speech anxiety', *Journal of Consulting and Clinical Psychology*, 36, 410–21. *149*

Melin, L. and Gotesman, K.G. (1981) 'The effects of rearranging ward routines on communication and eating behaviours of psychogeriatric patients', *Journal of Applied Behaviour Analysis*, 14, 47–51. *81*

Messer, S.B. and Winokur, M. (1980) 'Some limits to the integration of psychoanalytic and behaviour therapy', *American Psychologist*, 35, 818–27. *165*

Miller, N.E. and Bugelski, R. (1948) 'Minor studies in aggression, II: The incidence of frustrations imposed by the in–group on attitudes expressed towards the out-groups', *Journal of Psychology*, 25, 437–42. *66*

Miller, R.C. and Berman, J.S. (1983) 'The efficacy of cognitive behaviour therapies: a quantitative review of the research evidence', *Psychological Bulletin*, 94, 39–53. *158*

Miller, S. and Seligman, M. (1982) 'The reformulated model of helplessness and depression: evidence and theory', in Neufeld, R. (ed.) *Psychological Stress and Psychopathology*, New York, McGraw-Hill. *142*

Mineka, S. (1979) 'The role of fear in theories of avoidance learning, flooding and extinction', *Psychological Bulletin*, 86, 985–1010. *68, 69*

Mischel, W. (1968) *Personality and Assessment*, New York, Wiley. *105, 120*

Mischel, W. (1973) 'Toward a cognitive social learning reconceptualization of personality', *Psychological Review*, 80, 252–83.

Mischel, W. (1977) 'The interaction of person and situation', in Magnusson, D. and Endler, N.S. (eds) *Personality at the crossroads: current issues in interactional psychology*, Hillsdale, New Jersey, Lawrence Erlbaum. *153*

Mischel, W. (1980) 'Something borrowed, something new', in Cantor, N. and Kihlstrom, J. (eds) *Personality, Cognition and Social Interaction*, Hillsdale, New Jersey, Lawrence Erlbaum. *135*

Mischel, W. (1981) *Introduction to Personality*, 3rd edn, New York, Holt Rinehart & Winston. *2, 120, 123, 125, 128, 133, 137, 138*

Mischel, W. and Baker, N. (1975) 'Cognitive transformations of reward objects through instructions', *Journal of Personality and Social Psychology*, 31, 254–61. *138*

Mischel, W. and Peake, P.K. (1982) 'Beyond déjà vu in the search for cross-situational consistency', *Psychological Review*, 89, 730–55. *124, 128, 129, 130*

Mischel, W. and Peake, P.K. (1983) 'Some facets of consistency: replies to Epstein, Funder and Bem', *Psychological Review*, 90, 394–402. *128*

Mitchell, J. (1973) *Psychoanalysis and Feminism*, Harmondsworth, Penguin. *32*

Mitchell, K.M., Bozarth, J.D. and Krauft, C.C. (1977) 'A reappraisal of the therapeutic effectiveness of accurate empathy, non-possessive warmth and genuineness', in Gurman, A.S. and Razin, A.M. (eds) *Effective Psychotherapy: A Handbook of Research*, Oxford, Pergamon. *89*

Moore, D.R., Chamberlain, P. and Menkes, L.H. (1979) 'Children at risk for delinquency: a follow-up comparison of aggressive children and children who steal', *Journal of Abnormal Child Psychology*, 7, 345–55. *10*

Moos, R.H. (1969) 'Sources of variance in responses to questionnaires and behaviour', *Journal of Abnormal Psychology*, 74, 405–12. *132*

Mowrer, O. (1960) *Learning Theory and Behaviour*, New York, Wiley. *75*

Mowrer, O. (1969) 'Psychoneurotic defences (including deception) as punishment avoidance strategies', in Campbell, B.A. and Church, R.M. (eds) *Punishment and Aversive Behaviour*, New York, Appleton-Century-Crofts, 449–66. *67*

Munby, M. and Johnston, D.W. (1980) 'Agoraphobia: the long-term follow-up of behavioural treatment', *British Journal of Psychiatry*, 137, 418–27. *76*

Murphy, G.E., Simons, A.D., Wetzel, R.D. and Lustman, P.J. (1984) 'Cognitive therapy and pharmacotherapy', *Archives of General Psychiatry*, 41, 33–44. *152*

Murray, E.J. (1983) 'Beyond behavioural and dynamic therapy', *British Journal of Clinical Psychology*, 22, 127–8. *161*

Nay, W.R. (1979) *Multi-Method Clinical Assessment*, New York, Gardner Press. *20*

Nelson, R.O. (1977) 'Irrational beliefs and depression', *Journal of Consulting and Clinical Psychology*, 45, 1190–1. *147*

Nelson, R.O. (1983) 'Behavioural assessment: past, present and future', *Behavioural Assessment*, 5, 195–206. *72*

Nelson, R.O., Boykin, R.A. and Hayes, S.C. (1982) 'Long-term effects of self-monitoring on reactivity and on accuracy', *Behaviour Research and Therapy*, 20, 357–63. *144*

Nelson, R.O., Hayes, S.C. and Herson, M. (1981) 'Nature of behavioural assessment', in Herson, M. and Bellack, A.S. (eds) *Behavioural Assessment: a Practical Handbook*, 2nd edn, New York, Pergamon. *71*

Nicholls, J.G., Licht, B.G. and Pearl, R.A. (1982) 'Some dangers of using personality questionnaires to study personality', *Psychological Bulletin*, 92, 3, 572–80. *110*

Nisbett, R.E. and Schachter, S. (1966) 'Cognitive manipulation of pain', *Journal of Experimental Social Psychology*, 2, 227–36. *136*

Nisbett, R.E. and Wilson, T.D. (1977) 'Telling more than we can know: verbal reports on mental processes', *Psychological Review*, 84, 231–59. *154, 157*

O'Dell, S.L., O'Quin, J.A., Alford, B.A., O'Briant, A.L., Bradlyn, A.S. and Giebenhain, J.E. (1982) 'Predicting the acquisition of parenting skills via four training methods', *Behaviour Therapy*, 13, 194–208. *79*

Ohman, A., Fredrikson, M. and Hugdahl, K. (1978) 'Towards an experimental model of simple phobic reactions', *Behaviour Analysis and Modification*, 2, 97–114. *61*

Oliver, M.F. (1982) 'Does control of risk factors prevent coronary heart disease', *British Medical Journal*, 285, 1065–6. *118*

Olweus, D. (1977) 'A critical analysis of the "modern" interactionist position', in Magnusson, D. and Endler, N.S. (eds) *Personality at the Crossroads: Current Issues in Interactional Psychology*, Hillsdale, New Jersey, Lawrence Erlbaum. *133*

Olweus, D. (1979) 'Stability of aggressive reaction patterns in males: a review', *Psychological Bulletin*, 86, 852–75. *133*

Olweus, D. (1980) 'The consistency issue in personality psychology revisited – with special reference to aggression', *British Journal of Social and Clinical Psychology*, 19, 377–90. *127*

Osberg, J.W. III. (1981) 'The effectiveness of applied relaxation in the treatment of speech anxiety', *Behaviour Therapy*, 13, 723–9. *75*

Osler, W. (1892) *Lectures on Angina Pectoris and Allied States*, New York, Appleton. *113*

Owens, R.G. and Ashcroft, J.B. (1982) 'Functional analysis in applied psychology', *British Journal of Clinical Psychology*, 21, 181–9. *73*

Passini, F.T. and Norman, W.T. (1966) 'A universal conception of personality structure', *Journal of Personality and Social Psychology*, 4, 44–9. *123*

Patterson, G.R. and Reid, J.B. (1970) 'Reciprocity and coercion: two facets of social systems', in Neuringer, C. and Michael, J. (eds) *Behaviour Modification in Clinical Psychology*, New York, Appleton-Century-Crofts. *81*

Pavlov, I.P. (1927) *Conditioned Reflexes*, London, Oxford University Press. *57, 136*

Pawlik, K. and Cattell, R.B. (1964) 'Third-order factors in objective personality tests', *British Journal of Psychology*, 55, 1–18. *35*

Paxton, R. (1983) 'Incubation of anxiety: a theory prematurely hatched', *Behavioural Psychotherapy*, 11, 218–24. *62*

Pearce, S. (1983) 'A review of cognitive-behavioural methods for the treatment of chronic pain', *Journal of Psychosomatic Research*, 27, 431–40. *143*

Perri, M.C., Richards, C.S. and Schuttheis, K.R. (1977) 'Behavioural self-control and smoking reduction: a study of self-initiated attempts to reduce smoking', *Behaviour Therapy*, 8, 360–5. *145*

Pervin, L.A. (1980) *Personality: Theory, Assessment and Research*, 3rd edn, New York, Wiley. *2, 134*

Pervin, L.A. and Lewis, M. (1978) *Perspectives in Interactional Psychology*, New York, Plenum Press. *131*

Petty, R.E. and Cacioppo, J.T. (1981) *Attitudes and Persuasion: Classic and Contemporary Approaches*, Dubuque, Iowa, Brown. *156*

Piaget, J. (1963/1969) 'Language and intellectual operations', in Furth, H.G. (ed.) *Piaget and Knowledge: Theoretical Foundations*, Englewood Cliffs, New Jersey, Prentice-Hall. *149*

Pitcher, E.G. and Prelinger, E. (1963) *Children Tell Stories: An Analysis of Fantasy*, New York, International Universities Press. *31*

Plum, A. (1981) 'Communication as skill: a critique and alternative proposal', *Journal of Human Psychology*, 21, 3–19. *90*

Rachman, S. (1976) 'The passing of the two-stage theory of fear and avoidance: fresh possibilities', *Behaviour Research and Therapy*, 14, 125–31. *67*

Rachman, S. (1977) 'The conditioning theory of fear acquisition: a critical examination', *Behaviour Research and Therapy*, 15, 375–87. *59*

Rachman, S. (1978) 'Human fears: a three-systems analysis', *Scandinavian Journal of Behaviour Therapy*, 7, 237–45. *8, 68*

Rachman, S. (1981) 'The primacy of affect: some theoretical implications', *Behaviour Research and Therapy*, 19, 279–90. *156*

Rachman, S. (1984) 'Agoraphobia – a safety-signal perspective', *Behaviour Research and Therapy*, 22, 59–70. *69*

Rachman, S. and De Silva, P. (1978) 'Abnormal and normal obsessions', *Behaviour Research and Therapy*, 16, 233–48. *8*

Rachman, S. and Hodgson, R. (1974) 'Synchrony and desynchrony in fear and avoidance', *Behaviour Research and Therapy*, 12, 311–18. *68*

Rachman, S. and Hodgson, R.J. (1980) *Obsessions and Compulsions*, Englewood Cliffs, New Jersey, Prentice-Hall. *8*

Rachman, S. and Wilson, G. (1980) *The Effects of Psychological Therapy*, Oxford, Pergamon. *75, 79, 147, 152*

Raine, A. and Venables, P.H. (1981) 'Classical conditioning and socialization – a biosocial interaction', *Personality and Individual Differences*, 2, 273–83. *111*

Rapaport, D. (1967) *The Collected Papers of David Rapaport*, New York, Basic Books. *41*

Raps, C.S., Peterson, C., Reinhard, K.E., Abramson, L.Y. and Seligman,

M.E.P. (1982) 'Attributional style among depressed patients', *Journal of Abnormal Psychology*, 91, 102–8. *142*

Raush, H.L. (1965) 'Interaction sequences', *Journal of Personality and Social Psychology*, 2, 487–99. *131*

Raush, H.L., Barry, W.A., Hertel, R.K. and Swain, M.A. (1974) *Communication, Conflict and Marriage*, San Francisco, Jossey-Bass. *131*

Ray, J.J. and Brozek, R. (1980) 'Dissecting the A-B personality type', *British Journal of Medical Psychology*, 53, 378–81. *116*

Razin, A.M. (1982) 'Psychosocial intervention in coronary artery disease: a review', *Psychosomatic Medicine*, 44, 363–87. *118*

Rescorla, R.A. and Wagner, A.R. (1972) 'A theory of Pavlovian conditioning: variations in the effectiveness of reinforcement and non-reinforcement', in Black, A.H. and Prokasy, W.F. (eds) *Classical Conditioning*, 2, New York, Appleton-Century-Crofts. *62*

Richman, N., Stevenson, J. and Graham, P.J. (1982) *Pre-School to School: A Behavioural Study*, London, Academic Press. *10*

Rimm, D.C. and Masters, J.C. (1979) *Behaviour Therapy: Techniques and Empirical Findings*, 2nd edn, New York, Academic Press. *75*

Rimm, D.C., Janda, L.H., Lancaster, D.W., Nahl, M. and Dittmar, K. (1977) 'An exploratory investigation of the origin and maintenance of phobias', *Behaviour Research and Therapy*, 15, 231–8. *58, 147*

Robins, L.N. (1979) 'Follow-up studies', in Quay, H.C. and Werry, J.S. (eds) *Psychopathological Disorders of Childhood*, 2nd edn, New York, Wiley. *10*

Robins, L.N., Helzer, J.E. and Croghan, J. (1981) 'National Institute of Mental Health diagnostic interview schedule: its history, characteristics and validity', *Archives of General Psychiatry*, 38, 381–9. *88*

Rogers, C.R. (1957) 'The necessary and sufficient conditions of therapeutic personality change', *Journal of Consulting Psychology*, 21, 95. *11*

Rogers, C.R. (1959) 'A theory of therapy, personality, and interpersonal relationships as developed in the client-centered framework', in Koch, S. (ed.) *Psychology: A Study of a Science: Formations of the Person in the Social Context*, 3, New York, McGraw-Hill. *85, 88*

Rogers, C.R. (1974) 'In retrospect: forty-six years', *American Psychologist*, 29, 115–23. *91*

Rogers, C.R. (1977) *Carl Rogers on Personal Power*, New York, Delacorte. *88, 91*

Rogers, C.R. (1980) 'Client-centered psychotherapy', in Freedman, A.M., Kaplan, H.T. and Saddock, B.J. (eds) *Comprehensive Textbook of Psychiatry*, 2nd edn, Baltimore, Maryland, Williams & Wiggins. *85, 87, 88, 91*

Rogers, C.R., Gendlin, E.T., Kiesler, D.J. and Truax, C.B. (1976) *The Therapeutic Relationship and Its Impact: A Study of Psychotherapy with Schizophrenics*, Madison, University of Wisconsin Press. *90*

Roitblat, H.L., Bever, T.G. and Terrace, H.S. (1983) *Animal Cognition*, Hillsdale, New Jersey, Lawrence Erlbaum. *57*

Rorer, L.G. and Widiger, T.A. (1983) 'Personality structure and assessment', *Annual Review of Psychology*, 34, 431–63. *125*

Rosenberg, S. and Sedlak, A. (1972) 'Structural representations of implicit personality theory', in Berkowitz, L. (ed.) *Advances in Experimental Social Psychology*, 6, New York, Academic Press. *4*

Rosenhan, D.L. (1973) 'On being sane in insane places', *Science*, 179, 250–8. *14*

Rosenman, R.H. (1978) 'The interview method of assessment of the coronary-prone behaviour pattern', in Dembrowski, T.M., Weiss, S.M., Shields, J.L., Haynes, S.G. and Feinlieb, M. (eds) *Coronary-prone Behaviour*, New York, Springer. *116*

Rosenman, R.H., Brand, R.J., Jenkins, C.D., Friedman, M., Straus, R. and Wurm, M. (1975) 'Coronary heart disease in the Western Collaborative Group study: final follow-up experience of 8½ years', *Journal of the American Medical Association*, 233, 872–7. *114*

Rosenwald, C.C. (1972) 'Effectiveness of defences against anal impulse arousal', *Journal of Consulting and Clinical Psychology*, 39, 292–8. *30*

Ross, A.O. (1978) 'Behaviour therapy with children', in Garfield, S. and Bergin, A.E. (eds) *Handbook of Psychotherapy and Behaviour Modification*, 2nd edn, New York, Wiley. *79*

Rush, A.J., Beck, A.T., Kovacs, M. and Hollon, S. (1977) 'Comparative efficacy of cognitive therapy and pharmacotherapy in the treatment of depressed outpatients', *Cognitive Therapy and Research*, 1, 17–37. *152*

Rush, A.J., Beck, A.T., Kovacs, M., Weissenburger, J. and Hollon, S.D. (1982) 'Comparison of the effects of cognitive therapy on hopelessness and self concept', *American Journal of Psychiatry*, 139, 862–6. *152*

Rushton, J.P. and Chrisjohn, R.D. (1981) 'Extraversion, neuroticism, psychoticism and self-reported delinquency: evidence from eight separate samples', *Personality and Individual Differences*, 2, 11–20. *111*

Rutter, M. (1982) 'Psychological therapies in child psychiatry: issues and prospects', *Psychological Medicine*, 12, 723–40. *79, 80*

Rutter, M. and Garmezy, N. (1983) 'Developmental psychopathology', in Mussen, P.H. (ed.) *Handbook of Child Psychology*, 4, Chichester, Wiley. *8, 60, 128*

Rutter, M. and Giller, H. (1984) *Juvenile Delinquency: Trends and Perspectives*, London, Penguin. *10*

Rutter, M., Quinton, D. and Liddle, C. (1984) 'Parenting in two generations: looking backwards and looking forwards', in Madge, N. (ed.) *Families at Risk*, London, Heinemann Educational. *49*

Ryle, A. (1978) 'A common language for the psychotherapies', *British Journal of Psychiatry*, 132, 585–94. *165*

Sackheim, H.A. (1983) 'Self-deception, self-esteem and depression', in Masling, J. (ed.) *Empirical Studies of Psychoanalytic Theories*, Hillsdale, New Jersey, Analytic Press. *36*

Sandler, J. and Sandler, A-M. (1978) 'On the development of object relationships and affects', *International Journal of Psycho-Analysis*, 59, 285–96. *48*

Sandler, J., Dare, C. and Holder, A. (1972) 'Frames of reference in psychoanalytic psychology: II. The historical context and phases in the development of psychoanalysis', *British Journal of Medical Psychology*, 45, 133–42. *24*

Sarason, I.G., Smith, R.E. and Diener, E. (1975) 'Personality research: components of variance attributable to the person and the situation', *Journal of Personality and Social Psychology*, 3, 199–204. *132*

Schafer, R. (1976) *A New Language for Psychoanalysis*, New Haven and London, Yale University Press. *42*

Schanberg, S.M. and Kuhn, C.M. (1980) 'Maternal deprivation: an animal model of psychosocial dwarfism', in Usdin, E., Sourkes, T.L. and Youdin, M.B.H. (eds) *Enzymes and Neurotransmitters in Mental Disease*, New York, Wiley. *49*

Schostrom, E. (1966) *The Person Orientation Inventory: An Inventory for the Measurement of Self-actualisation*, San Diego, Educational and Industrial Testing Service. *91*

Schwartz, R.M. (1982) 'Cognitive-behaviour modification: a conceptual review', *Clinical Psychology Review*, 2, 267–93. *136*

Seagraves, R.T. and Smith, R.C. (1976) 'Concurrent psychotherapy and behavior therapy: treatment of psychoneurotic outpatients', *Archives of General Psychiatry*, 33, 756–63. *163*

Seligman, M.E.P. (1971) 'Phobias and preparedness', *Behaviour Therapy*, 2, 307–20. *60, 61*

Seligman, M.E.P. (1975) *Helplessness: On Depression, Development and Death*, San Francisco, Freeman. *140*

Seligman, M.E.P. and Johnston, J. (1973) 'A cognitive theory of avoidance learning', in McGuigan, J. and Lumsden, B. (eds) *Contemporary Approaches to Conditioning and Learning*, Washington, Wiley. *68*

Senatore, V., Matson, J.L. and Kazdin, A.E. (1982) 'A comparison of behavioural methods to teach social skills to mentally retarded adults', *Behaviour Therapy*, 13, 313–24. *80*

Shapiro, D.A. and Shapiro, D. (1982) 'Meta-analysis of comparative therapy outcome studies: a replication and refinement', *Psychological Bulletin*, 92, 581–604. *23, 167*

Shaw, M.L.G. (1980) 'The analysis of a repertory grid', *British Journal of Medical Psychology*, 53, 117–26. *100*

Shields, J. (1976) 'Heredity and environment', in Eysenck, H.J. and Wilson, G.D. (eds) *A Textbook of Human Psychology*, Baltimore, University Park Press. *109*

Sifneos, P.E. (1972) *Short-Term Psychotherapy and Emotional Crisis*, Cambridge, Mass., Harvard University Press. *53*

Silverman, L.H. (1983) 'The subliminal psychodynamic activation method: overview and comprehensive listing of studies', in Masling, J. (ed.) *Empirical Studies of Psychoanalytic Theories*, Hillsdale, New Jersey, Analytic Press. *32, 37*

Simon, A. and Ward, L.O. (1982) 'Sex-related patterns of worry in secondary school pupils', *British Journal of Clinical Psychology*, 21, 63–4. *10*

Simons, A.D., Garfield, S.L. and Murphy, G.M. (1984) 'The process of change in cognitive therapy and pharmacotherapy for depression', *Archives of General Psychiatry*, 41, 45–51. *155*

Skinner, B.F. (1974) *About Behaviourism*, New York, Knopf. *63, 64*

Slade, P.D. (1973) 'The physiological investigation and treatment of auditory hallucination: a second case report', *British Journal of Medical Psychology*, 46, 293–8. *75*

Slade, P.D. (1982) 'Towards a functional analysis of anorexia nervosa and bulimia nervosa', *British Journal of Clinical Psychology*, 21, 167–79. *72*

Slater, E. (1965) 'Diagnosis of hysteria', *British Medical Journal*, 11 June 1965 i, 1395–9. *9*

Sloane, R.B. (1969) 'The converging paths of behavior therapy and psychotherapy', *American Journal of Psychiatry*, 126, 877–85. *163*

Sloane, R.B., Staples, F.R., Cristol, A.H., Yorkston, N.J. and Whipple, K. (1975) 'Short-term analytically oriented psychotherapy versus behaviour therapy', *American Journal of Psychiatry*, 132, 373–7. *54*

Smith, B.D. and Vetter, H.J. (1982) *Theoretical Approaches to Personality*, Englewood Cliffs, New Jersey, Prentice-Hall. *2, 3*

Smith, M.L., Glass, G.V. and Miller, T.I. (1980) *Benefits of Psychotherapy*, Baltimore, Johns Hopkins University Press. *23, 167*

Smith, P.B. (1980) *Group Processes and Personal Change*, London, Harper & Row. *91*

Smith, P.B. (1981) 'Research into humanistic personality theories', in Fransella, F. (ed.) *Personality: Theory, Measurement and Research*, London, Methuen. *91*

Smith, T.W. (1982) 'Irrational beliefs in the cause and treatment of emotional distress: a critical review of the rational-emotive model', *Clinical Psychology Review*, 2, 505–22. *147*

Smith, T.W. and Brehm, S.S. (1981) 'Cognitive correlates of the Type A coronary-prone behaviour pattern', *Motivation and Emotion*, 5, 215–23. *147*

Solomon, R.L. and Wynne, L.C. (1954) 'Traumatic avoidance learning: the principle of anxiety conservation and partial irreversibility', *Psychological Review*, 61, 653–85. *67*

Spielberger, C.D. (1971) 'Anxiety as an emotional state', in Speilberger,

C.D. (ed.) *Current Trends in Theory and Research*, 1, New York, Academic Press. *103*

Spitzer, J.R. and Endicott, J. (1978) 'Medicine and mental disorder: proposed definition and criteria', in Spitzer, R.L. and Klein, D.F. (eds) *Critical Issues in Psychiatric Diagnosis*, New York, Raven Press. *20*

Spitzer, R.L., Endicott, J. and Robins, E. (1978) 'Research diagnostic criteria', *Archives of General Psychiatry*, 35, 773–82. *11*

Steinbrueck, S.M., Maxwell, S.E. and Howard, G.S. (1983) 'A meta-analysis of psychotherapy and drug therapy in the treatment of unipolar depression with adults', *Journal of Consulting and Clinical Psychology*, 51, 856–63. *23*

Steinmark, S.W. and Borkovec, T.D. (1974) 'Active and placebo treatment effects on moderate insomnia under counterdemand and positive demand instructions', *Journal of Abnormal Psychology*, 83, 157–63. *75*

Stern, R.S. (1978) 'Obsessive thoughts: the problem of therapy', *British Journal of Psychiatry*, 132, 200–5. *77*

Strupp, H.H. (1980) 'Contribution to "Some views on effective principles of psychotherapy" ', *Cognitive Therapy and Research*, 4, 271–306. *163*

Suinn, R.M. (1982) 'Intervention with Type A behaviours', *Journal of Consulting and Clinical Psychology*, 50, 933–49. *118*

Szasz, T. (1982) 'The psychiatric will: a new mechanism for protecting persons against "psychosis" and psychiatry', *American Psychologist*, 37, 762–70. *14*

Tausch, R. (1978) 'Facilitative dimensions in interpersonal relations: verifying the theoretical assumptions of Carl Rogers in school, family education, client-centered therapy', *College Student Journal*, 12, 2. *87, 91*

Teasdale, J.D. and Taylor, R. (1981) 'Induced mood and accessibility of memories: an effect of mood state or of induction procedure?', *British Journal of Clinical Psychology*, 20, 39–48. *156*

Tessler, R.C., Bernstein, A.G., Rosen, B.M. and Goldman, H.H. (1982) 'The chronically mentally ill in community support systems', *Hospital and Community Psychiatry*, 33, 208–11. *16*

Thoresen, C.E., Friedman, M., Gill, J.K. and Ulmer, D.K. (1982) 'The recurrent coronary prevention programme: some preliminary findings', *Acta Medica Scandinavica, Supplement*, 660, 172–92. *119*

Thorpe, G. and Burns, L. (1983) *The Agoraphobic Syndrome*, Chichester, Wiley. *70*

Tizard, B. and Hodges, J. (1978) 'The effect of early institutional rearing on the development of eight-year-old children', *Journal of Child Psychology and Psychiatry*, 19, 99–118. *49*

Torrey, E.F. (1972) 'What western psychotherapists can learn from witchdoctors', *American Journal of Orthopsychiatry*, 42, 69–72. *163*

Truax, C.B. (1966) 'Reinforcement and nonreinforcement in Rogerian psychotherapy', *Journal of Abnormal Psychology*, 71, 1–9. *164*

Truax, C.B. and Mitchell, K.M. (1971) 'Research on certain therapist interpersonal skills in relation to process and outcome', in Bergin, A.E. and Garfield, S.L. (eds) *Handbook of Psychotherapy and Behaviour Change*, New York, Wiley. *89*

Ullmann, L.P. and Krasner, L.A. (1975) *A Psychological Approach to Abnormal Behaviour*, Englewood Cliffs, New Jersey, Prentice-Hall.

Vaillant, G.E. (1976) 'Natural history of male psychological health: V.', *Archives of General Psychiatry*, 33, 535–45. *36*

Valentine, C.W. (1946) *The Psychology of Early Childhood*, 3rd edn, London, Methuen. *59*

Von Dusch, T. (1868) *Echerbuck der Herzksankheffen*, Leipzig, Wilhem Engelman. *113*

Wachtel, P.L. (1975) 'Behavior therapy and the facilitation of psychoanalytic exploration', *Psychotherapy Theory, Research and Practice*, 12, 69–72. *162*

Wachtel, P.L. (1977) *Psychoanalysis and Behaviour Therapy: Toward an Integration*, New York, Basic Books. *165*

Wachtel, P.L. (1982) 'What can dynamic therapies contribute to behaviour therapy', *Behaviour Therapy*, 13, 594–609. *162*

Wade, T.C. and Baker, T.B. (1977) 'Opinions and use of psychological tests', *American Psychologist*, 32, 874–82. *51*

Wahler, R.G. and Graves, M.G. (1983) 'Setting events in social networks: ally or enemy in child behaviour therapy', *Behaviour Therapy*, 14, 19–36.

Walker, S. (1984) *Learning Theory and Behaviour Modification*, London, Methuen. *63, 67, 135*

Waters, E., Wippman, J. and Sroufe, L.A. (1979) 'Attachment, positive affect and competence in the peer group: two studies in construct validations', *Child Development*, 3, 821–9. *49*

Watson, J.B. (1913) 'Psychology as the behaviourist views it', *Psychological Review*, 20, 158–77. *56*

Watson, J.B. (1930) *Behaviorism*, rev. edn, New York, Norton. *24*

Watson, J.B. and Rayner, R. (1920) 'Conditioned emotional reactions', *Journal of Experimental Psychology*, 3, 1–4. *58*

Watts, F.N. (1979) 'Habituation model of systematic desensitization', *Psychological Bulletin*, 86, 627–37. *78*

Watts, F.N. (1980) 'Clinical judgement and clinical training', *British Journal of Medical Psychology*, 53, 95–108. *20*

Watts, F.N. (1983) 'Affective cognition: a sequel to Zajonc and Rachman', *Behaviour Research and Therapy*, 21, 89–90. *156*

Weinstein, R.M. (1982) 'The mental hospital from the patient's point of view', in Gove, W.R. (ed.) *Deviance and Mental Illness*, Beverly Hills, California, Sage. *17*

Widiger, T.A. and Kelso, K. (1983) 'Psychodiagnosis of axis II', *Clinical Psychology Review*, 3, 491–510. *10*

Wiggins, J.S. (1979) 'A psychological taxonomy of trait-descriptive terms: the intepersonal domain', *Journal of Personality and Social Psychology*, 37, 395–412. *2*

Wiggins, J.S. (1982) 'Circumplex modes of interpersonal behaviour in clinical psychology', in Kendall, P.C. and Butcher, J.H. (eds) *Handbook of Research Methods in Clinical Psychology*, New York, Wiley. *105*

Wilkinson, F.R. and Carghill, D.W. (1955) 'Repression elicited by story material based on the Oedipus complex', *Journal of Social Psychology*, 42, 209–14. *36*

Williams, D.G. (1981) 'Personality and mood: state-trait relationships', *Personality and Individual Differences*, 2, 303–9. *110*

Williams, J.L. (1977) 'Implications of the rise of cognitive behaviourism', *American Psychologist*, 32, 895–6. *154*

Williams, R.B. Jr., Haney, T.L., Lee, K.I., Kong, Y., Blumenthal, J.A. and Whalen, R.E. (1980) 'Type A behavior, hostility and coronary atherosclerosis', *Psychosomatic Medicine*, 42, 539–49. *115*

Wilson, G.T. (1982) 'The relationship of learning theories to behaviour therapies: problems, prospects and preferences', in Boulougouris, J.C. (ed.) *Learning Theory Approaches to Psychiatry*, Chichester, Wiley. *69, 81, 136, 158*

Wilson, G.T. and Davison, G.C. (1971) 'Processes of fear reduction in systematic desensitization: animal studies', *Psychological Bulletin*, 76, 1–14. *78*

Wing, J.K., Bebbington, P.E., Hurry, J. and Tennant, C. (1981) 'The prevalence in the general population of disorders familiar to psychiatrists in hospital practice', in Wing, J.K., Bebbington, P.E. and Robins, L. (eds) *The Concept of a Case: Theory and Method in Psychiatric Community Surveys*, London, Grant MacIntyre. *6, 8*

Wing, J.K., Birley, J.L.T., Cooper, J.E., Graham, P. and Isaacs, A. (1967) 'Reliability of a procedure for measuring and classifying "present psychiatric state" ', *British Journal of Psychiatry*, 113, 488–515. *11*

Winnicott, D.W. (1953) 'Transitional objects and transitional phenomena', *International Journal of Psychoanalysis*, 34, 1–9. *45*

Winnicott, D.W. (1958) *Through Paediatrics to Psycho-Analysis*, London, Hogarth Press. *46*

Winter, D.A. (1982) 'Construct relationships, psychological disorder and therapeutic change', *British Journal of Medical Psychology*, 55, 257–69. *98*

Wise, E.H. and Haynes, S.N. (1983) 'Cognitive treatment of test anxiety: rational restructuring versus attentional training', *Cognitive Therapy and Research*, 7, 69–78. *147*

Witkin, H.A., Dyk, R.B., Paterson, H.F., Goodenough, D.R. and Karp, S.A. (1962) *Psychological Differentiation*, New York, Wiley. *103*

Wolpe, J. (1958) *Psychotherapy by Reciprocal Inhibition*, Stanford, California, Stanford University Press. *74*

Wolpe, J. (1978) 'Cognition and causation in human behaviour and its therapy', *American Psychologist*, 33, 437–46. *140*

Wolpe, J. (1981) 'Behaviour therapy versus psychoanalysis', *American Psychologist*, 36, 159–64. *78*

Woodruff, R. and Pitts, F.N. (1964) 'Monozygotic twins with obsessional neurosis', *American Journal of Psychiatry*, 120, 1075–80. *8*

Woods, P.A., Higson, P.J. and Tannahill, M.M. (1984) 'Token-economy programmes with chronic psychotic patients: the importance of direct measurement and objective evaluation for long-term maintenance', *Behaviour Research and Therapy*, 22, 41–53. *80*

Wortman, C.B. and Dintzer, L. (1978) 'Is an attributional analysis of the learned helplessness phenomenon viable? A critique of the Abramson-Seligman-Teasdale reformulation', *Journal of Abnormal Psychology*, 87, 75–90. *154*

Yarrow, M.R., Scott, P. and Waxler, C.Z. (1973) 'Learning concern for others', *Developmental Psychology*, 8, 240–60. *137*

Yates, A.J. (1981) 'Behaviour therapy: past, present, future-imperfect', *Clinical Psychology Review*, 1, 269–91. *70*

Yates, A.J. (1983) 'Behaviour therapy and psychodynamic psychotherapy: basic conflict or reconciliation and integration', *British Journal of Clinical Psychology*, 22, 107–25. *164, 165*

Zajonc, R.B. (1980) 'Feeling and thinking: preferences need no inferences', *American Psychologist*, 35, 151–75. *155, 156*

Zajonc, R.B. (1984) 'On the primacy of affect', *American Psychologist*, 39, 117–23. *155*

Zamansky, H.S. (1958) 'An investigation of the psychoanalytic theory of paranoid delusions', *Journal of Personality*, 26, 410–25. *37*

Zubin, J. (1967) 'Classification of the behaviour disorders', *Annual Review of Psychology*, 18, 312–35. *11*

Zuroff, D.C. (1980) 'Learned helplessness in humans: an analysis of learning processes and the roles of individual and situational differences', *Journal of Personality and Social Psychology*, 39, 130–46. *142*

Zuroff, D.C. (1981) 'Depression and attribution: some new data and a review of old data', *Cognitive Therapy and Research*, 5, 273–81. *142*

Subject index

The references section of this book serves as a name index. Names are included in this index only where there is no corresponding literature citation; in most cases these are the names of historical personages.

abreaction, 25
acting out, 36, 90
actualization, 85, 87, 91–2;
    self-actualization, 85, 91–2
affect, 8, 25, 32, 35–6, 107, 155–6,
    161, 163, 165
aggression, 10, 19, 28, 33, 37, 42,
    102–5, 112, 121, 127, 137, 141
agoraphobia, 2, 7, 69, 73
anxiety, 7, 34, 36, 46, 53, 58, 67–8,
    71, 74–9, 86, 96, 103, 108, 112,
    132, 139, 146–7, 150;
    measurement of, 18, 20, 22;
    anxiety state, 8; panic attack, 8,
    132, 148
appraisal, 138–40, 151, 165
arousal, 36, 108–10, 112–13, 117;
    cortical, 108–9
ascending reticular activating system,
    108, 112
attachment, 46, 48–9
attribution theory, 136–7, 142–3, 154
automatic thought, 151

autonomic nervous system, 71, 108,
    110, 117, 137
avoidance learning, 65–71, 75–9,
    138–9, 146; incubation in, 61–2;
    maintenance of fear in, 60–2, 72;
    safety-signals in, 68–9; two-stage
    theory of, 65, 75

behaviour therapy, 70–81, 112, 119,
    152–3, 158–9, 162–6
behavioural approach, 56–83, 101
behavioural assessment, 20, 71–3;
    functional analysis, 64, 66, 71–3,
    81–2; observation, 17–21, 66, 72,
    122, 125, 128–30, 164
behavioural specificity, 122
bereavement, 8, 141

categorization of mental disorder,
    10–12; DSM-III, 11; ICD-9, 11
catharsis, 25
classical conditioning: *see*
    conditioning

classification using prototypes, 12, 124

client-centred approach, 84–93

client-centred therapy, 87–91

cognitive restructuring, 145–52, 158, 165

cognitive therapy, 135, 144–5, 148, 151–9

conditioning, 57–70, 78–9, 80, 82; conditionability, 109, 111; conditioned fear, 58–9, 67, 78; conditioned response (CR), 57–8, 60–1, 67, 78, 135; conditioned stimulus (CS), 57, 61–2, 68, 75, 135; generalization in, 79, 91, 154; unconditioned response (UR), 57; unconditioned stimulus (US), 57–62, 109, 135

conscious: see system conscious

consciousness, 8–9, 25, 27, 34, 38, 156

consistency of behaviour, 21, 86, 122, 124, 127–30; cross-situational, 124, 128, 130; stability of personality, 102, 120–34; temporal, 127–30

constructive alternativism, 93

constructs (Kellian), 93–101; construct system, 94–8, 100–1, 165; impermeability of, 97; incongruence of, 86–8, 91; loosening of, 96–9; range of convenience of, 96; tightening of, 97, 99

contingency management, 79, 81, 158

coping strategies, 97, 118, 136, 146, 148–9, 165

coronary heart disease, 22, 113–19, 126; risk factors in, 114–15, 118

correlation coefficient, 20–1, 104

criminality, 111

curiosity, 38, 42, 63

defence mechanisms, 34–6, 51, 165–6; denial, 36, 165; displacement, 36–7, 46, 53; intellectualization, 36; isolation, 36–7; projection, 35, 37; reaction formation, 36–7; regression, 36; repression, 25–6, 31–2, 35–6, 52, 54, 96, 164–5; sublimation, 36; suppression, 36

definition of personality, 1–2

delinquency, 111

depression, 5–6, 8, 11, 17, 37, 44, 47, 65–6, 138, 140–3, 150–2, 165; neurotic/reactive, 8, 141 (see also manic-depressive psychosis)

depressive position, 44

developmental crises, 41

dreaming, 26–7, 54–5, 64, 96, 99, 160

eclecticism, 163, 167

EEG, 109

ego, 34–7, 40–2, 45

ego psychology, 40–3, 47

encounter groups, 90–2

expectancies, 138–9

exposure, 75–6, 78–9; with response prevention, 77

extinction, 57, 60–5, 67, 69, 75, 78, 82, 109, 164

Eysenck's personality dimensions, 102–13; extraversion, 18, 106, 108–13, 123, 126–7, 131–2; and Type A, 116; introversion, 106, 108–10, 112, 127, 131–2; neuroticism, 106, 108–11, 128; psychoticism, 106, 108, 116

Eysenck Personality Questionnaire (EPQ), 107, 112; E, 106, 111; I, 106; N, 106, 110; P, 106–8, 111

factor analysis, 35, 104–6, 122–3; oblique rotation in, 105; orthogonal rotation in, 105

field dependency, 104

fixed-role therapy, 100

flooding, 75, 77, 79, 150

Freud's models of the mind, 24–37; affect-trauma, 25; structural, 33–7; topographical, 25, 27, 33

good-enough mothering, 45–7

guilt, 10, 11, 34–5, 37, 44, 112

habitual response pattern (Eysenck), 106, 114

habituation, 75, 77–8, 110

humanistic approaches, 84–101, 162
hypnosis, 25
hysteria, 9, 25; dissociative hysterical
    neurosis, 9

id, 33–4, 40–1
implicit personality theory, 123
information processing, 136
insight, 7, 52, 54, 88
integration, 160–6
interactionism, 131–4, 137; scalar
    versus cross-over, 132
internal speech, 148–9, 153, 158
interpretation, 38, 52–3
interviews, 7, 11, 17, 19–20, 72,
    114–17
introspection, 34

Jenkins Activity Survey (JAS), 115–17

Kelly's fundamental postulate, 93

learned helplessness, 140–3, 156
learning theory (see also classical
    conditioning, operant
    conditioning, reinforcement), 3,
    56–8, 61–2, 64–6, 68–70, 72, 78–9,
    81–2, 84, 91, 112
libido, 32, 43, 45, 141
limbic system, 108
longitudinal studies, 36, 41, 127–8

manic-depressive (affective)
    psychosis, 5–6
medical models of mental illness,
    13–17, 74
mental disorders, descriptions, 4–11
mental impairment, 10, 79–81
mental retardation: see mental
    impairment
models of psychological abnormality,
    12–17
modelling, 76, 79, 158
multimodal therapy, 163

narcissism (psychoanalytic concept),
    50–1
narrow-trait theories of personality,
    113–19
neurotic disorder/neurosis, 7–10, 21,
    25, 32, 36–7, 43, 64–6, 87, 101,
    111
neurotic paradox, 65
neuroticism, general, 21, 33, 87; see
    also Eysenck's personality
    dimensions
neurotransmitters, 6, 14, 112
non-directive therapy, 87

object (psychoanalytic), 28, 31, 35,
    37
object-relations theory, 42–50
obsessive-compulsive neurosis, 8, 37,
    77, 81, 97, 101
Oedipus complex, 30–2
operant conditioning, 63–6, 68–9,
    71, 79, 80, 139, 167
outcome of therapy, 13, 15, 23, 49,
    89–90, 138, 140, 150, 152, 162,
    166–7

paranoid-schizoid position, 42–3
penis envy, 31–2
perceptual defence, 27
personal construct psychotherapy,
    98–100
personal construct theory, 84,
    93–101
personality assessment, 17–22, 51,
    71–3, 97–8, 107–8, 114–18;
    projective tests 17, 19, 32, 51
personality coefficient, 126–7
personality development, 27–31,
    41–3, 45–50, 109
personality disorder, 9–10, 50;
    psychopathy, 107; schizoid
    personality, 45
phobic disorder/phobia, 7–8, 37,
    58–63, 65–70, 73–7, 82, 138,
    146–8, 156, 162
placebo, 78, 136, 147, 150, 152, 167
positive regard, 85–6; positive self-
    regard, 86
preconscious: see system
    preconscious
preparedness, 60–1
primary process, 26, 55
problem-solving therapy, 136
programmed practice, 76

psychoanalytic theory, 24–55, 145, 161, 164–6; of fixation, 28–9; of instincts, 28, 42, 44–5, 48; of psychosexual development: general, 27–32, 41–2; anal stage, 28–30, 33, 42; oral stage, 28–30, 33, 42; phallic stage, 28, 30–1; childhood sexuality, 28, 32, 36
psychoanalytic treatment: psychoanalysis, 52–3; psychoanalytic psychotherapy, 53–4
psychosis, 5–6, 24, 80, 87, 106–8; functional, 6–7; organic, 6–7

questionnaires, 17–19, 21, 35, 72, 103, 107, 115, 121, 146

rational-emotive therapy, 147, 150
reality principle, 27
reification, 38, 121, 125
reinforcement, 61–7, 79–82, 109, 131, 139, 151, 158, 164; schedule of, 63, 79, 109; vicarious, 139
reinforcer, 63–7, 69, 79–80
relaxation, 74–7, 79, 99, 148, 165
reliability, 20–1, 101, 105, 116; equivalent forms, 21; inter-rater, 116; split-half, 21; test-retest, 20–1, 116
repertory grid, 97–8

satiation, 77–8
schizophrenia, 5–6, 9, 12–14, 17; catatonic, 5; paranoid, 5, 10, 37
secondary process, 277
selective perception, 150–1, 154, 165–6; see also perceptual defence
self, 35, 37, 42–6, 50, 85–8, 92, 94, 150
self-blame, 141, 143, 151
self-control, 30
self-efficacy, 139–40, 167
self-esteem, 42, 44, 149, 163
self-instructional training (SIT), 148–50; covert self-instructions, 148, 153
self-monitoring, 144–5
self-reward, 145
self-statement, 136, 148–9, 155
shaping, 63

silent assumption, 150
situationalism, 122–4, 131, 133, 137; criticisms of, 124–5
slips of the tongue, 26, 160
social learning theory, 135–40
social skills training, 80–1
socio-cognitive approach, 93, 122, 135–59
stimulus control, 138, 144
stress inoculation programme, 149
structured interview, 11, 20; Present State Examination (PSE), 11; for Type A behaviour, 114–17
superego, 33–5, 40
system conscious, 25, 27–8
system preconscious, 27, 51, 55
system unconscious, 26–7, 31–5, 37, 44, 51, 86–8, 92, 96, 165
systematic desensitization, 74–5; hierarchy in, 74–5, 95, 106

template-matching procedure, 129
test-taking attitudes, 18; acquiescence, 18; defensiveness, 18; response bias, 18
therapist attitudes, 88–90; empathy, 89–90; facilitativeness, 89–90; genuineness, 87–90; warmth, 89–90, 102, 104
thought stopping, 77–8
token economy, 80–1
trait, 4, 29, 32, 41, 102–19, 120–34, 137; anxiety, 103, 132
transference, 50–4, 166
transitional phenomena/objects, 46
trauma: in psychoanalytic accounts, 25, 27; in behavioural accounts, 58–9, 62–3
Type A behaviour pattern, 113–19, 147

unconscious: see system unconscious
unconscious conflict, 27–9, 32, 35, 37, 41, 43, 52, 54, 165

validity, 20–2, 39, 54, 64, 100, 116, 118; concurrent, 21–2; construct, 21–2; face, 21; predictive, 21–2, 121

Western Collaborative Project, 114